RENT VS. OWN

A REAL ESTATE REALITY CHECK FOR NAVIGATING BOOMS, BUSTS, AND BAD ADVICE

JANE HODGES

CHRONICLE BOOKS

SAN FRANCISCO

Hodges, Jane.
  Rent vs. own : a real estate reality check for navigating booms, busts, and bad advice /
Jane Hodges.
      p. cm.
  Includes bibliographical references and index.
  ISBN 978-1-4521-0253-5
1. Home ownership. 2. Rental housing. 3. House buying. 4. Landlord and tenant. I. Title.

HD7287.8.H62 2012
643'.12—dc23

                              2011018893
Manufactured in China

Designed by Eloise Leigh

This publication contains the opinions and ideas of its author. It is intended to provide
helpful and informative material about renting and buying a home. Every effort has been
made to present clear and complete information, however rules and regulations can change,
and every situation cannot be anticipated. If the reader is seeking legal, tax, investment,
real estate, financial, accounting, or any other kind of professional advice, the reader should
consult a competent professional who can appropriately address the nuances of the reader's
specific situation. The author and publisher specifically disclaim any responsibility for any
liability, loss, or risk, personal or otherwise, that is incurred as a consequence, directly or
indirectly, of the use and application of any of the contents of this book.

10 9 8 7 6 5 4 3 2

Chronicle Books LLC
680 Second Street
San Francisco, California 94107
www.chroniclebooks.com

DEDICATION

I dedicate this book to Dave, my long-suffering husband, who has put up with botched vacations, weekends, and nights as I've worked on bringing this book to fruition.

CONTENTS

PART 3: OPERATING INSTRUCTIONS
Reality Checks, Reality Bites

INTRODUCTION

Team Rent, Team Own

The year 2004 was big for me. At thirty-four years old, I bought a home for the first time and I left a job to resume my dream work arrangement: freelancing. I even had a plum gig: The *Wall Street Journal*'s real estate site asked me to write two columns about an emerging population of novice real estate investors trying to make money as landlords and rehabbers in the hot market. These gigs weren't just an interesting journalistic foray into the then-booming real estate market. They also offered what I saw as a kind of balm for the conflict I'd undergone while buying my own house.

You see, my ex-beau—I'll call him Team Rent—had vehemently opposed my becoming a homeowner from the minute I hit my first open house. I, Team Own, had vehemently favored it. It wasn't that I felt renting was some terrible racket—I'd lived happily at five rentals in New York and three in Seattle before I took a first-time-buyer class, talked to a mortgage broker, and started my search with an agent. My rental vita included a one-bedroom walk-up, a drafty turret in a professor's suburban Victorian, a roach-laden studio with hardwoods overlooking a crack corner, a librarian's sublet, a penthouse with a view, and a low-ceilinged in-law with garden access.

In New York I'd noticed that the people who'd "fixed" their housing costs either with hard-to-get rent-controlled apartments or by managing to buy had vanquished one of the great terrors of modern life—domestic uncertainty. In Seattle I'd noticed I could actually afford to buy. On the personal front, much of my life was uncertain—my preferred work style was freelance, my preferred men apparently noncommittal. It seemed homeownership was one commitment I could make, a new foundation that would lead me out of a period of volatility brought on by job upheaval from the dot-com crash, my mother's death from cancer, witnessing 9/11 from the roof of my Harlem high-rise, and a cross-country move to Seattle. Owning a home seemed like it would bind numerous loose ends, maybe even create a kind of learning lab for future writing endeavors.

In early 2004, the sting of my split-up was as sharp as the scent of the olive green paint still drying on my home office walls. But each time I put a byline on another article about someone else's real estate risk-taking, I felt a little more emboldened about my own: I'd bought a $225,000 asbestos-shingled Craftsman in an "emerging" Seattle neighborhood once known as Poverty Gulch. It had four bedrooms (one for me, one for an office, two for housemates if I got fiscally nervous), two bathrooms, a deck, rose bushes. Located downwind from a scrap metal recycler, it also had issues—a tilted front porch, a pink disco-style bathroom, rattling metal windows, and wacky neighbors I nicknamed The Pit Bulls, The Clampetts, and Off Their Meds.

I knew buying involved risks, and that I'd have to live up to the challenge of managing my sporadic income amid the steady expenses of owning. I wasn't afraid of those risks. But then, I also didn't understand them. Neither did my friends who were buying, nor the consumers and agents I kept interviewing or reading about in the media. The homeownership rate in America reached its all-time peak that year, hitting 69 percent. Indeed, other than a minority of antsy Team Rent types, bubble bloggers, and economists with nicknames like Dr. Doom, who wasn't willing to plant a flag on Planet Ownership? Lenders were flexible, loans were cheap, home prices were rising—*and how*, in some markets. At the time, it seemed that barriers to buy had vanished while the rewards for doing so just kept coming. We all know now these conditions were precursors to a bubble. But back then, life was still innocent.

Indeed, I spent much of my life in a red-faced Rent vs. Own debate. The debate, when I held my own version of it, was small potatoes—mainly about two incompatible people's views on commitment and money, and how real estate choices symbolized them. Team Rent and I certainly had differing real estate histories that colored our psychologies accordingly. I was raised in a 2,400-square-foot brick Cape Cod–style house my family had owned in Richmond, Virginia. Owning worked out well for us: My father sold the home three decades after he'd bought it, for $250,000 above its purchase price, and used it to launch retirement. Team Rent was raised in a small but pleasant rent-controlled apartment in Manhattan's huge Peter Cooper Village complex. Growing up, his family's rent was so cheap compared to renting at market prices that living otherwise wasn't really an option. His family stayed put and stashed their savings.

Team Rent was a wanderer, opting to work as a merchant marine and sometimes professor, keeping his "things" to a minimum and bags packed. I was a mental wanderer, willing to live in one city, apt to rearrange the furniture and résumé rather than relocate. I thought owning might be a good organizing principle for my peripatetic adulthood. Team Rent thought my idea of owning was code for wedding bells and babies. He also just had a thing against owners, against people who participated in matters he considered mainstream and capitalist, which he imbued with a more-disgusting layer of greed and materialism than was necessarily the case. He thought owners underwent a near-fundamentalist conversion, transitioning from interesting people to Stepford-like husks of their former selves, congregating with other joiners at backyard fences to act the part of homeowner, a role he saw involving conversations about contractors and dip recipes, gardening tips and bulk-buying at Costco. That they'd pay handsomely for this privilege was even more unfathomable to him: He thought all debt was bad debt, that a fixed-rate mortgage was as dangerous as a payday loan.

He already knew my stated personal reasons for buying, even if he didn't believe them, so I tried to make the economic case to him, while reminding him that buying a home wasn't a slippery slope of material silliness. First, I told him I was using a sensible FHA mortgage. I was planning to stay for a long time. I could afford my new monthly expense but had room for housemates if I needed rental income. I was saving. I had a home-repair strategy: When I had more equity I would borrow—carefully—to fix up my home's funk factor. And I was eligible for tax deductions on my mortgage interest, property tax, and even my home office. Team Rent wasn't convinced. He told me I didn't know what I was doing, that I was impulsive. I told him that I could do it without him. I liberated him, and he lined up a date with a renter.

Fast-forward to 2012, and the personal debate I went through with my now-ex is a quaint microcosm of a debate that's grown in size and scope and proportion—and is everywhere, writ large across the American landscape. It's a battle many adults are having with themselves and their families, and it's colored by the headlines: Politicians and industry leaders are debating the government's role in enabling affordable mortgage finance. Historians and students of sociology are studying the role of ownership and whether it is, or should be, a key ingredient in the American Dream. Under what circumstances does it still make sense to own? Is renting really such a bad deal after all? Which choice is riskier? Which choice makes more sense in a modern, mobile society?

In case you're wondering what became of my home in Poverty Gulch, bought at the height of a bubble, let me fill you in: From 2004 into 2007, my house rose in value, a boat rising with both Seattle's and the national market's tide, but also because Seattle funded two park projects nearby, giving the area an aesthetic injection. My new boyfriend (also on Team Own!) sold his place in 2006 to move in with me, and I told him that, assuming I could do it profitably, I'd sell the Poverty Gulch cottage in 2007 so we could buy our own place and start anew together. We both agreed that wherever we moved in 2007 was where we'd retire—period, and end of story.

So, as a self-employed person, I managed after three tries to take out a $60,000 home equity loan for renovations and I got to work making improvements—two bathroom remodels, a new roof, new windows, new electrical, exterior and interior painting, plaster work, et cetera. My agent listed it in June 2007 and I sold in one week, pocketing $85,000 in post-sale proceeds. I rolled that money into the purchase of a 1966 raised rancher, which I own with my now-husband (I married Team Own!) and where I'm typing these words. All in all, real estate was very good to me. It nudged my relationships into place, it made me think, it made me money. I ought to be a poster-child for owning, right?

And yet: As I continue reporting and writing about real estate within the broader business landscape, I'm keenly aware that it's turned out to be a very fickle partner for many Americans. Some of them, whose timing was just a little bit different from mine, were terrifically hurt by making the exact same assumptions I did. While I escaped Team Rent's doomsday claim that I'd go bankrupt from buying, it wasn't because I was particularly intelligent. Yes, I did standard-issue "careful" things—borrowing on a fixed-rate mortgage, renting to roommates and backfilling the savings account, seeking professional input before launching sale-related renovations. But mainly, I was lucky. Had I waited two months to list the home, my bulwark against modern uncertainty, I'd have run smack into the real estate downturn, the ultimate uncertainty.

Indeed, I'd have lived this nightmare: I'd have responsibility for two mortgages, the first ($1,560) and my half ($1,380) of the new home's, plus a monthly home equity payment ($300 minimum) for my former home's fixes. I'd have needed to choose whether to rent the Poverty Gulch pad at a loss, or sell it for one. My line of credit might've been called in by my bank due to my home's declining value, a new phenomenon in many markets and scary considering that the only bank willing to give me a renovation loan wound up federally shuttered and sold to another Wall Street giant. Maybe I'd have "walked away" from my first home, sending keys in "jingle mail" to my lender, a cynical gesture made by some owners who can't sell or modify loans. At best, I'd have drained my resources some time in 2009, around the time my income dropped 30 percent due to the recession and my credit cards were maxed out from prior-year wedding costs. I could've gone bankrupt.

And you know what? That's incredibly scary. What's scarier is that the mistakes many people made in the housing boom and bust are mistakes you can make in any real estate market. And no one but you is responsible for avoiding them. While at each step along the way the people who help you acquire real estate are responsible for keeping little pieces of your big picture on the up-and-up, you're ultimately responsible for the whole decision to rent or own, its consequences, expenses, and, of course, whether it makes you happy.

I'm still glad I bought one home, then another, and I'm not that disillusioned with homeownership as an institution. But maybe that's because I never expected buying to turn my life into something other than what it's been—a fair amount of work, but work I can do with a smile. I think if you want to buy, you should. If you want to rent, fine. But I also think that most of the information available for anyone considering the decision is tilted toward the assumption that—but of course—you want to become an owner. Do you?

Most first-time-buyer literature I've read subtly or overtly assumes that you've given owning a green light. Let me be clear: *This isn't that kind of book.* Nor is it a homeowner-hater book designed to feed your schadenfreude about foolish friends who bought places they couldn't afford. If you're convinced you're going to buy, please also turn to literature specifically for first-time buyers; while I've done my best to hit the high points of homeownership, you'll need to know more about financing a buy and additional variations among property and transaction types—there's more to say, and people who say it more thoroughly than I have here.

But if you're in an agitated state of advanced ambivalence (you've gone all Hamlet on homeownership), you want to line up your arguments and test them out, and you're not sold on what's for sale and the social sentiment surrounding it, stick with me. I'll try to explain where and how our attitudes to renting and owning originated, how the rules have functioned in the past, and where things seem to be headed. I'll share stories of renters and owners happy and regretful. I'm not a real estate agent, an economist, or a financial planner—though I've interviewed many. However, I am a person who believes we ought to question our institutions from time to time, and our assumptions about them.

The key to happiness in most relationships—with people, employers, housing—is figuring out what you expect from those relationships, then asking yourself if those expectations are realistic or have changed without your even knowing. If I've done my job, you'll come away with as many questions as answers. After all, the only thing you really own in this world is the one thing that can't be mortgaged or leased: The depth of your convictions.

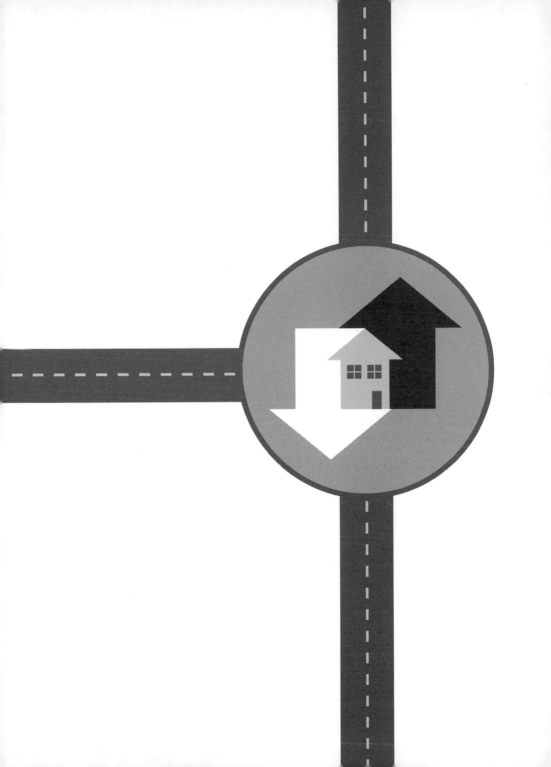

THERE'S NO PLACE LIKE OWN

REAL ESTATE AND THE AMERICAN DREAM

CHAPTER 1

APARTMENT THERAPY

What's a Person Like Me Doing in a Real Estate Market Like This?

Janna is a renter from the land of owners. A thirty-one-year-old freelance editor, she pays $500 per month to share a midtown Sacramento, California, flat with two roommates. She's managed to tune out the little voice inside of her that says she should *buy, buy, buy* a home, and when she writes the monthly rent check she refuses to wonder whether she's "throwing her money away" on rent, paying off her landlord's investment instead of her own, or missing out on the "forced savings plan" that is homeownership. Justifications to own loop like Muzak all around her: Plummeting mortgage rates! Tax credits and deductions for buyers! There's never been a better time to buy! They can all talk to Janna's hand—or, on a bad day, her middle finger.

Janna, perhaps like you, is surrounded by people—namely, most Americans—who have historically admired homeownership. And that admiration got her into trouble. Her parents instilled in her that owning is better than renting, and as the real estate market grew hot in the early 2000s they instilled in her that owning more is even better. During the nine post-college months when she lived with them, real estate talk dominated dinners. Family downtime involved rounds of Cashflow, a board game developed by motivational speaker Robert Kiyosaki, author of *Rich Dad, Poor Dad*[1.1] and other books seen as bibles by small-time real estate investors. Whereas some families play Nintendo Wii or tune in to *American Idol* for fun, Janna's family donned invisible eyeshades and cut fantasy real estate deals, then marked up their make-believe financial statements.

But now that Janna lives under a different roof, she's done listening to lectures on the virtues of owning and landlording. She's not interested in buying now, and is unsure about later. When her fiancé brings it up, she gently changes the subject.

"When he tells me he wants to buy, sometimes it makes me cringe," she says. "I ask him: 'Why do you want to have a $100,000 or $200,000 yoke around your neck?'"

There was a time not so long ago when she felt otherwise. Back in 2003, when she was planning to move out of her parents' place, she took her father's advice and instead researched buying. At twenty-three, she had a relatively short track record in the adult workplace, an even shorter one in the rental space; owning seemed like a decisive, if daunting, way to stake out her adulthood.

And yet, she did what so many tire-kicking potential home buyers do, operating on the general idea that owning is better than renting: She ran some basic math to see if she could afford to buy, and she realized that the monthly housing costs to own weren't that much higher than the monthly costs to rent. She wanted to live in a neighborhood like her current one, near friends and nightlife, coffee shops and indie boutiques. A one-bedroom rental there would cost $750 per month. If she was willing to live twenty minutes away, however, she could buy a two-bedroom townhouse for $128,000 in Cameron Park, a commuter village bordering the Sierra Nevada foothills. If she made a 3 percent down payment, her monthly housing payment would be $1,000. With a roommate paying half, she could own for less than it cost to rent in Midtown.

"To own a place that cost so little, that was just crazy," she says.

And so that's how a woman who wanted to rent in downtown Sacramento came to plunk $4,000 down on a townhouse in a suburb where she didn't really want to live.

A year later, when her townhouse had doubled in value (yes, this was 2004), she borrowed against its increased value—because, as she says self-mockingly, "I couldn't just let my equity sit there!"—and put $40,000 down on a $134,000 investment house in Fresno. She'd rent it for income.

Three years later, she was honest with herself: She wanted to live in Sacramento already. She'd actually wanted to live there all along. So what did she do? Yes, she bought again. She refinanced again, borrowing against her properties so she could pay her portion of a 10 percent down payment on a $300,000 home she was purchasing with a friend.

"I had this mentality that I should own any place where I live," she says. "Part of what started my whole financial spiral was my decision to move back into the city."

O—

$565,000 TWO WAYS: NEST EGG OR "YOKE OF DEBT"?

Soon Janna, twenty-six years old and living on a regional magazine editor's salary, had two investment rentals and a co-owned in-city home, properties with a combined value of about $565,000. It seemed like a fabulous nest egg: Three properties, a few hundred dollars' extra cash flow each month, and the expectation that future appreciation would help her homes' values and her financial position. But her last home purchase was a stretch—a big stretch—for her budget.

The positive trickle of real estate income that Janna had enjoyed began slowly reversing course due to the shifting real estate market. Tenant turnover and falling local rent prices meant she, too, had to lower her asking rent. She began losing $50 per month instead of gaining $150 in profit. Her mortgage payment on the Sacramento home was poised to adjust upward in 2007, adding another $200 to her expenses. Then there were pop-up maintenance expenses:

The townhouse needed a $5,000 plumbing and foundation repair—yes, a repair that cost more than her down payment—which she had to finance on an installment plan. Add to this pile unforeseen medical expenses.

Janna acted quickly to squash her mounting debt. She sold out of her Sacramento home share, figuring the resulting five-figure booty would help dam the growing flood of expenses, and she moved into an apartment.

But her troubles weren't over: When her Fresno renters moved out in early 2007, leaving the place trashed, she saw it as a sign—a For Sale sign. Busy at work and tired from all her moves and landlord duties, she decided to use the money from her Sacramento sale to pay the Fresno mortgage for six months, letting it sit empty while it underwent repairs. She assumed that when she sold the place, she'd be free of ongoing expenses connected to it.

By the time she listed the Fresno home, the real estate market had stalled nationwide, and the country was in recession—and so she had no choice but to rent her place again, this time at a $100 monthly loss. Now she was losing money on two properties and dealing with medical and home-repair debt. She fell behind on her homeowners' dues at the Cameron Park townhouse, and as she negotiated with her bank to sell the place for less than she owed on it— remember how she'd borrowed and borrowed against it on the assumption its value would keep rising?—her homeowner association slapped a $7,500 claim against her property for the unpaid dues.

An insomniac with panic, she consulted a lawyer about options. Long story short: She let her Cameron Park townhouse go in foreclosure and gave up her Fresno home in a personal bankruptcy filing during 2010. With her credit trashed, her idea of herself as a homeowner and real estate investor destroyed, and her housing hangover official, there is this outcome: She's finally renting in Sacramento. And then, there's also her accumulated wisdom: "Looking back on it, I think I had a really unrealistic view of homeownership."

WHAT IS A REALISTIC VIEW OF HOMEOWNERSHIP?

Janna's case is extreme. But her epiphany is collective, and it's the reason you're reading this book. What can you realistically expect of homeownership? No matter where you see yourself on the housing spectrum—buy-curious, a committed renter, someone who goes both ways depending on the market you're in or which martini you're on—wondering what we talk about when we talk about homeownership is the question du jour. If the 1990s and first decade of the 2000s represent the height of the government, lenders, and society at large pumping up the benefits of and easy access to homeownership in America, the coming decades will involve our collective reckoning with the havoc that this encouragement wrought. How did a once-sensible institution meant to instill stability and comfort come, instead, to undermine both? What have we come to expect of our homes financially, personally, culturally?

What's complicated here is that the principles Janna understood when she became a homeowner were widely accepted and, throughout much of American history, factually correct. Yes, a home is an investment and a savings plan of sorts, home prices typically appreciate over time, it's possible to make money from renting out property, and the monthly cost to rent and own can resemble one another in many local markets. However, the degree of truth in each of these principles and whether they are consistently true from year to year or from one market to another is where the generalities fall apart. As the Great Recession of 2007 to 2009 proved, the housing market's cycles don't always support the rosy case for betting the farm on, well, the farm.

Happy Homeowners: They're Still Around

Clearly homeownership, long considered the "given" choice for those able to cobble together a down payment, is up for review. Buyers like Janna who embarked on a leveraged debt spree, as well as old-school stay-forever owners, have watched nervously as values declined in recent years.

But even in the post-meltdown economy, not all homeowners regret buying, wound up overleveraged, or got stuck in property they couldn't sell. There's still a case for homeownership. And though she currently rents, Paige, a thirty-something interior designer, is interested in owning again. She comes from three generations of happy owners, all of whom have benefited from owning during the past six decades.

"I grew up hearing that real estate was a rock-solid investment, and in my family it was," she says. "I get an enormous amount of pleasure working on a new house. To the extent you can afford to do it, I think it's vital to make a space yours."

Her maternal grandfather, a Hungarian immigrant, served in World War II and, upon returning home, paid $8,000 for a 1,500-square-foot Cape Classic on a busy New Jersey street corner using a Veterans Administration loan made available under the GI Bill. That was more than sixty-five years ago. He paid off the house in less than ten years, stayed there for decades, and sold it, using the considerable proceeds to downsize into a condominium and also help fund his retirement.

Her mother and father sold their "starter home" in 1981 and paid $120,000 for a lot and the custom home a builder developed on it for them. At times making the mortgage was a struggle—its interest rate was in the high teens, typical of that era, and they had trouble refinancing. Eventually they succeeded in finding a more-affordable mortgage. Her parents still live in the 3,000-square-foot Colonial-style house. It's now worth about $600,000 and they, too, expect it to help fund their retirement.

Then there's Paige. She and her husband rent a house in Summit, New Jersey, a good place to raise kids. Since marrying in the mid-1990s, they have bought and sold property several times over, buying and renovating and selling several fixers in the Washington, DC, area, a home on the New Jersey shore, and so forth. With her DIY design skills and his ability to double as a contractor (he works by day in business), they enjoy fixing up old homes—and they're in it as much for the creative process as they are for the profit on renting or selling the places.

They approach owning like investors: Paige's husband has an MBA and handles what she refers to as their "complex matrix of leverage"—that is, their multiple mortgages on rentals—and, at times, they've been "highly leveraged." But to her, that's business as usual. They're still young, and will buy again, but she's not concerned about when. The trick, for Paige and her mobile family, is to choose their purchase carefully, with both livability and profitability in mind, since they move more often than did her parents. And sometimes the trick is renting instead.

"To my parents, having that big house in the suburbs and staying there a long time was worth it," Paige says. "But we get bored pretty easily and have a more mobile lifestyle. I guess I don't have the same American Dream as my parents. But I love owning a home."

Rethinking Renting

No inquiry into a new view of homeownership would be complete without a look at the other way to occupy housing: renting. Renting is seeing a handsome rebound. Maybe it was never such a bad option. But until recently in America, it was as if there were two kinds of people: Homeowners—and potential home-owners. Outside a few large and expensive cities where renting is a lifelong housing choice, renting was largely seen as a kind of backup plan, an interim life stage, a thing you did because you were too young or timid or noncommittal or financially disorganized to buy, a thing you did because you *didn't get it* about real estate and its many financial rewards.

Even now, amid the real estate market's reset, some of the old anti-renting sentiment still hangs in the air. After all, if owning is the American Dream, then what is renting? To some, renting is the waiting room for ownership. To others, renting is a perfectly lovely way to live. And to still another population, those who can afford to own but choose instead to rent are making a political choice—a refusal to participate in American life, a failure of character.

In 2008, supporters of a Minnesota politician named Erik Paulsen called out his opponent, Ashwin Madia, as unfit for Congressional office—because he rented. According to the *Minnesota Independent*,[1,2] Paulsen backers held a press confer-ence during which they cited Madia's lack of homeownership, his lack of familiarity with mortgages and property taxes, as traits that made him less understanding of his constituents. *Slate*, covering the spin, interpreted it thus: "A renter is a transient, unwilling to settle down, promiscuous when it comes to real estate and, the campaign implied, who knows what else."[1.3] It sounds comical. But it worked: Paulsen, the homeowner, won.

It's not just politicians who've paid a personal price for their status as renters in a nation steeped in ownership pride. David, a forty-five-year-old translator who's rented in five American states and also lived in Switzerland, says he has more money in the bank than most of his homeowner friends, whom he describes as "house poor," but nonetheless feels judged for renting. He recalls the chilly reception he got when he knocked on a homeowning neighbor's door one weekend morning to ask if a barking dog could be brought inside or otherwise quieted.

"The guy said, 'You're just a renter! You can get off my property,'" David recalls. "I'd asked very politely and he was extremely rude. Basically, I didn't count since I didn't own a home."

Matthew, a thirty-five-year-old who is married and a father, is a committed renter—a stance he described in an online essay dubbed "The Renter's Manifesto."[1.4] For him, the jabs about renting are subtler, mixed in with people's ideas about child-rearing and family.

"People who know we rent are always making the assumption that it's because we're saving for a down payment," Matthew says. "There's this idea that owning is what families do. People think kids need a yard and a stable place to call home, and that you can only have that if you own."

Meeting in the Middle: Reconsidering Real Estate

The conventional wisdom about owning and renting is changing. The big takeaways are that owning carries more risk and less reward than many people previously knew or believed and that, in a risky economic environment or for a mobile lifestyle, renting may make more financial sense than many people knew or believed. Of course, as the market repairs itself, the old arguments to buy will resurface: As home affordability improves, buyers may wonder if now's the time to get into the market. But there will also be new arguments to rent: Lenders may make it tougher for buyers to finance their purchases, and buyers may wait longer to enter the market because owning seems to require longer-term commitment—maybe too much commitment.

As of this writing, many consumers are ambivalent about their housing choices. Many who are in the market for a new place are looking into ownership and renting simultaneously, taking a "throw things at the wall and see what sticks" approach. Starting sometime in 2010, roughly 25 percent of all property searchers on real estate portal Zillow.com turned out to be "dual-track" shoppers, people who calculate what monthly payment they can swing and then search what types of rentals and for-sale homes are available at that price.[1.5] At Trulia, also a real estate portal, the volume of these shoppers—whom Trulia calls "crossover" shoppers—is 30 percent. If you're in the market simply for a new place, and you could go either way, you've got company—and plenty to consider.

"This represents a wholesale rethinking of whether the American dream includes homeownership," says Tara-Nicholle Nelson, Trulia's consumer educator.

In the future, home buying won't be as easy as it was just a decade ago. Homeownership rates may fall. The percentage of renters may rise. And the perceptions of both will continue to morph and change. And maybe that's okay. Remember Janna? She's in her own personal recovery. But when, and if, she returns to the home-buying market, she says she'll do it for different reasons: She'll look for a primary home she truly wants to inhabit, rather than one she wants to leverage.

"I do have traditional fantasies about the home I might own one day—I call them 'fantasies' now—but mostly it's an internal conflict. I daydream, and then I snap back to reality."

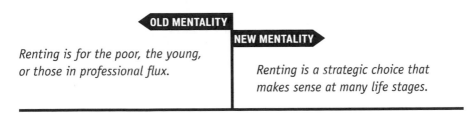

OLD MENTALITY

Renting is for the poor, the young, or those in professional flux.

NEW MENTALITY

Renting is a strategic choice that makes sense at many life stages.

Many adults who could buy opt to rent because doing so lets them live in neighborhoods or types of property they couldn't otherwise afford, or because despite their economic or job security they're looking around for new professional options that might require relocation. Aging adults may choose to rent rather than downsize to a smaller owned home.

OLD MENTALITY

If you can make a down payment and afford the mortgage, you should own.

NEW MENTALITY

Total cost of ownership includes mortgage, property taxes, utilities, maintenance, and commuting.

Many home buyers deplete their resources to buy, ignoring the reality that there's more to the housing cost than that monthly payment. If you buy deep in suburbia, commute costs and time can hit your wallet and lifestyle. If you've got no money left for replacement and repairs of home systems, you can go into debt soon after clearing the hurdle of buying. Owners have a fixed layer of cost topped with an unpredictable layer, much of which relates to maintenance. Many home fixes are expensive. Can you fund a $4,000 electrical-panel upgrade, a $15,000 sewer-line fix, or a $10,000 new roof? Owners don't face these repairs annually—but just one of them can take years to finance. Renters' total "cost of ownership" is straightforward.

OLD MENTALITY

NEW MENTALITY

Buying isn't risky; it's a guaranteed investment over the long haul.

Buying is risky and is subject to a shifting market, even over the long haul.

As home values rose precipitously during the early 2000s, people ignored warnings that such growth couldn't last forever (after all, it's not like incomes rose at this rate!) and stretched to buy as much home as possible. Some even borrowed against their home's increased value. But when the market stalled and prices fell, owners who'd poured all their resources into buying or who'd borrowed against their homes suddenly owned homes worth less than the debt on them—a situation known as being *underwater* or having *negative equity*. In the worst-case scenarios, owners sold at a loss or with debt to their lender (bye-bye, investment) or realized they could never climb out of their home-related debt and thus let their lenders foreclose (bye-bye, investment and credit rating and pride). As a result, many renters and would-be buyers are now aware that home values can drop—and that it's important to have a healthy down payment to provide an "equity cushion" against the market.

OLD MENTALITY

NEW MENTALITY

You always make money when you sell a home.

Profit on a home sale depends on equity, timing, and the home's condition.

Appreciation—gradual price increases typical in a normal non-recessionary market—is a factor in how homeowners make money at the time they sell. But it's not the only factor. How long you stay and the type of market you sell in can influence your takeaway. Also, putting a substantial down payment into your home and then staying in that home have a lot to do with how your home gains value. The fact that you can build equity by simply staying in place and paying your mortgage is why people call ownership a "forced savings plan," since the money you put in throughout the years comes back to you at the time of sale in a single, large chunk. Aside from a sizable down payment, if you invest to keep your home well maintained and up-to-date, it is more likely to hold or even gain value. But don't go overboard on remodeling just for the sake of returns.

◄ OLD MENTALITY

NEW MENTALITY ►

A mortgage is the bank's money— you can leverage it to work for you.

A mortgage is a form of debt. The more you borrow, the more you owe.

When people buy, they think of the home's price—say, $300,000—and then say to themselves, "I have a $300,000 condo!" But if they mortgaged the home (and the vast majority of buyers do), they don't have a $300,000 condo. They probably have a down payment's worth of condo—say, 10 percent of that $300,000 condo—and are making payments on the other 90 percent of it. Similarly, if that condo's value rises to $350,000, people tend to think, "I just made $50,000—now I can get my 'cash out' and use it." But if they do that, and the home's value retreats to $300,000 they've increased their debt. A home's value isn't a sure thing unless the homeowner has received an offer for that much. The moral of the story: Your mortgage is debt, and your equity is theoretical until the day you sell. As an exercise, replace the word *home* with the word *loan*. Being a loan owner is less glamorous than being a *homeowner*. The idea that there's *no place like loan* seems silly. But you get the point. Unless you own your home 100 percent, you're working on owning it.

CHAPTER 2

THE UNITED STATES OF HOMEOWNERSHIP

I Own, Therefore I Am

Having a safe place to live is important to any society, but in this country owning that place has been the historic goal. Asking which came first—Americans' hunger to own homes or policymakers' and banks' desire to find ways to feed it—leads to a circular debate. That's because in America, homeownership is an institution; and like all institutions—marriage, religion, business, government—others' emotions, values, and psychology about its importance run the gamut.

Homeownership fuels capitalism, and vice versa. In the wake of the real estate–related recession, the faith many Americans place in homeownership is under scrutiny, even among the most deeply converted. Have we come to expect too much from homeownership? Or is there a new way to look at housing that's more realistic, that reflects the needs of a changing society?

A HISTORY OF HOMEOWNERSHIP IN AMERICA

If you think the nation's fondness for ownership only recently reached crazy heights described as "Real Estate Lust,"[2.1] you're wrong: America has been deeply pro-ownership since the Founding Fathers' era. Whether granting pioneers land on which to set up the little house on the prairie, dispensing pro-ownership propaganda via the World War I–era "Own Your Own Home" campaign, or facilitating increasingly easy lending rules to make ownership evermore accessible in the 1930s and again in the 1990s, the American government and the American people have long embraced the feeling that ownership lends financial and emotional stability.

This American sentiment originates in Colonial times, and its overtones have shifted throughout the decades as America grew from a sprawling plot of land to an organized nation linked by a sophisticated transit system and bustling capitalist economy. Kenneth Jackson, writing in *Crabgrass Frontier,* his classic history of the rise of American suburbia, stated that in the nineteenth-century homeownership was an "anchor" against the instabilities of a growing urban society. While even then Americans were mobile, they still wanted to own homes.[2.2]

That feeling's still around today, writ large in the form of entire cable networks devoted to house hunting and interior decor, and in books like Meghan Daum's 2010 memoir *Life Would Be Perfect If I Lived in That House,* which recounts her relationship to real estate and homeownership in multiple cities.[2.3]

"What interests me is how people have used homes to express themselves. We all want to have a nest," says Daum. "If you own your home, you feel you own your own life."

What follows is by no means a complete history of homeownership in America; it's a partial glimpse into how the American psyche has come to consider ownership a key theme in the national narrative about success and fulfillment.

Declaration of Independence: Owning Sticks It to the Man

"The government has definitely had a role in promoting homeownership," says Robert Shiller, a Yale economist who studies housing markets. "We were founded and populated by emigrants who resented their former governments and their landlords, whom they associated with feudal society."

Land was seen as one of America's most valuable assets because land meant that settlers could build a home. Settlers wanted freedom in the form of property—and they were willing to work for it.[2.4] Thomas Jefferson, one of the authors of the Constitution, claimed that the so-called *yeoman farmer*—a land- and home-owning agrarian—was important to the national identity. Other founding fathers took a slightly different angle on ownership but agreed that, for Americans, owning land served as a literal and symbolic distinction between America and the Old World of life under feudalism.

Owning Makes You a True Citizen

As Americans made sense of the abundant property at their disposal, the colonies granted citizens who owned property more privileges—specifically, voting privileges—and set in motion a rhetorical loop that's still present in the case for homeownership today. Colonial laws required that voters have a certain amount of property (acreage) or assets (say, livestock). The big idea back then was that "freeholders" (or landowners) couldn't help but have a bigger stake in their community than renters because they paid property taxes and tended land. Therefore, they alone should get the vote. While suffrage laws (and, centuries later, mortgage-lending practices) eventually extended the vote (to renters) and broadened buying power to previously excluded groups—women, minorities—the idea of the owner as an "inevitably" superior citizen still persists.

O, Pioneers: Come and Get Free Land!

The abundance of land in America, the vast amount of frontier to settle, presented a new proposition to the country's settlers, many of whom came from a Europe developed in small, tightly packed cities. To drive home the message that America was the land of the free and the home of the brave, the government offered free land to those brave enough to go till, plant, and settle it.

The American Homestead Act of 1862 let American adults apply for ownership of large parcels of government land located outside the original thirteen colonies. Basically, if you improved upon it, stayed on it for at least five years, then filed for a deed, you had a decent—but not guaranteed—likelihood of gaining outright ownership in exchange for sweat equity. Historians might debate the success of this program, but if nothing else it glorified the notion of settling the frontier. "Go West, young man," is the phrase popularized in the 1860s.[2.5]

While not all homesteaders succeeded in earning their claims, the proposition was compelling—and the lore of the prairies and the West began. But farmland wasn't the only kind of land available in America. Advances in construction techniques and in transportation—street cars, trains, automobiles—meant that early suburbs began appearing around cities, offering a pastoral and even affordable appeal in contrast to crowded cities packed with tenements and apartment buildings. The idea of the single-family home as the place to raise a family was planted in this era.

Owning Is Democratic

Fast-forward to the early twentieth century, when ownership was linked to patriotism. Federal efforts at anticommunism messaging[2.6] included spin about how homeownership would prevent communism from reaching U.S. soil. And during the years immediately before and during World War I, homeownership was touted as a national virtue.

The U.S. Department of Labor as well as the National Association of Real Estate Boards both promoted homeownership through an "Own Your Own Home" campaign to encourage the virtues of the lifestyle. Ownership was masculinized (what men do to protect their families), feminized (what good mothers want for their kids), and popularized in newspapers, which ran essay contests about ownership as well as ads and coverage for low-cost building methods. Youngsters got flair—"We Own Our Own Home" pins.[2.7]

In 1922, the Better Homes in America movement swept the nation under President Warren Harding and Herbert Hoover, the future president who was then Secretary of Commerce. Encouraging affordable home construction and the virtues of homeownership and homemaking, the movement included week-long expos in multiple cities—as well as a demo home set up on the White House lawn. Hoover served on the advisory committee for the Better Homes movement and even authored an essay advancing the idea of "The Home as An Investment."

Historians and social observers acknowledge that homeownership was also designed to bring Americans into the so-called consumer class, since owners would have to shop for their homes and also pay their home loans.[2.8] Owning also made for obedient workers, because having a home loan to repay would give them a sense of corporate duty: Strikes and sloth would be less likely among people with a mortgage to pay and a home to maintain.[2.9]

Owning Is Government-Supported: Post-Depression Ownership

The Better Homes Movement and post–World War I patriotism helped spur growth in homeownership rates, which inched up from 45.6 percent in 1920 to about 48 percent in 1930. But the Great Depression dealt a blow to national morale and sent ownership rates back south again, as unemployed workers couldn't pay their mortgages and lost homes in foreclosure.

The government made several gestures to bolster the economy around the time of the Depression, such as forming the Home Owners' Loan Corporation to help consumers at risk of default to refinance and keep their homes. But two additional new organizations played a key role in making home buying easier and more affordable for future generations. First, the Federal Housing Administration (FHA) was formed in 1934 to provide insurance against homeowners defaulting on their mortgages. Second, the Federal National Mortgage Association (Fannie Mae) was formed in 1938 to provide financing so that lenders could make loans. These organizations are known as government-sponsored entities, or GSEs. (Freddie Mac, the other GSE, was formed in 1970. Freddie Mac's job is to facilitate lenders' ability to sell mortgage loans to outside investors, meaning lenders can maintain the proper finances to continue easily writing new loans.)

The FHA and Fannie were important for two reasons. First, prior to their formation, the typical home buyer had to front a 50 percent down payment to get into a home, and then he or she had to pay the rest of his or her loan off quickly, during a term of five or, at most, ten years. But with insurance against defaults now available, lenders relaxed their rules.[2.10] Soon, buyers could make 20 percent down payments and finance the remaining 80 percent of their home's purchase price—and do it during a twenty- or thirty-year period. This made buying much easier. Second, Fannie Mae's creation meant that lenders had a ready source of money to loan.

Ownership for All: The Post–World War II Boom

The GI Bill introduced under Franklin Delano Roosevelt was designed to spur economic activity and help returning vets score jobs, education, medical care, and—you guessed it—homes. Under the GI Bill, you could buy a home with 0 percent down using the Veterans Administration or VA loan program, still in existence. Meanwhile, builders such as Steven Levitt, developer of Long Island's Levittown neighborhood, created affordable suburban villages aimed at returning military. The typical Levittown home was about 750 square feet and cost about $6,990.[2.11]

Prior to World War II, the homeownership rate hadn't hovered above the mid-40 percent range, but between 1945 and 1950 it rose to 55 percent, and by 1960 it rose to 62 percent, as builders mass-produced middle-class housing. The United States had become a nation of owners, many of them living in suburbs and raising families (the "Baby Boom") during an era of prosperity, expansion, optimism. *It's a Wonderful Life*, the 1946 classic film produced by Frank Capra, showcased the virtues of homeownership for the common man, with hero George Bailey developing "Bailey Park" as an affordable place for working-class families to own—sidestepping the onerous rents of greedy local landlord Mr. Potter.

The Rise of Real Estate Lust: Bumping Ownership Levels Higher

Fast-forward to the 1990s. As the nation eased off a recession and the savings and loan industry banking crisis—which had catapulted mortgage interest rates to high double-digit levels—both Presidents George H. W. Bush and Bill Clinton expressed their intentions to grow the U.S. homeownership rate, especially among minorities. Clinton set "goal" percentages for Fannie Mae and Freddie Mac to fulfill under his National Homeownership Strategy, and the organizations responded by widening their view of acceptable lending standards yet again.[2.12]

After Clinton, George W. Bush took the pro-homeownership torch and ran with it, touting what he called his hope for an "ownership society." The government-related organizations created to support home buying allowed for more tweaks in lending criteria and rules to accommodate even more borrowers. But so, too, did nongovernment lenders who offered less-qualified buyers so-called subprime loans. It's a chicken-and-egg question whether the government, via the GSEs that insured against defaults (and, as such, outlined the criteria for loans they'd insure), or the rise of an entire cadre of new subprime lenders did more harm in encouraging looser lending standards.

As promotion of homeownership increased, and borrowing restrictions loosened, the homeownership rate rose. So did home values: Home prices rose 10 percent on an annualized basis each year between 1998 and 2005 (versus less than 2 percent annually in the prior seven years), according to Zillow. As home prices rose, buyers at all fiscal fitness levels got loans and some stretched, borrowing as much as possible to buy (or remodel) the most home they could—even if the loans they used were frighteningly funky—on the theory that home values would keep rising.

Investing in residential real estate by both amateur and established landlords came to account for nearly 20 percent of the market during the mid-2000s. Some investment-minded buyers, burned by stock portfolio losses related to the dot-com crash from 2000 to 2002, transferred the money they'd have kept in stocks into housing. People bought homes to flip—or hold for a short period of time before selling them to a higher bidder—and cashed out retirement accounts to invest in fixers, single-family homes, and small rental buildings,

WHAT'S A SUBPRIME LOAN?

Subprime loans are loans extended to people whose credit scores, debt levels, and other financial benchmarks used to determine loan-worthiness make them a higher loan risk. Typically, a subprime borrower must pay a higher interest rate or fluctuating interest rates—which can fluctuate to unaffordably high levels. During the late 1990s and 2000s, many lenders targeted subprime borrowers with new loan formats that, at first, offered compellingly low rates. In addition, less scrupulous mortgage brokers offered subprime loans to borrowers who qualified for less-risky loan products. On the one hand, these loans could let people with negative financial histories or improving financial lives get started on ownership, and in some cases the borrower could refinance out of them and into a better loan product. But on the other hand, borrowers who used these loans often found themselves in trouble later, or learned too late they had missed out on better options.

Subprime loans often included variable terms under an adjustable rate mortgage (ARM) structure, like initial low or "teaser" interest rates followed by rates that "reset" to new, higher levels the borrower often couldn't afford. During the boom, almost anyone could get a loan. There was the NINJA (no income no job no assets) loan, and the "stated income" loan (a.k.a., a "liar loan," frequently used by liars, investors, and self-employed people). You could get a pay-option loan, which let you choose what type of payment to make from one month to the next—just interest, for instance, if that suited your fancy—and the negative amortization loan, which actually increased your debt over time instead of the other way around.

aiming to make profit from rental revenue. The housing landscape had entered a cycle of easy loans, rising prices, more easy loans, and more rising prices— the definition, many began to say, of an unsustainable housing bubble.

The Twenty-first Century: Ownership Society?

Homeownership in America, which had held in the mid-60 percent range for decades, peaked in late 2004 at 69 percent. But eventually, home prices couldn't balloon any higher. In 2006 and 2007 they peaked in markets tracked by the Case-Shiller Index, which tracks home-price trends in major cities.

Around this time, the "subprime crisis" began unfolding. Buyers who had used adjustable-rate mortgages began facing resets to their mortgage payments that they couldn't afford, investors who had bought thinking they could sell at higher prices for profit couldn't, and buyers who had bought more home than they could afford also began confronting the downsides of homeownership. Foreclosures escalated, particularly in a cluster of high-speculation states including California, Florida, and Nevada, and in cities such as Phoenix.

Even owners who bought using traditional mortgages with more-predictable terms suffered, because home-value drops at the national and local level meant they suddenly owed more money on their home than it was worth. Between 2006 and 2010, the percentage of homeowners who owed more on their home mortgage than their home was worth on the market multiplied, rising from 5 percent of all mortgaged homes to 30 percent of all mortgaged homes, according to Celia Chen, an economist at Moody's Analytics. Some, assuming no price rebound and no other options, "walked away" (abandoning their homes to foreclosure). Others struggled to negotiate loan modifications directly with their lenders or government mediation organizations designed to curb foreclosure levels.

Some experts now argue that securitization—the ability for lenders to bundle mortgage loans and sell them as investments to Wall Street—helped contribute to poor lending standards. Since companies could collect fees for originating mortgages, yet not retain much risk once loans were sold off in a security, lending standards weren't properly policed.[2.13] Storied investment banks—Lehman Brothers, Bear Stearns—suffered losses from involvements in mortgage-related securities and were sold or bailed out by the government.

By 2009, the government had tripled the amount of money it normally spends on mortgage-related securities, all as part of a multiprong effort to help normalize financial markets damaged by the housing and related credit meltdown, which impacted consumer and corporate borrowing. The Federal Reserve balance sheet swelled to $2.3 trillion, a reflection of increased mortgage-related debt issued to rescue Fannie Mae and Freddie Mac, and to fund the Troubled Assets Relief Program (TARP), a government program that helps banks shed bad loans. Before the meltdown, government investment in such debt was about $800 billion, according to Robert Edelstein, a University of California, Berkeley, professor and cochair of the Fisher Center for Real Estate and Urban Economics there.

Not every market and not every homeowner was crippled by a wave of foreclosures. Many cities saw no "boom" in home pricing or housing speculation, and thus suffered little bust. But with rampant bank failures and the near-failure of default insurers Fannie Mae and Freddie Mac—government-sponsored entities rescued by government and now run as government-overseen entities—it's clear that the dream of pushing homeownership rates ever higher ignored several cold, hard, light-of-day realities. With consumers, banks, communities, and home values all suffering, the system's levers and pulleys had clearly jammed. The result is a reckoning that may unfold for several more years, till 2014 or 2016, depending on the expert consulted. Brookfield, Wisconsin-based Fiserv estimates, for instance, that many markets won't revisit 2006–2007 prices for a decade.[2.14] And after that, who knows?

ACROSS THE POND: NOT ALL NATIONS SHARE OUR JONES TO OWN

You'd think America, for all its support and sentimentality around homeownership, has one of the highest homeownership rates in the world. But actually, that's not so. The United States ranks seventeenth in homeownership levels among twenty-six developed nations, according to recent Senate economic testimony.

In some European countries (think Germany, where homeownership rates are below 50 percent), renting is far more the norm—even among the well heeled—and people devote money they'd direct to a mortgage elsewhere, like stocks. And in many places, especially Mediterranean countries, adulthood isn't synonymous with "striking out" on one's own, in a newly formed household. In Italy, Greece,

Spain, and Portugal, a high proportion of young adults live at home late into adulthood before striking out to form a separate household, owned or rented.[2.15]

Michael J. Lea, director of The Corky McMillin Center for Real Estate at San Diego State University, told a Senate banking committee that American home-ownership rates fall in the middle of 11 developed nations, but that in other countries there is "less intervention" by the government to support affordable owned housing. In comparison, in European nations and beyond there's more government support for affordable rental housing. The United States stands out in setting "goals" for ownership levels and is also among the few countries that allows tax deductions on mortgage interest. The process of securitization is also more dominant in America.[2.16]

Lea is an academic—and while popular culture debates in chat rooms and blogs whether homeownership means what it once did, a separate debate about homeownership's role in America is taking place in academic, political, and policy circles. It's a matter of philosophy: Some argue that the American government's involvement in encouraging (cynics might say "gaming") widespread homeowner-ship rates has reached past the tipping point of "supportive" and now falls some-where on the spectrum between "worth rethinking" and "dangerous" to society, like a lurking helicopter parent that hasn't prepared home-buying consumers the space to think for themselves. Even in the 1940s, when the homeownership rate was 50 percent lower than at present, observers were asking if the American system of home financing and the government role in it are prudent: *Home Ownership: Is It Sound?* written by Queens College professor John P. Dean in 1945, claimed ominously in closing that America is encouraging its consumers to "stride ahead through a field deliberately sown with booby traps."[2.17]

Others argue that the market simply needs a reset following a period of volatility. Karl Case, the Wellesley economist, suggested in a *New York Times* editorial that the American Dream isn't dead—it's just taking a "well-deserved rest."[2.18] Even NYU economist Nouriel "Dr. Doom" Roubini, who called the bubble before it happened, recently showed a faint sign of optimism about housing and the economy: He bought a Manhattan triplex in December 2010.[2.19]

UNITED STATES OF HOMEOWNERSHIP

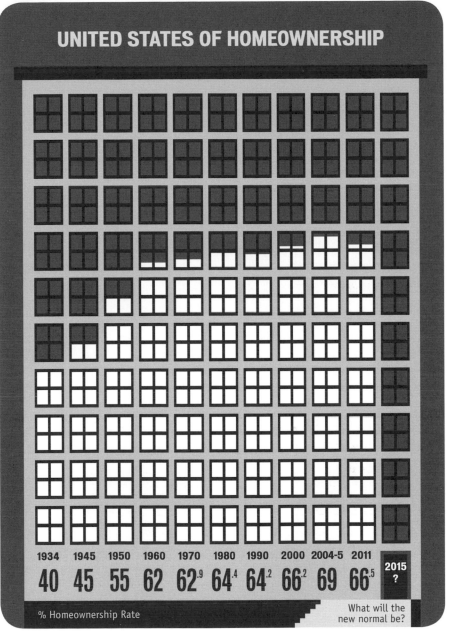

1934	1945	1950	1960	1970	1980	1990	2000	2004-5	2011	2015
40	45	55	62	62.9	64.4	64.2	66.2	69	66.5	?

% Homeownership Rate

What will the new normal be?

(Source: U.S. Census Data)

QUESTIONS TO CONSIDER

1. **What's your family housing history?** Did you grow up renting or owning, or both? What did it mean in your family when you moved from one rental to the next or one owned home to the next? What values did your parents and grandparents place on owning? Do you recall, as a child, knowing which of your relatives did and didn't own their homes? What were your early perceptions, if any, about their housing status?

2. **What's on your bucket list?** Is owning a home one of your life goals? Why? What does it mean to you to be an owner? Is it a financial achievement? Do you want to master your surroundings, or provide a certain type of environment for a future family?

3. **What's more important to you:** Living in a dozen cities and traveling to all the continents, or creating a nest and a community right in one zip code?

4. **How much home do you think a person really needs (whether rented or owned)?** Do kids need their own rooms? Do guests need a guest room or is a sofa okay? If you worked in a city, would you rather live in a smaller in-town space or a larger suburban abode that requires a commute? Why?

5. **What sorts of homes have you rented?** Do you think that renting is an interim-stage lifestyle, or a lifestyle in and of itself?

6. **Are you concerned about the environment?** Would you leave more or less carbon footprint in a home you rented or owned?

7. **Does owning a home make you more responsible as an adult, or should you consider buying only once you're capable of the responsibility?** Is renting the responsible choice given your life circumstances?

CHAPTER 3

TALK IS CHEAP; HOUSING IS EXPENSIVE

Reviving the Rhetoric

Mike, an engineer, bought a two-bedroom townhouse near New London, Connecticut, for $183,000 when he was twenty-four. He could easily afford his monthly housing payments, and his home was convenient to work. A few years after he bought, he renovated his basement and moved downstairs into it, then rented his two bedrooms to roommates. The extra income helped him fund a $35,000 graduate business degree without student loans—and, now that he's graduated, he's using rental income to help pay off his mortgage faster.

"I'm pretty positive about homeownership," Mike says. "For the most part, it's thumbs up."

If he has any regrets, though, they have to do with his home's location. New London is a seaside town with Yankee charm but with a decidedly settled-down feel. Mike, on the other hand, is a twenty-nine-year-old single guy who likes a little adventure and wouldn't mind more nightlife, access to a larger metro area, and access to an airport so he can travel more easily.

"I really didn't think about what I might be doing in five or ten years when I bought. I chose my place based partly on talks with my coworkers. I was the youngest guy in my workplace, and they were all in their forties and more settled down," he says. "If you listen to advice, though, you have to look at who's giving it."

When it comes to choosing housing, advice abounds. Mike was practical: He bought a home he could afford and that was near work. But he overlooked his personal life: Were the suggestions that forty-five-year-olds offered at the watercooler suitable for a recent college grad? Buying requires compromises. But if you want to avoid making mistakes, you need to understand the biases behind advice—solicited and not—available to you.

You can play with rent vs. buy calculators online, modeling different scenarios. But they're not exactly accountable, and they ask you to enter assumptions about variables even Nobel economists can't predict (like future home price appreciation) and life basics you haven't yet nailed down (like how long you'll live in your L.A. place before you get a job offer in NYC). The tools can be illustrative, but only if you understand the variables you're entering. For instance, if you're not aware that a realistic rate of home-value appreciation in your market is about 2 percent per year, you might assume that the 5 percent rate set as a default in an online tool is the norm. Or if you don't know your credit score and wrongly assume that it's top-shelf, the calculator might model a mortgage payment that's a few hundred dollars lower than your poor score would permit.

You can certainly ask the experts—real estate agents and mortgage lenders or brokers. But these are the folks who make commissions when you buy. While the good ones will counsel you on your timing, credit, budget, and expectations in the hopes that their honesty brings you back later, the ones who put their own interests first will usher you toward purchasing something—anything: a shoe box, a meth lab, a place you can't afford—and doing it now.

And while many parties are around to help you during the run-up to home-ownership, once you've bought, all those friendly, helpful people who held your hand as you took that big step will vanish—and you'll be left alone to manage both your property and your finances. None of these folks will think ahead for you; if you know that as soon as you move in you're going to quit a job or have a baby or face a major expense that didn't go into the loan workup, it's not their job to say, *Hey, maybe you're overstretching*. Indeed, it's no one's job but yours.

If you're the rare analytical breed who asks a financial advisor whether to rent or own, you may confront a harsh view of reality—or a very different view on how much (or little) you should pay for housing. While a loan officer's calculator may enable you to borrow three or four or five times your income to buy, depending on interest rates, advisors will rightly point out that if you plan to ever retire you probably shouldn't blow your budget on housing. Some may tell you owning is more like stashing money in a low-interest savings account than it is ascending the S&P 500. Of course, a home is more than an investment. But if you buy for emotional gains alone, investment gains may not follow. So here's most of the contemporary advice you're going to hear on the topic, who dishes it out, and why you can take it all with a grain of salt.

YOU SHOULD BUY!

1. *"Owning a Home Is Vital to the American Dream."*

WHO SAYS THIS: *real estate agents, advertising, research surveys, politicians, and lobbyists*

The phrase *The American Dream* was coined by James Truslow Adams, an author whose 1931 book, *The Epic of America*[3.1], discussed the dream in terms of the possibility of freedom and upward mobility. That dream has become associated with homeownership—and then with great wealth and procurement of possessions like cars and TVs. The American Dream, some cultural observers and historians argue, has become an excuse for Americans to overstretch financially, for the United States to live in a perpetual red it can't escape, and for people to buy not just more home than they can afford but more everything than they can afford.[3.2] Does owning a place, or borrowing to buy, make you an American? Comedian George Carlin put it this way: "It's called the 'American Dream' because you have to be asleep to believe in it."

2. *"Owning Your Home Is Always a Great Investment!"*

WHO SAYS THIS: *real estate agents and successful real estate investors*
Real estate agents make commissions off your transaction. Commissions vary by market and type of agent, but, generally speaking, when you buy a place your agent makes up to 3 percent. That means for every $100,000 you spend, your cheerleading agent could make $3,000. So, sure, real estate is a great investment—*for agents*. Your luck may vary, but not your agent's. And FYI, home values *fluctuate*. Yes, they generally rise over the long haul. During a hot market—think the mid-1990s to mid-2000s—real estate was a nice, stock-like investment even for short-term owners, and many armchair investors who did their homework made handsome money buying, selling, and renting out property. But in a normal market—one in which home prices appreciate at percentages in the low single digits—owning is a longer-term proposition if you want to exit with gains. In 2007, the typical home buyer expected to stay in his or her home for eight years, but as of 2010 the typical buyer plans to stay for a decade, according to National Association of Realtors[3.3] research. Will you stay a decade?

3. *"Homeownership Makes for Better Communities."*

WHO SAYS THIS: *real estate agents, research, and, indirectly, the government*
Some research indicates that homeowners are more likely to participate in civic activities, voting, volunteering, and community service. That may be true, but in today's entrepreneurial information age, homeownership can hamper community-building in one major respect: Job mobility and flexibility. Richard Florida, writing about the impacts of recession in *The Great Reset*,[3.4] cites research indicating that high rates of homeownership have presaged higher

rates of unemployment in some markets, because when a regional economy falters or experiences a wave of job loss, owners can't sell and, thus, can't move to where new jobs await. While ownership may allow for slow savings throughout a lifetime, it can also force owners to remain in communities or jobs they're best to leave. Do renters have more time to devote to entrepreneurial work and the mobility to snag the best gigs, while homeowners are stuck mulching and reading the want ads?

4. "You're Making a Good Living and Are a Grown-up, so You Should Own."

WHO SAYS THIS: *peers, pushy parents, that little voice inside of you*

The average first-time buyer in America is typically in his or her early thirties, according to Walt Molony, spokesman for the National Association of Realtors. Depending on your market and social set, as you hit the third decade your crew may pursue big-people things like finishing grad school, settling down with partners, climbing the career ladder, having kids—and, so logic dictates, buying homes. Just because you're a certain age or you're a doctor/lawyer/celebrity apprentice with a nice paycheck doesn't mean you s*hould* buy a place. Your income and financial position today may change tomorrow, expectedly (due to a job change, sudden debt, little mouths to feed) or not (for all those same reasons). Maybe you don't believe in owning and prefer to keep your funds invested elsewhere. That's fine! If you can't focus on the purchase, and can't predict what neighborhood would accommodate your needs, why buy because someone else deemed it *smart*?

5. "Owning a Home Is a Forced Savings Plan."

WHO SAYS THIS: *middle-class homeowners, creative types who want to use their home as an "asset"*

There's some merit to this argument: If you buy a home you can afford, maintain it properly (and/or invest in remodeling and repairs to sustain or boost its value), develop equity through either a big down payment or staying there a good, long while, and sell it in a normal market, you will likely make some money when you exit. That's an awful lot of "ifs," isn't it? William Wheaton, an MIT economics professor, puts it this way: Renters face small risks—of a rent increase—every twelve or twenty-four months at lease renewal. Owners face one big risk—how much their home is worth—just once, when they sell. Do you want to bet the financial farm on a future sale? And if you can't motivate to save money on your own, consider this: How will you put up thousands of dollars for a down payment, make a mortgage payment, and set aside funds for home maintenance and upkeep, not to mention other life emergencies?

6. *"Homeowners Get Special Tax Deductions and Perks."*

WHO SAYS THIS: *agents, mortgage lenders, accountants, the IRS*

Homeowners get a variety of tax deductions, including a deduction for their mortgage interest as well as for their property taxes. You can take deductions for matters as esoteric as your home office (a deduction available to renters, FYI) and, as of this writing, private mortgage insurance. You can get credits for adding "green" and energy-efficient improvements to your home, which could in turn reduce your energy bills, and occasionally the government will offer temporary tax credits to own, such as $8,000 credits extended to buyers during the soft housing market in 2009 and 2010. However, if deductions are your main motivator for buying a home, stop and think. Buying a home to get a tax break is like starting a family just so you can get the child tax credit. It's a mountain of responsibility for a foothill of fiscal advantage. As political leaders grapple with how to address the American economy, it's likely that some of these deductions will be reduced or even erased, especially for higher earners who, some research shows, are the folks most likely to use and benefit from them. By the way, taxes are a two-way street: If you make mad profit ($250,000 for singles, $500,000 for couples) selling, you need to pay capital gains taxes.

7. *"Home Prices Are Changing—Get in While You Can!"*

WHO SAYS THIS: *real estate agents, investors, friends and family, manic Zillow users*

Everyone's an amateur economist, right? If you're already interested in buying, watching prices start to rise or fall in your local market can motivate you to finally act, and that's legitimate. Who doesn't want to feel "smart," either getting a good deal before prices rise further or thinking like an investor and "buying on the dip" before they start rising again? Home prices rise and fall for complex reasons. But one gauge of whether you—and your neighbors—can really afford to buy is how much it costs to buy a home relative to how much most people earn. If median home prices exceed three times your area's gross median income level, that may be a sign that a market is becoming too expensive for buyers, according to the 2011 Demographia International Housing Affordability Survey.[3.5] According to the study's research methodology, when prices exceed five times your area's gross median income, that's a sign of a severe affordability problem—or a sign that you live in certain hot markets like the San Francisco Bay Area, New York, or Los Angeles.

8. *"Interest Rates Are Shifting! You Should Pounce!"*

WHO SAYS THIS: *mortgage lenders and brokers, real estate agents*
While it's true that low interest rates mean you'll spend less on interest when paying your mortgage—or can borrow a higher amount because the interest part of your monthly payment is lower—it's also true that low interest rates are often a sign of economic funkiness. Mortgage brokers and bank loan officers make nice commissions when you buy, no matter what the interest rate, and rates can change on a daily basis. Also, there are two kinds of interest rates: The "best-advertised" rates (i.e., if you have perfect credit and satisfy other criteria) and the "real" interest rates (i.e., add 0.25 percent to the rate here for imperfect credit, add 0.5 percent there because you're not making a down payment). Interest rates have been at historic lows since some time in the mid-1990s, meaning in the single digits. Are you actually getting more home (based on a low interest rate)—or are you getting *more loan*?

YOU SHOULD RENT!

1. *"You Need Your Flexibility—Don't Get Tied Down!"*

WHO SAYS THIS: *nervous significant others, envious friends, commitment-phobes*

It's true that many people rent. If you're in the early years of your career, new to the workforce, new to the country, or if you've got complicated financial circumstances (exiting a marriage, for instance) renting may be easier while you sort out your new landscape or if you're not sure how you'll want to live one or two years down the line. If you really wanted to own, though, you could make it work if you apply a little foresight. Many people who know their lives are in flux have valid reasons to own and don't mind the extra steps required to sublet their place while they're on that overseas assignment, to get roommates to make ends meet, or to simply take their chances once they've signed up for a mortgage. Some people even see owning as a way to create a foundation or structure for their lives, rather than an impediment to freedom. Do you think flexibility is over when you own?

2. *"You Can't Buy, You Don't Have Six, or Eight, or Twelve Months of Income Saved!"*

WHO SAYS THIS: *fiscal conservatives, financial advisors, your Depression-era grandparents*

Financial advisors—and your forebears—may have a point. If you had six months' salary parked in savings and no mortgage, you could invest some of it in stocks and park some of it in an interest-bearing savings account. While in an ideal world you could buy, invest, and save all at once, you may have to pick and choose your priorities as you balance the competing demands of adulthood. Who profits when you forego buying to beef up investing? Your money manager, who may make commissions on handling your money. If you can afford to buy a place, maintain it post-purchase, and continue to put money in a rainy-day fund as well as in retirement investments, then you're probably in decent shape. How much of a financial risk-taker—or nail-biter—are you?

3. "Renting Is Cheaper Than Owning, the Best Way to Start Out."

WHO SAYS THIS: *other renters who don't want to hear your home-shopping stories*
Renting isn't always cheaper than owning, not in some markets where either there's low rental inventory or a glut of cheap for-sale homes. Rents rise and fall with the economy and the local employment picture, so each time you renew your lease you may pay a little more—and, depending on local laws, how much more can vary. Builders in denser downtowns are increasingly finding creative ways to make ownership more affordable—either through smaller-footprint or pick-from-a-range-of-finishes spaces. If you can afford a place on your own but want to soften the monthly housing expense, you can get a roommate. (Beware, though, that if he or she vanishes you're still responsible for the lease.) Another option: Co-buying a place with a friend, partner, or family member can also offer a cheaper monthly payment than renting—albeit with maintenance responsibilities. With co-buyers, there will be added complications—such as choosing how to take title (or structure the ownership) and making legal agreements about how you and the other party or parties can exit the investment. Can you handle planning ahead and the paperwork?

4. "You're Single. What if You Meet Someone?"

WHO SAYS THIS: *girlie girls, guys who think you buy when you get married*
Ladies, conservative Aunt Millie and your sorority sisters from Delta Sorta Silly need to get with the times. Single women have been buying at a faster clip than any other demographic during the past twenty years. Meet someone? Move 'em in, move out and sublet, or sell. Sure, you can also rent and meet a partner. But don't forego owning just because you're single.

The other argument bandied around about women home buyers is that, because women historically earn less money than men, they're more likely to be at-risk borrowers. Research shows that women opt for more stable and conservative mortgages, though, meaning they're safeguarding their money in that regard. Guys, anecdotally it appears you're more likely to view real estate as either an investment (a place you can flip, or where roommates can help you pay off the mortgage) or as a thing you do when you marry (a place that makes the spouse happy, but maybe isn't such an investment anymore). You know what? You're allowed to enjoy your bachelor pad—owned or rented—simply for the quality of life it gives you. Does housing carve your relationship status in stone?

5. *"The Apocalypse Is Nigh! Greedy Capitalists and Homeowners Pay!"*

WHO SAYS THIS: *the stoned guy at the organic co-op, people who obsess about politics*

Everyone has that underemployed Doomsday friend who fancies himself "global," smokes some dope, reads the alt-weeklies, and says that American capitalists (read: the employed) and the real estate and stock markets are a giant conspiracy scheme. But eventually everyone starts screening his calls. Alternatively, people who talk politics incessantly tend to wax on about homeownership and the government—granted, with some reason. Still, if you want to live in an owned home, can afford it, expect to be able to afford it in the future, and will enjoy it for years to come, there's no reason to forego these joys because the neighborhood crank or the punchbowl politician thinks you're bowing to convention. How guilt-prone and paranoid are you?

6. *"You? You Definitely Can't Handle the Work."* Or: *"I Don't Miss the Yard AT ALL."*

WHO SAYS THIS: *exhausted homeowners, people who think you can't operate a weed whacker*

Renting's biggest advocates are often former owners. They rush back to renting as if to a lover's embrace, relieved and ecstatic to regain a landlord who'll resolve their domestic problems. But dig below the surface and you'll realize that many owners who go reactionary on owning are really lamenting the particular property they chose to purchase, the financing they used to buy, or their own lack of realism about maintenance tasks and costs. If you expect the unexpected and have the savings and willingness to learn a few new things, homeownership's learning curve isn't insurmountable. If you're nervous about upkeep, you can buy a condo or a newer or yard-free place that lets you sidestep "old house" or landscaping challenges. Also, renting isn't entirely maintenance-free: Ding the walls and spill a little coffee on the carpet, and it comes out of your security deposit. And hiking to your parking spot or doing coin-op laundry in the basement of your complex during "laundry room hours" can be inconvenient. How handy and flexible are you?

7. *"Renting Is the Only Option if Your Credit Sucks."*

WHO SAYS THIS: *people familiar with your rubber checks, black-and-white mortgage calculators*

What's considered a "hot" or "not" credit score varies from one minute to the next. While scores below 600 are pretty much always bad and scores in the mid-700s and north are always great, when you score in the 600s or low 700s the bell curve moves around a bit on what's considered doable for lending purposes. For the real scoop, ask a mortgage lender how your scores will impact loan options. If they're low, you may be able to get a loan but at a higher interest rate. If you're confident you can improve your score and refinance to a better loan later, this may be an option. You might be able to get a guarantor. If you're buying with a partner, it's possible that his or her credit will qualify for the loan and you could make separate arrangements—a legal transfer of shared ownership from him or her to you—later. If your score is abysmal, you could "rent to own" a property. In this scenario, a landlord gives you the option to buy at the end of the lease. These are all complicated options, but they refute the myth that you have none. What makes more sense—waiting and fixing credit, or fixing credit while you own?

8. *"Renters Are Healthier and Happier Than Owners."*

WHO SAYS THIS: *academic research, homeowner haters*

Strangely enough, a recently published Wharton School study reveals that the image of homeowners as happy, more civically involved citizens isn't necessarily true.[3.6] While owners may regard their neighborhood more favorably than renters, they also spend less time with friends and also weigh more. It's not surprising: Owning can be stressful—if you let it, or if you buy more home than you can manage. However, keep in mind that most owners band together in a kind of virtual and backyard fence brotherhood, sharing tools, tips, names of handy hires, and giving each other advice on everything from getting rid of gophers to how to nix that dog smell in the ducts. Can you at least talk to your neighbors?

O━

READING THE REAL ESTATE NEWS

There's another source of advice you'll have to interpret: Blogs and the news. You can't hit the Internet or turn on the radio without seeing or hearing updates about the stock market, the economy, and major "indicators" of the nation's fiscal health—like information on geeky stuff such as housing starts (code for new construction), housing supply, monthly home sales data, the homeownership rate, and so on. But even if you're not trading real estate stocks, or your own local real estate market doesn't seem topsy-turvy with foreclosures or ghost-town subdivisions abandoned by bankrupt builders, does any of this matter? In a word: Yes. While it's true that real estate is local, what's happening nationally may eventually wend its way into your local market, so even if your city follows different cycles than other cities, you still need to understand how the national real estate market is behaving in addition to benchmarking your own market.

Many people considering buying follow home prices in their market, which are typically published on a regular basis (monthly) by the local multiple listing service or released via regional real estate organizations. Price trends are valuable and can help illuminate a market or particular neighborhood that's promising, but they're not the whole story. Interest rate trends are also telling: When rates inch lower, buyers can borrow more and may finally get into the market. Conversely, if rates suddenly start inching north, buyers may pounce while they can or back off their goal to own.

If you're trying to benchmark the overall health of the national or a local market, Zillow Chief Economist Stan Humphries recommends that you follow and also learn to understand these metrics and how they're trending—and then become aware of how they're spun by economists, agents, and media reports.

National Housing Supply or "Monthly Inventory" Level

WHAT THIS TELLS YOU: *whether there are enough (or too many homes) to fulfill consumer demand*

National and local housing inventory is expressed in months' worth of inventory. Basically, this is the total number of homes for sale in a given month divided by the number of home sales completed during the prior month. The result is a number representing how many months it would take to "clear" those homes through sales.

3 months or less
It's a tight housing market, with little supply and competition to buy.

3–6 months
This is a balanced market. Enough supply for buyers, but not an oversupply.

6 months or more
It's a slack housing market, with oversupply and competition to sell.

Days-on-Market Data

WHAT THIS TELLS YOU: *how long it takes to sell a home nationally and locally*

Data about "days on market" can tell you which neighborhoods are hot or not, and can also reveal how your market functions versus others in your state or in the nation. Keep in mind that your local market may have norms different from the national numbers that follow, so once you learn them watch for a quickening or slackening pace in your market. In general, it takes about thirty days for a home's sale to close after an offer has been made. The lower (or closer to thirty) the days on market, the faster homes are selling. The higher the days on market, the slower they're selling. It's important to benchmark local data regarding days on market. Some markets (resort towns, smaller communities) may move slowly all the time, yet hold their price levels. Other markets may move quickly because of local incentives or employment trends, but revert back to more balanced numbers in the next quarter.

45 days or less
The market is brisk, good for sellers but competitive for buyers.

45–90 days
The market is balanced, with push-pull between buyers and sellers.

90 or more days
There is housing oversupply, bad for sellers but good for buyers.

100 or more days
The market is incredibly slow, tough for everyone.

Rent Vacancy and Prices
WHAT THIS TELLS YOU: *whether it is a renter's or landlord's market*
Vacancy rates—how much rental housing sits empty—provide a lens into how landlords will behave toward their clients. *High vacancy* means landlords may cut deals or offer more for the money via "concessions" (free parking, extra amenities, one month free on a twelve-month lease, etc.) and *low vacancy* means you may compete or pay more for rentals. Mark Obrinsky, chief economist at the National Multi Housing Council, says that the national market's vacancy figures indicate the following:

4 percent or less
This is a landlords' market. Renters pay a premium for hard-to-get units.

4–6 percent vacancy

This is a fairly balanced rental market.

6 percent or higher

This is a renters' market. Renters can get deals and incentives.

On a local level, however, Obrinsky says that vacancy benchmarks can vary, so it's important to learn your market's norms and watch for changes. A 4 percent vacancy level in New York or San Francisco is very high, while in Atlanta a 6 percent vacancy level isn't a big deal, he says.

The "Price-to-Rent Ratio"

WHAT THIS TELLS YOU: *whether it is cheaper to rent or own the same property in your market*

This old-school census bureau formula reveals the relative price of renting vs. owning in a market. If rent prices are rising faster than for-sale prices, fence-sitters might opt to buy—but if prices to own are rising faster than rents, it suggests renting may be more sensible. Price-to-rent data is available from the census bureau and may wind up in your local news. It's calculated by taking a property's list price (the "price to own") and dividing it by twelve months' rent on a similar property. It's important to look at how the ratio trends (are ratios rising or falling?) to get the nature of a market. Here's how responses are often interpreted:

15 or below

It's inexpensive to own relative to renting.

15 to 20

You can make the case for either option, so also consider other factors.

20 or higher

It's more expensive to own than rent here.

FOR EXAMPLE: *If a two-bedroom condo costs $240,000, and a two-bedroom apartment rents for $12,000 per year ($1,000 per month), the ratio would be 20, meaning owning is a bit expensive. If the rent rises to, say, $16,000 per year ($1,450 per month), then the ratio would be 15, which makes the case to own look better.*

CHAPTER 4

WHAT KIND OF INVESTMENT IS A HOME?

Financial vs. Emotional Rewards

Bill Valentine, a certified financial advisor in the affluent resort town of Bend, Oregon, bought a house with his wife in 2000 for $235,000. But as investor speculation descended on his small city—at one point in 2005 a local developer told him that one third of all home sales in a new subdivision had sold to out-of-town investors—he got an uneasy feeling about where his local market was headed. Homes on his street were selling for multiples of what they were worth just a few years earlier. What if he sold, got out while he was ahead, and did something else with his cash?

There was just one problem: His wife liked the house and the neighborhood, and the couple didn't want to disrupt their kids' lives. So in 2006, he tried a different approach to see if he could have his equity and a place he liked living, too: He put his home on the market for $699,000—a price resembling what similar homes in his neighborhood were fetching—and sought an investment-minded seller who would buy his house and then lease it back to him for two years.

He got no takers—but an abundance of local press. By looking to get out of his mortgage, yet not move out, he was essentially calling Bend an overheated market. His story, however, illustrates that a home, while an investment, also has an emotional, sentimental value. As an investment, he'd grown uncomfortable with his home's unsustainable value. Yet he and his wife liked living there and knew finding a comparable rental in their neighborhood was unlikely. In the end, the family stayed and the home's value dropped back down to Earth—to the mid-$300,000s range in 2011. He doesn't have any regrets about not "selling high." After all, a home isn't a stock. But in an ideal world, a home provides both personal and financial shelter.

"How much value do you assign to a home as an investment versus a sentimental purchase?" Valentine asks. "That's where there's a disconnect for the average consumer."

INVESTMENT VS. SENTIMENT

If you're even thinking about buying, eventually the idea that your home isn't just a great place to live, *but also a great investment,* crops up. It sounds too good to be true: Something you want to buy (a home) might be *good for you financially*? Many people use their vague understanding of a home's financial benefits or the extent of those benefits to justify overbuying. And some research shows that owners over age fifty, the demographic nearing retirement, and most likely to need their equity to pay for it, typically overestimate their home's value by an average of 5 to 10 percent.[4.1]

What do you get from housing? Renters know what they're getting: They get the space between four walls, at a certain price, for a certain amount of time. Renters don't get any direct investment benefit from their property, unless of course rent is so cheap relative to owning that they can add extra money to their investment portfolios. According to the most recent American Housing Survey from the U.S. Census Bureau and U.S. Department of Housing and Urban Development, median monthly rent in America is $808, almost 20 percent less than the $1,000 per month owners pay on their mortgage. Renters typically spend more of their monthly income (31 percent) on housing than do owners (20 percent), the survey notes, meaning using the rent "savings" to invest may be hard for some.[4.2]

But owners get both emotional satisfaction as well as an investment. They can also pat themselves on the back when they read statistics about the fact that they have a higher net worth than renters: Owners' worth has ranged from 31 to 46 times that of renters between 1998 and 2010, according to analysis of the Federal Reserve's Survey of Consumer Finances by the National Association of Realtors, which currently pegs owners' net worth at 41 times that of renters—$200,000 or so, versus the renter's ballpark $5,000.[4.3]

But it's hard to deduce whether owners are wealthier *because* they own, because owning made them behave differently as investors (i.e., saving more because they're responsible for home upkeep or because a fixed-rate mortgage makes for predictable housing payments), or because owners tend to be older than renters and are thus going to have higher net worth simply by virtue of having been in the workforce longer. Some 31.7 percent of all owned homes are owned outright, with no mortgage.[4.4] Often, such owners are older and have paid on a mortgage for decades. Many renters, however, tend to be young people who may be establishing themselves financially. Does renting make them worth less, or is it youth?

HOME AS ASSET: ILLIQUID AND EXPENSIVE

A home-as-investment is different from the basic securities—stocks, mutual funds, exchange-traded funds—that the typical consumer buys for his or her retirement or other long-term savings accounts. While you probably think of a home as a personal nest, your special place to live, follow along: This discussion is meant to separate out the investment case so you can set realistic expectations for what a home contributes financially.

Real estate is an illiquid asset—one that is not easy to exit or convert to cash. You can sell stocks and mutual funds swiftly, and it's easy to withdraw cash you've parked in a money market or savings account. You can also exit a rental home relatively quickly, paying to end a lease early, subletting it, or switching to a month-to-month routine that allows escape on short notice. But buying and selling can each take a few months.

A home's illiquidity may seem obvious: When you buy you own a building on a hunk of land, or a unit within a large building. It's certainly more complicated to sell a home than to log on to your online brokerage account and move some money around. But there's another layer to the illiquidity factor: Financing a home buy is expensive. This means if you don't stay in the home for a decent length of time, the fees to buy and sell it will cut deeply into whatever financial benefits owning has bestowed. Aside from the down payment, when you buy you'll probably pay 3 to 6 percent of the asset's cost in closing fees,[4.5] and when you sell you typically pay anywhere from 6 to 10 percent of its cost in fees. Other investments come with minor transaction trade or management fees, depending on whether you hire a pro to advise and handle trades or use low-fee online services.

And to the extent you can compare a home's behavior to a stock's, it performs positively, but not necessarily as well. Generally speaking, homes in America have risen in value during long periods of time. Home values rose from the mid-1970s to the mid-2000s, offering a 6 percent rate of return each year from 1978 to 2008, according to research by economists Jack Clark Francis and Roger Ibbotson. However, these researchers pointed out that top-shelf stocks in the S&P 500 during that period had annual returns of 11 percent.[4.6] Measure returns during smaller or different time frames and the comparisons vary. But if you're looking long-term, the data suggests that owning real estate and owning stocks can both pay off. Owning real estate, however, offers the benefit of not having to pay rent.

HOME VS. MUTUAL FUND

For the sake of argument, pretend you inherited $200,000 and had to decide whether to invest it all in stocks or all in real estate. What would happen to your money? Here's a hypothetical look.

WHAT IF YOU PUT $200,000 IN A MUTUAL FUND AND HELD IT TEN YEARS? (YOU COULD MAKE $30,764 OR MORE.)

You'd pay 7 basis points (0.07 percent) in management fees, or $140. The cost of the trade is $10. In ten years you'd pay $1,400 in management fees and $20 in trade fees ($10 to buy, $10 to sell), and you would get dividend income. An annual dividend of 2 percent, even if the fund's share price declines or doesn't change, would mean $4,000 per year—or $40,000 during ten years. This means that your $200,000 plus $40,000 equals $240,000. If the price of the shares remains the same, you'd have that $240,000 minus $1,420 for management/trade fees, or $238,580 at the end of ten years. You'd likely pay state and/or capital gains tax of up to 20 percent on this $38,580 gain, leaving you with a minimum of $30,764.

WHAT IF YOU BOUGHT A $200,000 HOME OUTRIGHT AND HELD IT TEN YEARS? (YOU COULD MAKE $25,000 TO $37,000.)

Assume you'd pay up to $5,000 in fees to make a mortgage-free purchase. For maintenance, you'd pay about 2 percent annually, or $4,000, which during ten years is $40,000. Selling the home costs about 10 percent (agent fees, repairs, excise taxes, etc.), or $20,000. If the home doesn't rise in value, the $200,000 investment, minus maintenance and sale-related fees turns into $135,000. The home's value would have to rise between 50 percent and 60 percent during the ten-year period—in the single digits on an annualized basis, which is possible based on historic data—to where it's worth $300,000 to $320,000 to provide a result resembling the fund's. (These final values adjusted for maintenance and fees to buy and sell would produce $25,000 to $37,000 worth of post-sale profit.)

It may look initially like the mutual fund is a slam dunk, since it provides dividends even if the fund share prices don't rise in value (and if they did, you could make much more than that $30,000). But if you had this money and chose to invest it in the mutual fund rather than buy the home, you'd still have to pay for rent—and your rent would likely rise gradually during the decade.

If you bought a home, however, your "investment gains" are lower but your living space is included in your monthly payment. If you bought a home and it didn't rise in value, and you wound up exiting with $135,000, the $65,000 you "lost" on your initial investment (due to maintenance spending and the costs to buy and then sell the home) isn't that much if you look at it as a decade's worth of rent averaging $541 (plus utilities) per month. If you sold the home at the profits modeled in the example, walking with a few tens of thousands of dollars, and converted the roughly $75,000 paid for maintenance and purchase/sale fees into a monthly rent, you paid about $625 per month (plus utilities) and exited with some change.

REAL ESTATE: A LEVERAGED INVESTMENT

When you buy a home using a mortgage, you're making a leveraged investment. A leveraged investment is one whereby you borrow money to make an investment, and in so doing amplify your risk. Say you put 20 percent down on the home's asking price and then borrow the rest. If the home's value rises, your benefit rises—that's because borrowing let you buy more home than you could afford using your initial resources (whatever that 20 percent was). But if the home's value falls, your benefit may too—and it's possible to lose not only your initial investment but also some or all of the funds you borrowed as well.

Say you buy a $500,000 home using a 20 percent down payment (or $100,000), and borrow the remaining 80 percent (or $400,000). If the home rises in value and you want to sell, you keep the difference between the higher-sale value and what you owe on your mortgage loan (after subtracting sales-related fees). But if the home in this example falls in value—say, to $300,000—and you want to sell it, you're still obligated to pay both sale-related fees and the $400,000 you borrowed to buy. If the home fell to $0, you could lose both your $100,000 investment and the remaining $400,000 you borrowed. While it's unlikely any home would fall in value to $0, you get the point: With leverage, it's possible to lose more than your initial investment (here, $100,000).

Unlike a home, most stocks and mutual funds are not leveraged investments: When you pay $50 for a share, you own 100 percent of that share. If the value rises, you benefit. If the value falls, you lose. But unlike a leveraged purchase, *you can't lose more than your original investment amount*. (A caveat: It is possible to make leveraged purchases of stocks and funds using strategies such as buying them "on margin" from a brokerage, and you can lose more than invested if you "short" a stock, making bets against its price behavior. But these are strategies you'd have to pursue, not scenarios you'd unknowingly encounter.)

The expectation that home values rise over time motivates many people to stretch to get into the best address they can afford. Many buyers reason that the more you borrow, the more you can possibly gain. In theory, this is true. Additionally, purchasing a home is costly in terms of fees, so some buyers reason that it's wise to buy as much home as possible rather than risk outgrowing a smaller, cheaper place and paying fees again to "move up" within just a few years.

In the Great Recession, the fact that home values fell precipitously after several years of gains showed lots of surprised buyers—particularly those in high-speculation markets who bought during the Boom, or who used loans they couldn't refinance—the downside of leverage. Leverage isn't always bad: If you have access to low-interest home equity and use it to pay off higher-interest debt, that's smart. But if you use it to beget more leverage and lack the sophistication to manage the related risk, that's dangerous. When people pursue loan modifications so their principal—or loan amount outstanding—is lowered, they are in essence trying to get out of the leverage they signed up for when they bought. This is the basis for much moral hand-wringing over personal responsibility for understanding mortgage products and housing-related risks.

THE TAX FACTOR

Taxes are a major issue for investors. If you can trim the taxes related to your investments or your profits from your investments, you keep more of your gains. (This is why the Roth IRA was invented—so investors can pay taxes on contributions upfront, but forego taxes on the future, higher balance they withdraw during retirement.) Renters don't get tax benefits related to their housing. But homeowners can tap several tax benefits that relate both directly and indirectly to the investment case for ownership. The biggies include the following:

- **Capital gains exemptions**[4.7]: When you sell a home or an investment at a profit, you are supposed to pay capital gains taxes on the profit. When you sell securities (stocks, mutual funds), you pay steep capital gains if they're held less than a year and varying rates if you've held them longer. When you sell a home you've lived in for two of the past five years, you can pocket a substantial amount of profit tax-free before capital gains kick in: You're exempt from capital gains tax on the first $250,000 (if single) or first $500,000 (if coupled) of profit on the property. You only pay capital gains on the amount above those thresholds. For many, this makes a home a compelling investment.

- **Mortgage interest deduction**[4.8]: If your home is mortgaged, you can deduct mortgage interest. The interest you pay on your mortgage each month doesn't contribute to your equity in your property. However, to soften the blow, Uncle Sam lets you deduct it. How much you can deduct varies by tax bracket and how you file and, of course, mortgage amount. The IRS indicates that in *most* cases you can deduct all of your mortgage interest. It's a definite discount on owning, but no freebie.

- **Mortgage interest deduction on home equity/second mortgages**: The mortgage interest deduction applies to home equity debt, too, so if you've borrowed against your home the interest you pay is deductible up to $100,000. This is a significant perk on two fronts: Not only are home equity–related lines lower interest than traditional lines of credit, but they have the added benefit of tax deductibility. (Interest on non-equity linked lines of credit, such as consumer credit cards, ceased to be deductible as of 1986.)

- **Other tax benefits**: Property taxes are deductible. Private mortgage insurance (charged to borrowers who make less than a 20 percent down payment) is temporarily tax deductible, though the future of its deductibility is uncertain. Owners may also be eligible for tax credits for making energy efficiency-related home improvements.

HOW MUCH HOME? HOW MUCH INVESTMENT?

Depending on your current and potential financial situation, real estate and financial professionals may discuss different rationales for how to regard your home as an asset within your overall financial picture. Here are some of the themes you may hear:

1. *Owning a Home Is a Forced Savings Plan!*

Edith, a retired teacher in New York City, has had a good life. But to her daughter-in-law Lisa, one aspect of Edith's life serves as a cautionary tale: Edith never bought a home.

"My poor mother-in-law is facing retirement, and even with a below-market rent, she can't really afford to stay in the apartment she has lived in for fifty years. I find that really sad. She gets no equity or security out of paying rent for *fifty years*," Lisa says. "But her best friend bought an apartment when her building became a co-op in the 1970s. She can sell her place and take the money and do with it whatever she wants. I find this story kind of tragic; my mother-in-law would have something to sell if and when she needed to move to assisted living or a place in Florida."

Historically, the investment argument against renting goes something along the lines of Lisa's story: When you write a check to the landlord, you are throwing your money away from an investment perspective. This argument claims that when you write a check to your mortgage lender, you are in essence writing a check to yourself, since when you eventually pay off the mortgage you'll be able to live rent-free. (You'll still owe property taxes, utilities, and maintenance, but zip to the mortgage company.) Or if you choose to sell a home you've lived in a long time, you'll likely get a healthy chunk of post-sale profit—and, depending on your local market and how long you stayed, the amount can be sizable, possibly years' worth of household income.

What about renters who stay somewhere awhile? According to "forced savings plan" logic, if you're a lifelong renter when you reach your senior years you won't own your home outright, thus haven't "fixed" your housing costs. This means that during the part of life when your income drops you'll still need to come up with funds to pay for market-rate housing (unless you qualify for cheaper, assisted living or live in a property where rent is capped at below-market prices). In addition, opting out of owning means you don't ever get any money back in the form of a sale-related mini-windfall.

Supporters of the argument that a home is a forced savings plan often note that Americans are terrible at saving, so if their housing payment has a future investment or savings function, it's a good thing—even if the savings rate is modest. You have to pay someone each month for housing anyway, this thinking goes, so if you're going to write a check you might as well make it out to a mortgage lender.

Forced savings plan detractors, however, argue that renters—especially those whose monthly payments are lower than the mortgage payment on an equivalent property—may have more disposable income to invest in non–real estate assets. This means renters could save their way to the nest egg that owners supposedly get from their forced savings plan, thus building future funds to pay future rent. In addition, local markets and life circumstances (job security, etc.) play a big role in which decision makes more sense.

2. *Homeownership Produces Dividends.*

If you found a home you loved and had the option to rent it or own it, which choice would make the most financial sense? Two economists suggest that you consider calculating the potential "dividend" that owning delivers versus renting. To follow along, you'll need to find some figures and do some math, but this is, after all, a financial decision.

"A lot of people just look at the monthly payment to rent versus the monthly payment to own, and compare the two," says Gary Smith, an economist who coauthored the book *Houseonomics*[4.9] with his partner, Margaret Smith, an economist and investment advisor. "They forget that what it costs to rent will be higher five or ten years from now than what it will cost to own with a fixed-rate mortgage."

So if as an owner you can see financial benefits—a specific numerical dividend—from the outset, you can justify owning from a financial perspective. The duo's research, originally conducted for the Brookings Institution, presents a formula that prospective buyers can use to find out if the home they're eyeing provides an actual "return" compared to renting the equivalent property.

The *Houseonomics* model does make a handful of assumptions. It assumes, for instance, that you plan to stay in your home awhile (say, a good five years or so) in order to justify the costs to buy and sell the property; these costs aren't used in the home dividend formula. It assumes that you're in a fixed-rate mortgage so your monthly payment won't rise as precipitously as renters' payments at like properties. The formula also compares renting and owning the same property, which not all consumers would do if given that choice: Some renters deliberately spend below their means to save money (or save for a down), and many buyers choose a place nicer than what they've rented because owning offers investment promise. But by comparing renting and owning equivalent properties, the formula lets you look objectively at your housing options from a financial point of view.

Ideally, the dividend is positive, meaning this is how much money you'd save, adjusted for the financial benefits of owning. Compare your investment, that is, your down payment ($55,000), to this first dividend, and you can see

DOES YOUR HOME OFFER DIVIDENDS?

HOME DIVIDEND

1 YEAR'S RENT	**+**	TAX DEDUCTIONS APPLICABLE TO YOU FOR OWNING	**−**	1 YEAR'S MORTGAGE PAYMENTS

−	ANNUAL PROPERTY TAX	**−**	HOMEOWNER'S INSURANCE	**−**	MAINTENANCE (assume 1 percent of purchase price, or model more as you like)

= YOUR DIVIDEND

FOR EXAMPLE, DOING THE MATH ON A HOME IN

AUSTIN, TEXAS:

A four-bedroom, two-bath ranch-style home listed for **$275,000** and with **$6,100** in annual property taxes. For dividend purposes, should you rent it (at **$1,811**/month, according to Zillow.com) or buy it with 20 percent down and a 5 percent thirty-year fixed loan?

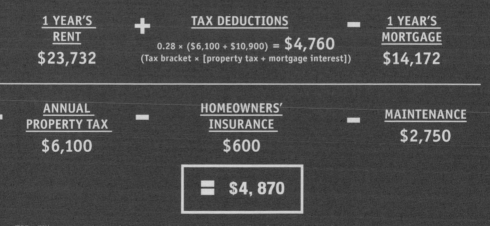

1 YEAR'S RENT	**+**	TAX DEDUCTIONS	**−**	1 YEAR'S MORTGAGE
$23,732		$0.28 \times (\$6,100 + \$10,900) = $ **$4,760** (Tax bracket × [property tax + mortgage interest])		**$14,172**

−	ANNUAL PROPERTY TAX	**−**	HOMEOWNERS' INSURANCE	**−**	MAINTENANCE
	$6,100		**$600**		**$2,750**

= $4,870

TIP: *Zillow.com, the real estate portal and data site, lists both rental and mortgage payment estimates for properties on its site, which you can use if you're stumped on how to find out what the rent price would be on a home similar to one for sale. To figure out how much of your mortgage payment is interest in your first year in a home, visit www.amortization-calc.com. And to figure out your tax bracket, visit the IRS (www.irs.gov). Generally, your multiplier will be 0.25, 0.28, or 0.33.*[4.10] how your $4,870 dividend is like an investment return (here, it's 8.9 percent). This return is a "dividend" because you can (ideally) reinvest it elsewhere—in an interest-bearing savings account, in stocks or funds—and you'd not only have your "rent" covered but your home would provide you with a source of wealth.

3. *Your Home Is an Investment, but It Shouldn't Be Your Only Investment.*

They say a home is the biggest investment you'll ever make. That's true for two reasons: First, that's because it's leveraged and a mortgage is about the only leveraged purchase you can make as a consumer. Second, if you overinvest in your home then you won't have any money left to invest in other types of assets because you'll be "house poor"—meaning your home will be your only investment because you overspent on it. If you subscribe to the theory that a home is a forced savings plan, this may not worry you much.

But it probably should. The interest rate or "investment return" you get from a savings account (or a savings-like rate of return) will be lower than that you get on other types of investments. As the recent real estate downturn demonstrated, one of the basic tenets of investing is that you shouldn't put all your money into one kind of investment. When you buy stocks or mutual funds, you typically build a portfolio that includes assets from different industries, nations, and company sizes (small, medium, monolithic); even if you don't know what you're doing, and you pick and choose from an employer's 401(k) menu, you'll likely hunt and peck your way to a mix of diverse asset types that your company's plan manager has chosen for you.

So if you agree with the idea that a home shouldn't be your only investment, then if or when you buy a home, that means you need to choose one that's sufficiently affordable so you've got money left to fund your retirement accounts and other expenses. While many home buyers are tempted to use leverage to the fullest and buy as much home as their lender will allow, another school of thought cautions that if you want to own a home but also retire comfortably, you need to curb your real estate enthusiasm and spend less on housing so that you can also invest elsewhere.

Charles Farrell, a financial advisor with Northstar Investment Advisors in Denver, writes in *Your Money Ratios*[4.11], his retirement savings book, that home buyers should *never* have outstanding mortgage debt worth more than twice their household income—and even then, only when they're under thirty. As you age, that multiple should decline gradually until it hits zero, preferably around the time you turn sixty-five. His belief is that when you hit retirement age you don't want to pay a mortgage anymore. (For more detail, see www.yourmoneyratios.com.)

This ratio has nothing to do with the price of your home, mind you, but the amount you're borrowing to buy it. Using Farrell's math, if you and a partner are under thirty and have a combined household income of $80,000, your loan debt shouldn't exceed $160,000, or twice your $80,000 income. This means that if the two of you put 10 percent down on a $180,000 home, or 20 percent down on a $200,000 home, you'd buy within ratios that leave you room to invest beyond your own address.

Depending on your overall financial picture, age, and philosophy, there are pros and cons to this approach. For instance, if mortgage interest rates are low, and you can borrow money inexpensively from home equity (perhaps at 4 percent) and invest it at higher interest rates (maybe 8 percent) elsewhere, you could potentially benefit by *not* paying off your mortgage in such a rush. After all, why hurry to pay off a loan with a 4 percent interest rate if you could instead invest money in an account capable of earning twice that rate? On the other hand, if mortgage interest rates were higher (perhaps 6 percent), and the sorts of investment options available didn't provide much better returns, then remaining aggressive about paying off the loan might make sense.

4. *It's an Investment That Requires Participation.*

Some people argue that running a home is like operating a business. That's partly what makes homeownership so complicated: Just as corporate figureheads can use dozens of strategies to tease profits out of their businesses, if as a homeowner you're counting on future financial returns from owning, you will have to keep on top of all of the investment, debt, risk, and returns you get from owning—and understand how to make adjustments as your financial life changes so that you meet your goals.

For instance, as an owner you'll have to decide how much to spend on capital improvements (repairs and maintenance), how much to reinvest in the business to improve its value (i.e., remodeling), whether to leverage it further (borrowing against its equity to fund other expenses), when it makes sense to refinance debt (i.e., paying to refinance your mortgage), and how to prepare for and price it for sale. Each of these moving parts has broader impacts on your household finances. Renters, too, have to make decisions about how to accumulate investment funds for the future, and do so in an environment where their housing costs can change based on landlord whim.

Bottom line: A home has investment features, but it's a complex investment whose rewards are based on risk. As the twenty-first century has progressed, consumer sentiment about how safe a home is as an investment has declined: In 2003, 83 percent of Americans thought buying a home was a safe investment, versus 64 percent during 2010, according to a Fannie Mae survey.[4.12] However, a majority of Americans—as polled by Fannie Mae and many other organizations—still think owning is a good idea. Maybe, with a better understanding of risks and investment principles, renters and owners alike are tempering their expectations about what a home contributes financially to their lives.

QUESTIONS TO CONSIDER

Whether and how well a home performs financially is open to interpretation, and is also impacted by local market dynamics. On what grounds do you believe a home can pay off financially? Answer the following:

1. How rapidly are rent rates and home prices rising in your market?

2. How long can you commit to your next living situation?

3. Is an owned home an investment only if it appreciates?

4. Is it an investment if you pay the mortgage off 100 percent and own it outright?

5. Is it an investment if, at the end of several years, you can sell and walk away with a little chunk of money and the knowledge that having some equity allowed you to tap low-interest home-related loans (versus high-interest alternatives) to fund big expenses (your small business, a kid's education)?

6. Is it an investment by virtue of allowing you to avoid paying rent?

7. Is it an investment because you're inclined to save more, knowing you're responsible for funding home maintenance?

8. Is your rental the wisest investment choice because it shields you from the risks of owning and allows for mobility—key if you think you may need to move around for your job?

CHAPTER 5

THE S-WORD: SUSTAINABLE HOUSING

Pay, Move, Live, Repeat

Danielle and Jeremy, newlyweds, began shopping for a home in suburban Minneapolis during 2008. Both of them are successful small-business owners—she runs a marketing and PR firm from home, he runs a car-customization boutique—and they wound up qualifying to jointly buy a home priced at up to $600,000. As they drove through neighborhoods filled with larger, new construction at the top of their price range, Danielle kept wondering who lived in all the new homes.

"We felt like we were doing well with two good, full-time incomes and could consider a more-expensive home," she says. "But we wondered, 'How many people can afford these homes?' "

She got a glimpse of who could buy those homes when the couple revisited their mortgage lender to learn more details about how it had financed homes in those price ranges: People who were willing to borrow to the max. Their lender clarified how it would work for the couple to buy a $600,000 home, explaining that they'd have to pay higher interest rates for a jumbo mortgage loan (a loan with a balance above $417,000) *or* they'd have to take out multiple loans, a first for up to $417,000, and a second at a higher rate for the remainder they needed to borrow.

"That was a reality check for us. We didn't want to have to get two loans to qualify for a home," Danielle says. "Once we found that out we started looking at cheaper homes."

Way cheaper homes, in fact. The more the couple crunched the numbers and thought about their options, the more they thought that maybe they should spend substantially less than their maximum borrowing potential. They reasoned that since they're both small-business owners whose service businesses are easily impacted by the economy and clients' shifting budgets, they'd be wise to buy a home they could afford on one income. That way, if one or both hit a rough patch, it'd still be easy to pay the bills.

The couple wound up buying a four-bedroom, two-and-a-half-bath contemporary home for under $400,000. It has the amenities they wanted, like a ground-floor office for her, bedroom space for Jeremy's two teenage children from a prior relationship, and a "walk out" basement for easy backyard entertaining. But more important, by not stretching to buy it, the couple can enjoy it no matter what's happening with their businesses.

"When the recession was at its worst, I did take a hit to my revenue," Danielle says. "That made us very happy we weren't in a fully extended financial situation with our mortgage."

And those other newly built homes the couple avoided because of their higher price tags?

"I'm guessing some of the buyers there had stretched to get a home, and they couldn't afford the effect of the recession," she says. "I've seen foreclosure signs on those streets."

TEMPTED BUT SAVING

Across the county, Sheree, a recently divorced mother of two, is renting a three-bedroom townhouse in Minnetonka on a street that's within walking distance of three good public schools. She and her ex-husband sold their former home in the divorce, and in between her self-employed status and a hit she took to her credit score after she maxed out credit cards paying for legal fees, she knows it doesn't make sense to buy now—no matter how much she wants to. Between her lowered credit score and what she considers a low income from self-employment for a family of three, she doesn't think she'd get a good loan.

"In general, I still feel people should own if they can," Sheree says. "I'm a renter right now, mainly because of divorce."

Lately, she's seen townhouses similar to her rental hit the market, at attractive prices. One just sold for $143,000, and another just dropped its price to $129,000. Sheree's tempted, especially since her rent is $1,250 and she could conceivably get a mortgage with a similar or lower monthly payment. But she also wants to put down 20 percent, which isn't an option with her own resources just now—although she might be able to ask a relative to contribute.

"I believe in putting down 20 percent," she says, in part to sidestep the costs of private mortgage insurance that accompanies loans made for lower down payments. "Coming up with $20,000 doesn't seem so bad to me, to make sure you avoid the expense of PMI."

It's hard to watch good deals float by, especially considering she's been a homeowner before and has chosen the school district she thinks is best for her children. But she's also exercising self-restraint, knowing that until she increases her income and raises her credit score, her loan choices will be expensive.

"You know what they say about going to the grocery store? Don't go shopping when you're hungry," she says. "I'm reminding myself of that as I see these homes hit the market."

MEET THE SUSTAINABLE CONSUMER

Choosing one-third less home than you qualify to buy? Renting till you can come up with a 20 percent down payment? Renting altogether instead of stretching to own? These choices reflect a new ethic some adults are displaying as they consider housing—and an old ethic some say could resuscitate the housing market. Sheree, Danielle, and Jeremy embody thinking sustainably—making housing decisions not based so much on immediate gratification but based on how those decisions plug into their bigger personal, financial picture.

Sustainable is a word typically associated with the green movement, with conserving natural resources through the intelligent manufacture or design of products. But it's a word that's now wending its way into speeches by political, economic, and housing leaders. Their definition of *sustainable* refers to offering consumers choices that they can afford not just initially but later as well. And for consumers, this means that if you can barely afford to get into a home, chances are it'll be hard to sustain your living situation after you sign your closing papers or lease.

It's not that you can't stretch to make that initial down payment or deposit, and eat a little ramen for a month or two. It's that you need to have a plan so that scrambling isn't a permanent lifestyle—because if it is, you'll be in trouble when the inevitable home repair or other life expense crops up, or if you experience a loss of income or temporary inability to work.

With the loosening of lending standards in the 1990s and 2000s, renters and buyers with little demonstrable talent for money management (no savings, low credit scores, precarious incomes) could easily get into homes they couldn't afford either from the outset or once a few minor financial setbacks—or loan resets—occurred. But those days are long over. While some argue that lenders have swung too far in the other direction, making it too hard for relatively qualified renters or buyers to get into appropriate homes, some consumers themselves are taking a cue from the economic downturn and proactively choosing a more careful approach to their housing spending.

While in the United States a home is often called a forced savings plan, meaning that if you buy it and make mortgage payments you are *saving*, elsewhere you need to prove you can save before you buy. Both *Newsweek*[5.1] and Congressional transcripts[5.2] pointed out that, in Germany, one way buyers can qualify for mortgages is a forced savings plan—with a bank. There, some banks offer customers what's known as *savings contracts*, whereby customers commit to opening and funding a savings account that becomes a down payment, then apply for a mortgage loan through the bank where they demonstrated their ability to save. That may not fly in America, but the idea of proving you can save before you buy is wise—and something you can do yourself.

The National Association of Realtors' President Ron Phipps discussed sustainability at an annual convention held in New Orleans, saying that while some people should rent, those who decide to buy homes need to be able to "support them over the longer haul."[5.3] That means they need to be able to understand all the costs associated with owning.

The government, which has historically encouraged homeownership both directly and indirectly, is showing signs of a sentiment shift away from the old emphasis. Sheila Bair, the former chair of the Federal Deposit Insurance Corporation (FDIC) responsible for rescuing hundreds of banks bogged down by botched home loans, floated in a mid-2010 speech that maybe the government should deploy more resources toward rental housing and devote less time to pushing ownership.

"Even as we emerge from the crisis, it is worth asking whether federal policy is devoting sufficient emphasis to the expansion of quality, affordable rental housing," she said, setting off thousands of tweets and bubble bloggers. "Sustainable homeownership is a worthy national goal. But it should not be pursued to excess when there are other, equally worthy solutions that help meet the needs of people for whom homeownership may not be the right answer."[5.4]

Warren Buffett, the billionaire investor, put it this way in an address to his company's shareholders: "Putting people into homes, though a desirable goal, shouldn't be our country's primary objective: Keeping them in their homes should be the ambition." He updated his thesis in his 2011 address to shareholders, saying ownership can be a good investment, but that the goal shouldn't be helping consumers buy the home of their dreams but instead a home they can afford.[5.5]

Doug Duncan, chief economist of Fannie Mae, described the new sustainable consumer this way: "They are rebalancing their attitudes toward housing and homeownership by adopting a more realistic, long-term approach, and are less willing to take risks. This focus on sustainable housing is better for the economy, better for the housing market and better for America's families."[5.6]

CAN YOU SUSTAINABLY RENT OR BUY A HOME?

Sustainable housing refers to housing—rented or owned—that you can afford to get into, stay in, and maintain. Before you sign a lease or show up at an escrow office, ask yourself if the place where you plan to live gets a green light on all of these questions.

1. *Does It Make Sense for Me Personally?*

Can I live here awhile or am I already mentally shopping for the next place? Is this someone else's idea of what's right for me? Would a job change or promotion require a new commute or out-of-state move? Can I accept the responsibilities here, whether homeowner duties like landscaping and repairs, dues owed a homeowner association, or renter scenarios like battling for street parking?

2. *Can I Afford It Right Now?*

Can I move in without pillaging every drop of savings? If I raid every last drop of my reserves, can I replenish it quickly? Will I need to borrow or pay beyond my comfort zone to live here? Am I willing to take on additional work—or roommates—to generate funds required to live here comfortably?

3. *Can I Continue to Afford It?*

Am I expecting positive or negative changes to my income, expenses, family size or status, or medical expenditures? (The top three reasons for bankruptcy and foreclosure are loss of income, divorce, and unanticipated medical expenses; these factors also figure in homelessness.) Is my ability to afford the place contingent on having roommates or financial help? Is my home a "ticking time bomb" needing repairs I can't afford to make any time soon? Can I fix my fixer?

4. *Do I Have an Exit Strategy?*

If I leave a rental and look for another, can I afford the going rental rates elsewhere? If I were to sell my home, can I make enough money so that when I subtract roughly 10 percent of the sale price and my outstanding mortgage balance, I come out in the black (i.e., above $0)? If I'm in the red as I approach an exit, can I improve my situation, wait to sell, sublet, or pay off home-related debt? If I wanted to rent out my home, could I fetch a rent that covers my mortgage?

5. *After Paying for Housing, Am I Also Saving and Investing?*

If I rent, am I saving for retirement? If I buy, is my home my sole "investment" or am I—or will I soon—begin saving elsewhere too? How does my housing payment cut into my ability to handle debts and also save for emergencies, fun goals, and my senior years? Can I improve it?

6. *What Do I Expect to Gain? How Much Am I Willing to Lose?*

If I have to move out of this home sooner than expected, am I willing to pay the rest of the lease or take steps to find my replacement so that the landlord won't charge me the remaining rent? If I have to sell a home sooner than expected, how much money can I afford to bring to closing if I'm selling for less than I owe my lender? If I need to move and would have to take a loss on a sale, can I afford that loss—and what, in the future, may be taxes I'll face on the loss?

Am I willing to buy a home knowing its value might falter? Is the experience of having lived here so worth it that I don't care if I lose money when I sell, or worth it because of the living experience itself?

o—

WHAT IF YOU CAN'T SUSTAINABLY RENT OR BUY?

Living sustainably isn't easy coming right out of the gate—or in a country where credit card usage and debt are a persistent burden for many consumers. If you're a recent college graduate making recent grad wages, if you're in the early years of your career, if you work in a career that pays modestly but live in an expensive city, or if you're recovering from one of life's many financial shocks—a job loss, the arrival of children, a divorce, the need for unpaid time off—it can throw you off your game or make you feel you can never ever play.

You can choose not to live sustainably—but the risks of doing so may be as considerable as the rewards. For some people, spending heavily on housing—rented or owned—is worth it because of factors like location, school district, commute, or living in a desirable-enough neighborhood to where they could easily attract a roommate or turn their entire home into a rental if need be. Other people feel like they *should* live in the most housing they can possibly get.

If you don't keep a budget, or have never mocked up your monthly income and outgo, it's time to take the pulse on how you're spending money—or hit up the personal finance literature.

Chances are that, with respect to housing options, you'll find out one of several things:

- **You can move in without raiding your resources,** have some savings for living expenses, and can continue to save or invest for the future. In other words, you're impressively rational and responsible. *What you can work on:* Making sure you're saving for major goals and that, where you are investing, you're making the most of your choices.

- **You'll raid your resources to move in** but can easily afford housing payments after move-in and then resume saving. You're like lots of people. *What you can work on:* First, replenish your savings. Then, repay any money borrowed from retirement accounts. Make sure you're not leaning on credit cards—or, if you are, make a plan to pay more than the minimum each month while also repaying your savings.

- **You've got no resources but someone is helping you, after which you can handle payments, but you won't really be able to set aside much for a while.** Sounds like you have a little bit of an appetite for risk, mixed with a lot of self-confidence. *What you can work on:* Look for ways to cut corners in your budget so that you can save responsibly. Avoid splurging or increasing your debt. Set a specific goal date and amount you'll start saving, and stick to it.

- **You've got no resources but someone is helping you, after which you can handle payments.** You can save, too, if you are willing to "get creative." You're probably in debt, or young, but a partner or parent is offering to help you buy—or is carrying the weight. *What you can work on:* If you're not financially self-sufficient, or if you're receiving a gift to buy an asset you might not be easily able to handle, think twice—and be honest about your situation with anyone who's helping you. If you want to get creative, consider working overtime or extra, taking on paying roommates, or using services like Airbnb (www.airbnb.com) or Roomarama (www.roomarama.com) to rent out rooms on a short-term basis. While in your twenties you may need roommates, don't set yourself up to need them for life. A future partner, child—or you—may not want them forever.

- **You'll raid your resources and can only afford housing payments if you "get creative."** And even once you're creative, you've got no savings and won't really be able to save for a while. *What you can work on:* A reality check! You're in a bit of a danger zone and may want to reconsider moving into this home. While some compromises are required of almost any move, you're making too many considering how insufficiently they'll position you for sustainable living. You're totally unprepared if emergencies hit. Consider cheaper living, and take a look at your budget to address where you owe or where the fat is.

- **You'll raid your resources and can only afford housing payments if miracles happen.** You've got no savings and not even any available credit on your cards. You're living paycheck to paycheck. *What you can work on:* Be someone's roommate while you pay off debt and start saving, live with family for free until you've got a job, or get a guarantor if you must rent. You're at the beginning of a journey to self-sufficiency, but you first must get out of debt.

If this sounds harsh, keep reading: As you learn more about the differing expenses to rent and to own, and how they scale over time, you'll start to understand why you need to take charge of your own financial literacy before buying or biting off a pricey monthly payment. You need to develop your own sense of how much money you're willing to spend on housing within a life where you'll likely use debt or savings for other purchases, such as education, a car, and everyday expenses. As you age you'll encounter competing demands for your money. Do you want housing to hog it all?

BUDGETING TOOLS: HOW'S YOUR BUDGET?

Have you taken a look lately? It's best to assess your budget over a period of several months so that you can see patterns and how the impact of occasional major expenses forces you to adjust the big picture. Run the numbers using services such as **GoSimplifi** (www.gosimplifi.com), **Mint** (www.mint.com), **Yodlee** (www.yodlee.com), **moneyStrands** (www.moneystrands.com), **Lendingtree's moneyright** (www.lendingtree.com), or **HelloWallet** (www.hellowallet.com).

PART 2

RENT VS. OWN

BUDGETING AND SHOPPING FOR PROPERTY

CHAPTER 6

WHO IS THE *REAL* REAL ESTATE CONSUMER?

You, All the Time

Just because you can finance a home buy, should you?

Elaine, a forty-two-year-old marketing executive in New York, remembers the crisp November day in 2001 when she realized she wanted to buy a home. She'd been moonlighting to stockpile emergency savings, correctly anticipating that she'd eventually be among the masses laid off by her dot-com start-up. After losing that job—and another just like it—within a ten-month period, she was mulling a move to the West Coast when she scored a position at an established ad agency unlikely to disappear. Strolling through SoHo on a sunny Saturday, relieved about work, she had an epiphany.

"It suddenly just became so crystal clear to me that New York was my home and I should buy a place here," she said. "9/11 was part of it, too—I was walking around in an area of the city that had been blocked off and had just been reopened. It wasn't like me to feel sentimental, but after being in the city throughout that whole ordeal I guess I wanted to commit to New York."

She was thirty-three, had a year's worth of income set aside in savings, and parents who were willing to help her as well. She'd been living in a rent-controlled studio apartment—a hard-to-score form of housing whereby her $900 rent was far below the $2,000 rent on a comparable place. But despite the good deal, her 350-square-foot home had drawbacks. Her place was too small to host overnight guests or even a tiny dinner party, and while bargain rent let her save money, she also felt like she was still living in a dorm room and wasn't really a "grown-up." The cost increase to move into a bigger rental, though, was so steep that to her it didn't justify the emotional benefits.

So in early 2002, she bought a $360,000 one-bedroom condo on the city's Upper West Side. She could finally spread out in 850 square feet, with a proper bedroom, dining area, and office nook. She emptied out her $80,000 in savings to put 20 percent down on the home, and got additional assistance from her parents for closing and fees. While her new monthly housing payment was in the mid-$2,000s, far more than before, she felt that the abundance of space she now had for nesting and entertaining meant she was no longer forced to leave home to socialize. She also continued freelancing outside of work to rebuild her savings reserves.

"I've got no regrets at all," she says. "I've thought a lot about the emotional benefits of owning your home, and for me owning has made a big, positive difference."

DOES IT FEEL RIGHT?

Most people who buy a home do so because owning a place feels right to them, or seems like part of the next stage of their lives. They wander into the process with a general feeling about why they want to own—to nest, create permanence, choose a physical space that plays a role in a growing relationship or family, because they're confident they'll stay in a particular job or market for many years to come, or as a step toward financial security. And in the best scenarios, like Elaine's, the experience lives up to the buyer's expectations of it. For Elaine, buying a home and creating a new personal space seemed like a practical next step. It felt right—and, lucky for her, she had available resources to finance the purchase.

But not everyone feels that owning is a necessary step in their own life narrative—and, in fact, renting may sometimes serve a life's purpose better. Across Manhattan, Stephanie, a forty-three-year-old screenwriter and film instructor, has held on to the same apartment for almost eighteen years. With her apartment priced at less than $1,000 per month, she knows she has a very good deal in a safe neighborhood and is lucky to have her hands on one of the thousands of rent-controlled apartments in New York, meaning her rent is fixed at a below-market rate. She briefly flirted with buying in 2004, when she was earning top dollar as a corporate publicist and could make the purchase jointly with her then-boyfriend, but in retrospect she realizes owning a home would have been more trap than foundation.

Discussing a real estate purchase and then getting preapproved to buy with her boyfriend brought up deeper conversations about what they both wanted out of their futures, as individuals and as a couple, and ultimately they decided to end the relationship rather than cement it with a mortgage on a $610,000 two-bedroom. The relationship's end led to other changes in her life—such as her newfound appreciation for renting. Soon Stephanie began de-emphasizing publicity work so she could spend more time screenwriting. Her income began to shrink, but her happiness grew. Had she taken on a Manhattan mortgage with her ex-boyfriend, she would've emptied out her savings and her half of the monthly housing payment would have been double her rent. She would've never been able to pursue her film ambitions.

Now dating another man in Brooklyn, she's found that her well-located and reasonably priced apartment is an asset that helps support her creative life. When times are good, her place remains comfortable and affordable. When money's tight, she can decamp to her boyfriend's or her mother's place and rent it out to travelers who pay roughly $250 per night for short-term stays.

"The decision I made lets me pursue the things that are my priorities right now," Stephanie says. "That's worth more to me than owning my place. If I came into some money, I'd be interested in buying. But there's no way I could buy in my current situation without giving up the work I care about and going back to the work I left."

REAL ESTATE'S TARGET MARKET: EVERYONE, ALL THE TIME

You are a consumer of real estate, whether you rent or own. The word *dream* appears again and again in real estate advertising, and the idea that owning is the American Dream and thus must be protected is often trotted out by the very people who defined the dream for you that way.

You have a right to dream, and (sorry, renters) generally speaking, in America, your dream should be to own. If you're lucky you can have your dream home. What dream home? If you haven't figured out what your idea of a dream home is, start dreaming. But if you don't have an idea of what your dream home is like, there are a variety of dreams to choose from: You can win a dream home from the occasional builder sweepstakes, go to any home show and see the latest "dream home" model on the show floor, flip on a TV, check shelter blogs and magazines, or look at property porn—celebrity home coverage. Many cities have "Street of Dreams" homes tours each year. You may not be able to afford them. But you can dream.

As you're already aware, the American government and many Americans (generally more than 60 percent, according to surveys) view homeownership positively, even in light of the real estate meltdown and even if getting into a home is harder than it once was. While in recent years a larger subset of people stated in surveys that they may adjust to the market by waiting a bit longer to own or putting down more when they buy, they still have a sense that it's a good thing. So if you subscribe to the idea that owning a home is fundamentally good, you're not alone.

There's nothing wrong with feeling good about where you live—as long as good feelings about where you live don't spin so far out of control that they run counter to other aspects of your well-being. Jonah Lehrer, a neuroscience researcher and author of a book about how people make decisions, told the

Washington Post that when people are looking at homes to buy, their dopamine levels can often override their rationality, making them justify expenses or choices that may be unwise later. While you may have good intentions—choosing a suitable home—the next thing you know you may be considering more home than you need, and rationalizing its benefits.[6.1]

Real estate agents tease out what motivates you or excites you about a home—and what you dislike about certain homes—so they can show you more of what you want to see. If you're easily swayed—by the senses, what's new, a good deal, competition, or status—you're in a kind of emotional zone that could make you pounce on any number of homes for sale. Some agents will help you curb your enthusiasm so you're happy during the long term, while others will encourage your enthusiasm to keep you dreaming—or, cynics might say, asleep. Is this good or bad? You went shopping to satisfy a feeling, and the agent is just helping you. Why shoot the messenger?

That said, the messenger is working in an industry filled with tricks to keep you feeling good about buying and keep you away from the scary thought that you're about to borrow a huge amount of money to acquire a several-hundred-thousand-dollar illiquid asset whose future value (while likely higher than your purchase) and maintenance requirements are both uncertain. The selling of a home involves a series of carefully calculated acts in many parts: From airbrushed online photos and videos to carefully researched listing language, the big idea is to make you imagine what it'd be like to live your particular life in a particular space. Many listings also practice the now-widespread art of "staging," or merchandising a home for sale using a mix of furnishing and decorating techniques designed to make you, the buyer, feel more at home—a kind of sales feng shui to get you to buy faster and for more money, too.

Yes, real estate is primarily a consumer purchase—one you're making for personal satisfaction—but it's also a major financial decision that impacts your overall financial position. It's fine to daydream and react emotionally to potential homes, but at some point in the process it's wise to reality-check your fantasy of a future lifestyle in a particular property against the rubric of sustainability. Like going to premarriage counseling to examine the hard questions, visiting your doctor before triathlon training, or checking in with a financial advisor or fiscally conservative friend before splurging on a big purchase, it's important to listen to your head as well as your heart. Need proof that home buying is an emotional act? Consider this: The typical home buyer spends a median of three months looking at properties and looks at a median of twelve homes, according to NAR data. Yet buyers spend about five hours shopping for a mortgage loan, according to Zillow Mortgage Marketplace data.[6.2]

O—

FROM RENTER TO FIRST-TIME BUYER

Who's the typical American renter? Often, it's someone who's young: A whopping 70 percent of all renters are between the ages of twenty and thirty.[6.3] Renters also tend to include lower-income workers, a large population of immigrants, and people who, young or not, are getting on their feet financially and may rely on social assistance (government voucher programs, charitable aid) in order to pay for their housing. Increasingly, renters also include prior owners: those who lost a home to foreclosure, those who sell and decide to rent until further notice, and people nearing retirement who have downsized.

Renters tend to deploy a slightly higher amount of their monthly income for their housing payment, spending a median of 31 percent of income per month and a median $808 monthly payment, versus owners who pay a median of 20 percent of income and have a median $1,000 monthly payment, according to the most recent U.S. Census data (see pages 59–60).[6.4] Presumably, renters' higher spending on housing is attributable to the fact that most young people (who dominate the renting population) earn less in early adulthood and thus their housing payment may account for a larger percentage of their income. Also, because renters don't have to fund maintenance and repairs, they may choose to spend more on housing, since rent includes these fees, which owners must pay beyond their mortgages.

"FIRST"-TIME BUYER

In the real estate world, *first-time buyer* is a very loose term. If you've never bought before, you're obviously a first-time buyer. But if you've bought three or more years ago, you're regarded as a first-time buyer for lending purposes, meaning that all the low down payment loans and other breaks made available to first-timers are also options for you as well. In addition, if you previously owned with a spouse but got divorced, you may qualify as a first-time buyer without having to wait three years. In its surveys of recent buyers and sellers, the National Association of Realtors doesn't ask consumers to distinguish which kind of first-time home buyer they are—a true property virgin, or a repeat buyer using first-time financing—so it's not surprising that the first-time buyer population is large.

Some housing policy critics say that perpetual requalification of experienced buyers as first-timers isn't doing them or the housing market any favors—as it means experienced owners are endlessly exposed to favorable loan terms (like low down payments), keeping them in a kind of financial feedback loop that never incentivizes them to develop the level of equity that represents the financial benefit of owning. But other observers, and owners themselves, see these rules as valuable, especially in a mobile society where job changes and relocations may force owners to periodically sell and rebuy, or where young buyers whose fortunes improve throughout the years may want to trade up while they still have time to pay down their newer, more expensive purchase.

The typical first-time buyer, not surprisingly, picks up where the renter leaves off. If you're in the market to buy your first place, you're probably between thirty and thirty-two—the median age range for first-time buyers during the past thirty years, according to Walt Molony, spokesman for the National Association of Realtors. NAR reports that first-time buyers represented 50 percent of the housing market in 2010, up markedly from norms of about 40 percent in recent years in part due to first-time buyer tax credits available in 2009 and 2010 and, perhaps, because some existing owners couldn't "move up" due to issues with the sluggish market or home equity. The majority (58 percent) are married, while 20 percent are single women, 12 percent are single men, and 8 percent are unmarried. These buyers pay a median of 4 percent down to get into a home.

REAL ESTATE CONSUMER: RENT VS. OWN

Renters rarely hold housewarming parties for themselves. Happy to have located a lease, they move in, set up shop, and go about the business of living in their new neighborhood. Sure, as far as consumers go, renters have to buy things for their homes: New furniture, storage items, a few cleaning and hardware devices. They get hit up by door-to-door sales folks or find the occasional flyer for pizza delivery in their mailbox just like owners. But generally speaking, marketers aren't pitching the renter with the same fervor they use to pursue the home-owner. You see, homeowners not only need the same items as renters, but more of them. They also need a broader array of tools and hardware to maintain their property, and may have more storage to stow pantry items and other necessities (not surprisingly, warehouse clubs like Costco and Sam's Club mainly count home-owners among their membership). Owners have a lot more money to spend, theo-retically, as well. Their perceived or actual wealth from owning may mean their credit lines are increased, or they may choose to take out a "just in case" line of credit with their home equity, which means they've got big spending power. The owner, in essence, becomes a super-consumer.

Your choices about real estate don't end once you become an owner. If anything, they expand: You need to protect your home, and you'll wind up period-ically upgrading it so that it's structurally sound and, thus, also has future resale value. You'll also want to customize and furnish it for your own personal enjoyment. You might do a major remodel. And later, if or when you begin planning to sell, you may wind up spending to undo your personal touches so that your home has broader appeal to potential buyers. You'll have to decide whether to pay out of pocket for these costs or to finance them with home equity.

In addition to shopping for materials and furniture, you can continue to shop for an altogether new mortgage. You can refinance your mortgage (in effect, rebuying your existing place on different terms) to shorten or lengthen the time frame in which to pay it off or to get a better interest rate that makes for a cheaper monthly payment. You can seek out a line of credit against your home's equity (a second mortgage, or a home equity loan) or do a "cash out" refinance, in which you subtract a little of your equity in exchange for a chunk of cash. These latter gestures are moves many owners make when funding big-ticket expenses like college tuition, small-business expenses, repaying higher-interest debt, or embarking on a home renovation.

Paradoxically, as soon as some owners attain equity, they want to burn through it again by pulling it out and playing with it. In some cases, this makes financial sense. After all, using home equity for value-enhancing activities such as replacing a failing HVAC system with an energy-efficient heating and cooling system might be rational; dipping into home equity for consumer purchases like plasma TVs or vacations isn't necessarily smart. But in other cases, owners tap equity because they're in a pinch and lack savings to fund emergencies like medical costs or lost income.

So while homeownership is seen as a financial security blanket and during the long haul tends to produce a savings effect, for a certain kind of buyer owning can serve as a kind of gateway drug to a seemingly infinite low-interest line of credit. For people who have trouble managing money, this can lead to trouble. Between 2003 and 2007, homeowners in America went on what Harvard University's Joint Center for Housing Studies referred to as a "debt binge," withdrawing $1.2 trillion from their homes' equity during refinancing, and using it to whack credit card and other debts or for other purchases.[6.5] In 2007 and 2008, many lenders shut down, froze, or requested paybacks on these lines of credit due to declines in the home value against which it was offered. When home values fell, many owners who had borrowed against equity at the peak of home value, or who had remodeled their homes to unsustainably expensive new dwellings, soon owed more than the homes were actually worth and/or couldn't sell the homes profitably. While this equity availability isn't likely to happen again in the near future, you get the idea: You play, you pay.

For a look at the worst-case effects of real estate consumerism, consider what has happened to some of the owners featured on ABC's hit show *Extreme Makeover: Home Edition*. The show features down-on-their-luck families who get sent away on vacation while a crew of builders swoop in and do a sensational remodel—or outright raze and rebuild—on their home. The family returns to a big reveal, often to a home customized for each resident's preferences. The home is larger, and it's worth more—but more expensive to operate. The home's swollen value means the owner has equity against which to borrow—and for some owners, this equity became a double-edged sword.

The *Wall Street Journal* in 2010 reported on the first of what became a cluster of "Extreme Foreclosures"—homes that became too expensive to operate for owners who either lost income, couldn't handle the increased tax and utility bills, or who simply wanted to get their money out for other reasons. The story cited show reps as saying future remodels' sizes would shrink and feature less-expensive and more energy-efficient appliances.[6.6]

No doubt, the show wanted to prevent stories like this one: In Florida, the *Times-Union* reported on the expected 2011 foreclosure of a 1,300-square-foot home featured on the show. Once an army barracks, the makeover more than tripled the home's size. Within three years of the remodel, the owners took out mortgages worth $192,600 against the home, and then fell behind on payments. While the makeover no doubt improved the home, it also made unprecedented debt available to the owners. Its operating costs also skyrocketed: Annual property taxes jumped ten-fold, from $500 premakeover to $5,200, and monthly utility bills that once averaged $60 cost $400.[6.7] Moral of the story: Bigger isn't always better.

THE MOVE-UP BUYER: REMODEL OR RELOCATE?

As time passes, you may debate whether to remodel your existing place to suit your changing needs or whether it makes more sense to sell and buy another home offering the features you want. Those who buy a smaller home often "move up" (i.e., buy bigger or better) from their "starter" home. Typically, move-up buyers are in their mid- to late forties, according to NAR. Most of them can afford moving up to a pricier place because they can use the profit from the sale of their first property to provide a down payment on their new home. They may also be moving geographically for job reasons.

But for those who are staying local, the decision whether to remodel or move is a classic homeowner conundrum—and a major financial decision. On the one hand, remodeling is expensive and disruptive to live through. But on the other hand, you can hire architects or contractors to design and build exactly what you want. Some owners, however, decide that moving makes more sense: If what they need is so drastically different from what they have, they reason, why not start over? The stakes may be even higher than when you first bought: Now you're looking for the next "dream," but you're also selling the old one—and learning what needs to be done to attract buyers. Yet another option remains: You can hire a builder to construct a new home for you, but that can be expensive and require years of planning and permitting once you have located and bought a lot. You could also buy new construction in a planned community, choosing from among multiple home models and a menu of customization options.

As your equity, financial strength, and income grow, you'll have other choices around real estate: You might buy a second home or vacation home. Or you might decide to invest in rentals—or become a landlord by default if you move elsewhere and opt to rent your old place. Likewise, you might relocate and can't profitably sell or want to wait to sell your home and decide to rent until the market improves. This leads to yet further real estate decision-making: How will you finance these purchases, handle them as investments, and address them on taxes? These decisions are beyond the scope of the rent versus own debate, but they're part of the spectrum of real estate choices that crop up the longer you own and the more established you become financially.

If you've stayed in your home awhile before moving up, you might be among the lucky 14 percent of repeat buyers who don't finance their home at all—meaning they pay cash or don't have to borrow. But among the 86 percent of repeat buyers who do get a new mortgage, more than half make a down payment below 20 percent, according to data from NAR. For some, this makes sense in an environment where mortgage interest rates are low, but for others, it raises the question of whether the buyers will achieve substantial equity positions that will translate to substantial post-sale proceeds later.

Based on the most recent data on household composition in the United States from the U.S. Department of Housing and Urban Development, only 28 percent of primary residences are owned mortgage-free, and among owners only 40 percent own homes outright.[6.8] This means the American Dream—owning a home, outright—can take a long time to come true. But it happens. Roger, a West Coast publicist, says that homeownership was crucial to his mother's retirement: His parents bought a home in 1977 for $29,000, and his mother owned it free and clear by 2010, when it became apparent that, at seventy-four, she needed to sell and move to a retirement community. She sold it in 2010 for $325,000, and after paying sales fees and entry dues to a senior community, she still has $270,000.

"For the past five years, we had planned on that home being a health fund for my mother," he says. "It was absolutely understood that this was how she'd pay for uninsured medical costs and to help fund her retirement."

At its best, the homeownership story ends like this: An owner buys, stays, accumulates equity, and can use the home's value to fund his or her retirement. The owner can sell the property to fund a new life elsewhere, or refinance the property (via a reverse mortgage or other form of financing) in order to finance aging in place. But in a mobile, changeable society, where employees move more frequently than in the past, the odds of staying in one place a long time are lower. So the real estate consumer—of rented or owned housing—must consider home-related spending carefully.

CHAPTER 7

CONFRONTING YOUR CREDIT HISTORY

Know Your Numbers

Teri, a forty-something mother of two teenage boys, had always enjoyed a high credit score—until her divorce. During the divorce process, her husband filed for a Chapter 7 Bankruptcy, and because of the timing, her score sank alongside his. Initially, this didn't effect her housing options. As part of their divorce agreement she'd kept the home they'd owned together outside San Antonio, Texas, and continued to make payments on it.

But raising two kids and maintaining a house as a single mother overwhelmed her, and so she decided to sell. After a brief stay with her mother, Teri and the kids struck out to find their own rental. That's when she learned the real impact of her lowered score. Her ex's bankruptcy—in effect, also hers—still lurked over her credit report like a dark financial cloud. Now, seven years later, her score remains in the low 600s, still low enough to scare some landlords.

"I recently got turned down for an apartment I wanted because of my credit score," says Teri, who was looking to move closer to the call center where she works. "I thought that they'd check my landlord references, but instead they said the building goes strictly by credit scores. I wish I'd known that. There goes my $50 background check, straight down the drain."

Fortunately, Teri was able to find a rental. She recently moved into a two-bedroom detached garden home managed by a landlord who cared more about her references from prior landlords and her demonstrated ability to pay her bills on time than about her numbers. The property was advertised "for rent by owner," a tip-off to Teri that she'd be dealing directly with the property's owner and not an employee of a large management company who lacked the ability to show flexibility with renters.

Whether you're in the market to rent or own, your credit history and resulting credit scores play a big role in determining your housing options, so you need to know your numbers—and how they're perceived—before starting a home search.

Before the recent move, Teri had briefly considered buying again, in part because the mix and type of rental properties available in the area around San Antonio where she wanted to live were "rinky-dink" and poorly maintained, she says. Intrigued by a newly constructed community of homes whose ads promoted monthly costs resembling the roughly $1,000 she pays for rent, Teri applied for a loan. However, as she suspected, her credit—again—hampered her options: She'd have to pay higher interest rates and private mortgage insurance rates if she bought, and the monthly payment would run about $1,200, not $1,000.

For renters, scores control access to particular buildings and possibly your deposit size, but not the monthly rent price. But for potential buyers, the stakes are higher. Scores influence the interest rate you pay on your mortgage loan and, if applicable, your mortgage insurance rates. For a buyer, in a nutshell: *Low score? Then it costs more.* As of this writing, borrowers with a 760 or higher credit score can get a 4.68 percent annual percentage rate on a traditional (thirty-year fixed) mortgage loan for a median-priced home.[7.1] Lower-scoring borrowers would pay incrementally more—up to a 6.3 percent interest rate, for instance, for borrowers scoring in the 620 to 639 range. This translates to hundreds of additional dollars for each monthly payment, and tens of thousands of dollars worth of added interest payments during the life of a loan.

Before you can worry about dilemmas like Teri's, you need to actually have a credit history—a record of your behavior as a borrower. Along with that history you'll accumulate a set of credit scores that mark how well you handle credit. Each month as you make—and miss—payments, and as you open and close accounts, the data in your report and the score associated with it will shift accordingly.

In America, the clock on your credit begins ticking about six months after you've taken out a loan or been approved for a line of credit. Whether you have an auto loan, a student loan, a store charge card, or a "revolving" credit card (Visa, Mastercard, American Express, Discover), once you've had at least one account open for six months, lenders and creditors will start reporting your account activity and payment behavior to the credit bureaus—organizations that collect consumer credit data and provide reports to you and to companies offering you additional loans, lines of credit, or financial contracts (such as a lease for a rental home, automobile, or computer). The largest bureaus are Equifax, Experian, and Transunion.

Fair Isaac Corporation, a Minnesota-based company, develops scoring formulas that these three bureaus use to evaluate your credit activity and turn it into a so-called FICO score. These scores range from 300 to 850—but because each of the three bureaus uses FICO scoring methods slightly differently or may have differing data about you, you can have a different score at each of the three bureaus. You need to find out before you apply for a lease or a loan how your numbers look to develop realistic expectations about your chances with landlords and lenders.

○━

HOW TO IMPROVE YOUR CREDIT SCORE

There are dozens of ways to improve your score—and dozens of credit score improvement programs and credit score monitoring programs. According to Fair Isaac's www.myfico.com consumer site, scores are weighted according to the following elements within your credit reports:

- **Payment history** (35 percent). Have you paid on time or late, and on how many accounts? If late, how late (30, 60, 90 days) were you? For how much money were you late? How long since you were last late, and on how many accounts? Which accounts have you paid on time?

- **Total amount owed** (30 percent): What proportion or percentage of total credit available to you are you actually using? What proportion or percentage of credit, by credit type, is in use? Are balances at the max or minimum? Which accounts have balances?

- **Length of credit history** (15 percent): How recently were your accounts opened? How long have you had to demonstrate responsibility with these accounts and with certain account types?

- **New credit** (10 percent): Have you been shopping for and applying for more credit or loans? What proportion of your credit lines and loans are newer?

- **Type of credit in use** (10 percent): What type of credit are you most often using? Are you mainly repaying a loan and occasionally using a charge card, or do you display other patterns?

It's pretty obvious that paying on time helps, paying beyond the minimum due is smart, and keeping your balances from running up to (or over) their limits is beneficial. Letting your credit accounts season (or age) can help if you're young or transitioning from underbanked to "more banked," which means that closing old accounts isn't always the best idea. Since part of your score includes an analysis of what percentage of your available lines are in use, closing a line of credit can reduce your potential total credit available—and make what credit is in use look higher on a percentage basis; this can have a negative impact on your score. Applying for every credit line offered to you is also counterproductive, as it tilts your credit mix toward youth versus maturity. If you don't have a major credit card but do have a card from a single store (say, a credit card good only at a clothing or electronics retailer), demonstrating responsible use can help you land a big-brand revolving credit card account.

SCORE SEARCH

The three major credit bureaus are legally required to let you view your credit reports for free once annually. (For a nominal fee, you can look more often.) Credit reports include your name (and aliases), address, employers, social security number, and a list of accounts that will include revolving debt (where your minimum monthly payment isn't required to pay off the total debt balance) and installment debt (where you're on a set payment plan until the line of credit or loan is entirely paid off). Also included are judgments, unpaid child support, and account collections activity, and foreclosure or bankruptcy proceedings. When you apply for credit or loans, it shows up on your report (and impacts your score), but when others (e.g., marketers) ask to see your credit in advance of marketing credit to you, it's considered a "soft" request that doesn't affect your score.

ANNUAL CREDIT REPORT

www.annualcreditreport.com
This portal provides a one-stop shop for checking credit reports free once annually from the three major agencies—Equifax, Experian, and Transunion.

EQUIFAX

www.equifax.com
Free Credit Report: (800) 685-1111

EXPERIAN

www.experian.com
Credit Report Requests: (888) 397-3742

TRANSUNION

www.transunion.com
Free Credit Report: (800) 888-4213
Purchase Credit Report: (800) 888-4213

FAIR ISAAC CORPORATION

www.myfico.com
You can also get reports and scores here for a small fee, plus useful tips for interpretation.

WHAT'S "GOOD" CREDIT?

Assuming you have a credit history, and a set of scores, you should know that, as of this writing, if your scores are below 600 you may be better off renting. If your scores are over 760, then buying a home may be a viable option for you. And if you're somewhere in the middle, you've got some thinking to do.

One of the most confusing concepts in the credit market is the fact that lender sentiment about what credit score ranges are good enough for various types of loans changes constantly. The vast swath of score territory between 600 and 760 is where lenders tend to continually adjust the screws on access to credit and loans. And even on the low end, lenders vacillate between how restrictive they are with borrowers.

In a bustling economy, lenders may extend credit and loans to lower-scoring borrowers and do so for fairly reasonable terms: This rising-tide-lifts-all-boats approach helped fuel the housing boom from the mid-'90s to mid-2000s. In a slower economy or "tighter" (i.e., stricter) credit market, lenders may only make credit available to best-scoring borrowers or layer restrictions onto loans for low-scoring borrowers. That's what's been happening from 2007 to the present, and while would-be buyers are salivating at the chance to get good deals and loans with low rates, the reality is that some won't qualify.

Freddie Mac and Fannie Mae data indicate that the average credit score for conventional mortgages was 760 as of 2010, up from 720 in 2007. And FHA loans show an average credit score of 700, up from around 630 in 2007.[7.2] You now need a 760 to get the kind of loan you used to get for 40 points less. Contrast that with the mid-2000s, when 680 was good enough for best-advertised rates, and the picture becomes fuzzy: Are score requirements now too high as an over-reaction to the real estate bust? Or were previous score requirements too low, and new score requirements appropriate?

The housing-related recession and lenders' about-face on who does and doesn't get credit has coincided with a tough economy, where high unemployment, a rethink on health insurance, and consumers' already-tenuous grasp of personal debt have meant millions of people have declared bankruptcy, defaulted on loans, entered foreclosure, or struggled to pay bills. Many former homeowners who have undergone a foreclosure are returning to the rental market, their credit scores battered from failing to keep up with mortgage payments. Some may have separately, or additionally, declared bankruptcy—an inability to address an overwhelming debt load. Bankruptcy and foreclosure are two of the worst things that can happen to your credit.

In Chapter 7 Bankruptcy, you keep some assets for yourself and liquidate others to repay your creditors; this bankruptcy remains on your credit report for a decade and makes it very difficult for you to secure loans and credit at affordable terms. In Chapter 13 Bankruptcy, you arrange to repay creditors according to a plan, and while the bankruptcy appears on your credit history its impacts ease faster, after seven years.

Foreclosures can be personally wrenching for many reasons, but in financial terms when you go through foreclosure you relinquish property to a lender because of your inability to pay an installment loan to that lender. While the dollar amount of debt you're reneging on in foreclosure may be way higher than the credit cards or unpaid medical bills that sent you to bankruptcy, because a foreclosure is tied to an asset you can actually return to a lender, it effects your scores in a different way than does a bankruptcy.

HOW DO FORECLOSURE AND
BANKRUPTCY IMPACT SCORES?

Depending on your initial score, Fair Isaac research indicates that a foreclosure can lower your numbers by 85 to 160 while a bankruptcy can lower them by 130 to 240, according to Barry Paperno, consumer operations manager at myFico, Fair Isaac's consumer Web site. Indeed, this may be why some owners decide to pursue what's known as strategic default. They forego their largest creditor—a mortgage lender—but continue paying their other debts, knowing that once they lose their home they'll need to be able to persuade a landlord to rent to them or keep credit available for other reasons.

CHARACTER + CREDIT: THE RENTER'S CURRENCY

Renting requires more "character" reference than owning. That's because you're living in a property that someone else owns. Landlords vet you by using a rental application, references, and character assessment. Most rental applications ask for a credit check, criminal background check, prior addresses, rental history, if you've been evicted, your work history or proof of employment (such as a pay stub), your income and financial position, and personal references. They'll also ask if you've previously declared bankruptcy or been subject to liens on debt, and how many credit requests were made in your name in recent months.

Got a thin credit history or low credit score? Be prepared to offer evidence of income and responsible financials via the following: Recent pay stubs (proof of income and employment), a nominal fee for the landlord to run background checks, your social security number for credit checks, phone numbers of references, and possibly a deposit check (cashed if you're approved as a tenant). You may also need to tally credit card balances, funds available in checking and savings accounts (and the numbers on those accounts for verification), and provide information about debts.

Under the Fair Housing Act and other laws, landlords cannot legally reject your application due to race, religion, ethnic background or nationality, gender, age, family status, or disabilities. However, landlords can use business or financial criteria—credit scores, income minimums, or references—to reject you. Landlords may also legally enforce their own rules about no smoking, no pets, maximum numbers of occupants in a particular unit, and other factors important to you.

Credit Scores: The Buyer's Tool

As of late 2010, Experian began tracking on-time rental payments as reported by rental management companies. If you're establishing credit and paying rent on time, this is a plus—assuming your management company is among those reporting. If you're counting on a lax landlord who doesn't mind if the rent's a little late, you might have to change your behavior or else prepare to see your late rent payments turn up on Experian reports.[7.3]

When it comes to buying, "character" is entirely financial. You can have the charisma of the Unabomber and a trail of angry landlord references, but if your credit score, debt and income ratios, and salary and assets look good on paper, you could be a contender for a nice loan. That's the good news for high-scoring borrowers. There's a reason that low-scoring borrowers pay more: Government research shows that a low credit score is one of the most significant predictors of a potential mortgage default. While a low down payment (little invested) or minimal equity (little to lose) may also be factors in predicting default, many people with low credit scores have a checkered past with managing loans and lines of credit, and therefore may also have similar difficulties handling a mortgage. According to data cited in a U.S. Department of Housing and Urban Development report to Congress on causes of the foreclosure crisis, borrowers with scores below 600 were more than twice as likely to default on loans as borrowers with scores of 700 and above.[7.4]

For instance, in 2011, amid the continuing housing correction, low-scoring borrowers (with scores below 580) must make higher down payments than the 3.5 percent normally permissible on popular FHA loans. And borrowers who make a less-than-20 percent down payment must pay proportionately higher private mortgage insurance (PMI) rates as part of their monthly housing payment than would healthy scorers with the same down. This is a far cry from the mid-2000s, when low-scoring borrowers could get 0 percent down loans, sometimes with sidecar lines of credit, and what were (initially, anyway) favorable terms.

There may be fewer options now if you have a low score than there were before, but there are probably *some* options. Keep in mind that lenders aren't going to tell you what to do about your scores. That's why you need to take a look at them and then weigh the pros and cons of *working with* what you've got versus *working on* what you've got and acting later.

Fair Isaac and Informa Research Services offer an up-to-date modeling program on the myFICO Web site that demonstrates how a borrower might fare with a loan based on his or her score—and his or her potential, improved scores. Taking Teri as an example, here's what would happen had she wanted to borrow

$194,000 to buy that tempting new construction home with a theoretical $1,000 monthly payment, according to the Fair Isaac and Informa tool.

To get that payment, she'd need a top-shelf score that would qualify her for a very low interest rate. But Teri's reality—a score in the low 600s—is very different from the land of best-advertised rates, made available only to best-scoring consumers. She'd wind up paying the most of all these categories:

760–850 / 4.685% APR: **$1,004**   680–699 / 5.09% APR: **$1,052**

700–759 / 4.91% APR: **$1,031**

680–699 / 5.09% APR: **$1,052**

660–679 / 5.31% APR: **$1,078**

640–659 / 5.75% APR: **$1,132**

620–639 / 6.3% APR:

$1,201
TERI'S SCORE

As Teri's buy-versus-rent tire-kick shows, when considering buying, you have to weigh several choices related to your credit score: Should you spend time improving your credit score before applying for a mortgage but risk that home prices might increase while you're improving that score? If you want to own, should you use the financing that's available to you given your particular score but pay higher fees for financing as a result?

Teri says she's decided to wait a few more years to revisit the decision. By then, both her children will be out of the house and school district choices won't impact her thinking, and her scores ought to improve. While home prices could in theory rise, she's not worried: Her expenses will decrease during the next two years as her sons reach financial independence and she spends less to support them, meaning she'd have more money to meet the future, higher cost of owning a home if and when she tries to buy.

"There are ways in which owning a home is a positive. It bothered my kids a lot that I felt I had to sell our house. But a home is what you make of it," says Teri. "I would own again. But my credit score is a big factor for me. I felt like the monthly payment that was advertised was a teaser."

RENTERS COPING WITH CREDIT PROBLEMS

Got a low score or short credit history?
These approaches may help win over a skeptical landlord.

CONSIDER A SMALLER BUILDING OR INDIVIDUAL LANDLORD

Often, individual landlords who've met you in person or own only a few units may show more generosity toward lower scores than do corporate owners of larger buildings, where tenant selection is up to a building manager.

MAX OUT THE SECURITY DEPOSIT

Many landlords will ask for higher deposit if credit is poor.

BRING REFERENCES

Former landlords who will tell your future landlord what a model tenant you were are gold when you have a low credit score.

TRY A TRIAL PERIOD

Propose a three- or six-month lease, to prove you can make the rent.

GET A GUARANTOR

Find someone you trust (and who's better off!) to cosign. Keep in mind that he or she will need to have a financial profile that you lack, that is, sufficient income, credit, etc.

RENT WITH A ROOMMATE

If you can share space with a better-scoring roommate, that may improve your chances—if the roommate has good credit to offset yours. Alternatively, you could sublet a room from a better-scoring roommate whose name is on the lease and is ultimately responsible for the rent getting paid.

LOOK AT THE MARKET

With high vacancy, landlords may be more flexible. If your score is low, you may have the most options in areas of town where there's high vacancy.

ARE YOU A FORMER HOMEOWNER?

Many landlords view low scores from former homeowners more generously than low scores held by non-homeowners. If you could get and pay a mortgage, they reason, you can pull it together to rent, even if you're in recovery mode.

CHAPTER 8

DEPOSITS
AND
DOWN PAYMENTS

Entrance Fees

When Alex, a twenty-six-year-old publicist, set out to buy a condo, she had a few requirements: She wanted to buy within Chicago's city limits, pay no more than $150,000, and make a big down payment—ideally for 20 percent of her home's price.

Living in downtown Chicago was a no-brainer: She'd spent her postcollege years making a two-hour daily commute there from Skokie, Illinois, a small city where she could share a home inexpensively with her boyfriend and focus on paying off college loans. After she paid off her undergrad debt, she wanted to live downtown near work while she was still in her twenties and could enjoy city life. Yet with a serious relationship and likely future awaiting her in the suburbs, she also wanted a place that she could sell or turn into a rental within five years. To her, the best way to prepare for either scenario was to buy an inexpensive condo with a big down payment.

"This is a very transitional point in my life," Alex says. "Part of the whole calculation about whether to rent or buy is the question of how long you plan to stay in a place. But I figured a tipping point was that if I made a large down payment I'd have the option to either sell or become a landlord in four or five years."

Alex was fortunate enough to have a father willing to give her money toward her down payment—about 27 percent of first-time buyers get a cash gift, according to the National Association of Realtors, and she also had a Roth IRA retirement account from which to withdraw funds. So during the summer of 2010, she put $30,000 down on a $150,000 one-bedroom condo in Chicago's Old Town neighborhood. Her good credit qualified her for a 4.75 percent mortgage interest rate, and her monthly payment—including taxes, insurance, and condo dues—is $850.

$1,000 TO GET ROLLING IN A NEW COMMUNITY

Meanwhile, Erin, a forty-two-year-old adjunct college professor, spent her savings to rent and drive a U-Haul truck cross-country from Brooklyn to southern Oregon. She arrived with less than $1,000 to get into a new rental home. She'd chosen to move to Ashland for a change of lifestyle and proximity to family. But after nearly two decades working in gratifying but low-paying literacy and teaching jobs in New York City, she didn't have a big cash cushion for the transition. Indeed, the high cost of living in New York City and the difficulty of saving there were the other reasons she chose to move away.

Because she arrived short on cash, her options for finding a rental were limited to landlords who would let her pay her first month at move-in and then pay up the deposit over time. Ultimately, with references from her family, she found a two-bedroom for $700 a few miles outside of Ashland. She splits that with a roommate and is working part time while she works on building up a full-time teaching load.

"I definitely had to work those terms with my landlord, and he didn't make it easy," Erin says. "For a lot of people who live paycheck to paycheck, coming up with first and last months' rents and deposit is prohibitive. That's why some people I know can't move."

While she transitions—and until she gets full-time work—owning is out of the question. It may remain so for a long time.

"It's in the back of my mind," she says. "But I've got a lot of debt and savings to tackle before I can even start thinking about it."

WHY CASH OUTLAY MATTERS

Ultimately, Alex's and Erin's monthly housing payments aren't so different, $700 versus $850. But the cash outlay they each made to get into their homes, and their financial situations, couldn't vary more. A major difference between renting and owning is how much money you typically need on hand to get into your new home. Often, down payments are a deal breaker for people who like the idea of buying but not how much money it takes upfront.

Alex bought because she wanted to, she had a down payment available, and she has an exit strategy that she's factored into her financial planning. She could also make a down payment without depleting her emergency savings or touching her employer-offered 401(k) plan. Erin rented because she's getting to know a new community, working to establish herself professionally there, and lacks savings. And she knows her financial situation isn't going to change anytime soon. Her community's small size and high unemployment rate, and her arrival in the middle of an economic downturn, all mean she's working less than full time. She moved for lifestyle, not career.

So what can you expect if you're debating renting versus owning from a "money upfront" angle? Generally speaking, when renting, your deposit is a multiple of one month's rent—often one to three months' worth representing the first month of rent, last month of rent, and a deposit. In some markets, you may also need to pay up to two months' worth of broker fees just to gain entrée to the right properties.

When you buy a home, upfront costs can vary. That's because a home's listed price can be negotiated (or, in a hot market, driven higher by multiple offers) and then financed in dozens of different ways depending on the size of the down payment you make. You know a home's probable price tag at the outset, but math with a mortgage lender is what sets your monthly payment.

Take Alex. Her 20 percent down payment produced an $850 monthly housing payment. Had she made a 3.5 percent, or $4,250, down payment on her condo at the same interest rate, her monthly payment would fall between $1,050 and $1,100 (a figure that includes private mortgage insurance, required on mortgages originated with less than 20 percent down). If she put down 50 percent, as in the olden days, she'd pay $620 per month. She might not qualify for all of these options. But ultimately, if you're debating renting and owning the big idea is this: When it comes to renting, no matter how large your deposit is the rent remains the same. With owning, the bigger your down is, the smaller your monthly housing payment.

Understandably, renters with some—but limited—resources may feel that the kind of down payment required to produce a reasonable monthly housing payment simply costs too much.

"Sure, rent can seem high. But to get a low monthly payment in a home you own, you have to tie up all your money in a big down payment," says Chris, a twenty-five-year-old grad student at Kansas State University. Like Alex, he says he'd be leery of buying unless he had a very high down payment. He'd almost prefer a life of renting, but his fiancée is interested in owning, so he expects to eventually wade into homeownership.

The 20 Percent Goal

So how come Alex—and many buyers—want to make a 20 percent down payment to buy? When the Federal Housing Administration formed in the late 1930s as an agency that guaranteed mortgages in the event of default, thus spurring lenders to loosen up on their underwriting rules (lender-speak for lending criteria and formulas), typical mortgages required a 50 percent down payment and a short repayment term. But FHA's creation soon meant that lenders were willing to let people buy with a 20 percent down payment and longer repayment term. Over time, that was dropped to a 3 percent (currently 3.5 percent) down payment, but with the proviso that people paying under 20 percent pay private mortgage insurance (PMI).

These days, making a 20 percent down payment is more of a rarity than a norm: Four out of five first-time buyers make a less-than-20 percent down payment, according to NAR's Walt Molony. But those who strive to make one frequently are doing so to avoid paying PMI, an insurance whose cost varies based on your home's price and your credit score. Making a low down payment and getting a loan with PMI can lower your borrowing power, because PMI is factored in by lenders to your monthly housing costs. Many people feel paying PMI is like throwing money away since PMI is a payment that lowers borrowing power and doesn't add to equity.

Large downs may be eligible for better interest rates, give you a better "equity cushion" in the event of an unplanned near-term sale or market downturn, and may make you a more competitive home bidder, since some sellers see buyers with large down payments as more likely to succeed at closing on their loan. In addition, some housing types may require certain types of financing. For instance, some co-op communities require down payments as high as 25 percent to 50 percent. And during the height of the recent housing-related recession, some lenders required condo borrowers to make 25 percent down payments under the assumption that condos appreciate at a slower rate than single-family homes, therefore a higher down was needed to provide an equity cushion.

Is Bigger Always Better?
Rental deposits are typically easier to cobble together than down payments on a purchase. At a maximum, they're typically three months' worth of rent—first, last, and deposit—although in some markets there may be extra fees. Putting more deposit down on a rental doesn't really influence the monthly price of rent. Renters don't voluntarily pony up more money in the hopes of getting a cheaper rent. Where they do offer more deposit, it's at the request of a landlord who wants

UPFRONT COSTS

RENT

ONE TO FIVE MONTHS' WORTH OF RENT

DEPOSIT: Assume half to two months' rent, possibly higher for low credit scores

PET DEPOSIT: Most landlords charge an extra deposit for pets, often $300 to $500

FIRST MONTH'S RENT: Due upon lease signing or move-in

LAST MONTH'S RENT: Due upon lease signing or move-in

EXTRA FEES: Some landlords charge fees for storage, car/bike parking, etc.; these may be annual fees paid upfront, or may be charged monthly atop the rent.

BROKER FEE: In some cities, like New York, you may have to pay a fee to the broker who helped you find your place—one to two months' rent, or up to 15 percent of the annual rent. This is nonrefundable. If you plan to stay in a place several years, the broker fee hurts less. (Consider: If you pay 15 percent of annual rent to a broker for a $2,000/month apartment, but stay six years, the fee spread over six years averages $50 per month. Stay one year and it's equivalent to an extra $300 per month.)

SAVINGS: Some landlords will want to see that you have a certain amount of savings reserves, but this is less important in renting than in owning.

RENT VS. OWN

OWN

EARNEST MONEY: When you make an offer on a home, you typically write a check for several thousand dollars to prove you're serious about pursuing the purchase; this is known as earnest money, and if the seller accepts your offer the funds are placed in escrow and become part of your total down payment on the home.

DOWN PAYMENT: 0 percent to 30 percent, or more, of the home's price. It's rare to finance a purchase with a 0 percent down payment (VA loans are possible with zero down), common to do a 3.5 percent down payment via the FHA loan program, and also common to make down payments of 10 (FHA loans to borrowers with FICO scores under 580) to 20 percent or more of a home's purchase price. You can use gifted money, withdraw from retirement, or use a down payment assistance grant to fund a down payment, but special rules may apply.

CLOSING COSTS: Typically anywhere from 2 to 6 percent of the purchase price. You can negotiate that the seller pay closing, or possibly finance it. But it's better to assume you'll pay it than someone else will. Prior to 2010, sellers could pay up to 6 percent of a buyer's purchase price in closing costs (i.e., all of them) on an FHA loan, but this was lowered to 3 percent in 2010 so that buyers bring at least 3 percent of closing to the table.

SAVINGS: Many lenders want to see that buyers have a certain amount of money sitting in reserve, say two to six months' worth of housing payments.

more deposit because of your background check results. However, some state laws may restrict how much deposit a landlord can demand or accept, so offering more deposit may not help you much if you're in a competitive rental market.

With owning, on the surface of things, it seems like the goal is to put down the biggest down payment possible. But determining how much money you want to put toward a down payment is more complicated than that. The more money you put down on real estate, the less money you invest in other important personal assets, like emergency savings and retirement savings. While this isn't necessarily a bad idea—if, like Alex, you have money left in retirement funds after you pull out down payment money—it's also not necessarily a good one if you're transferring all of your assets into just one, a home.

Since in America borrowing to buy a home is viewed as beneficial and a mortgage is considered "good debt," you can dig deep into many otherwise untouchable resources to fund a home purchase. You can make a one-time withdrawal (known as a "distribution") of up to $10,000 from an IRA account to put toward your down, borrow from your 401(k) if your employer allows it, or accept cash gifts from friends and relatives. You certainly can't borrow from an IRA or 401(k) to pay rent. But if a benefactor wants to help with rent, most landlords—like lenders—won't object.

If you're buying and receiving a cash gift toward your down payment, you need to be aware of the "all or something" rule: Lenders want your white knight to either front all 20 percent of a down payment for you, or, if your gift giver can't do that, then lenders will want you to provide at least 5 per-cent of the home's down payment and then use the gift you've received atop that. You can also borrow from friends or family members through a personal loan, or via a social lending or microlending site. In addition, you can take advantage of down-payment-assistance programs offered through city, county, or state programs; generally, these programs provide you down payment help in exchange for your attending home buyer education classes and may require small fees if you move within a short window of time.

HOW TO PAY $2,000 LESS
TO MOVE INTO A CONDO THAN TO RENT

Here's a hypothetical example of how it could actually be cheaper in terms of upfront money to buy one stop across the Hudson from New York City than to rent there. Keep in mind that if the renter and owner here remained in their spaces for a long time period, some of these variables would change. The owner, for instance, would have to pay pop-up maintenance costs for the Hoboken unit that aren't included in the example below. The renter's monthly payment could go up with each lease renewal.

RENTING
IN HARLEM
$16,360 upfront + $3,700/month ongoing

BUYING
IN HOBOKEN, NEW JERSEY
$14,315 upfront + $3,185 per month ongoing

Take a $3,200/month two-bedroom apartment that charges $500 per month for parking. If the landlord or management company wants two months' deposit ($6,400) and a pet deposit ($500), and the broker charges a fee of 15 percent of the annual rent (or 15 percent of $38,400, which is $5,760), that comes out to $12,660. On top of that, you'll still need to pay your first month's rent and parking fee ($3,700).

YEAR ONE OUTLAY: $16,360 (includes deposits, broker, first-month's rent and parking) + $40,700 (eleven months' worth rent and parking) = **$57,060.**

YEAR TWO OUTLAY: $44,400 for rent (and parking), assuming no rent increases.

Take a $409,000 two-bedroom condo that includes a parking spot and charges $425 monthly dues. Say the buyer makes a 3.5 percent down payment of $14,315 (and has a 5 percent interest rate, thirty-year fixed mortgage). Assume the buyer has excellent credit and negotiates that the seller pays all closing costs, which are 3 percent of the asking price ($12,270). The buyer's monthly mortgage payment would be $2,694 (includes mortgage insurance and property tax), plus $425 per month for dues. Assume $66 per month for homeowners' insurance.

YEAR ONE OUTLAY: $14,315 (includes first payment) + $35,035 (eleven monthly payments of mortgage, insurance, taxes) = **$49,350.**

YEAR TWO OUTLAY: $38,220 for monthly payments, assuming same dues.

All that said, a low down payment may make sense even when you can afford a higher one if interest rates are low or if you're concerned about keeping cash reserves available, expect but haven't yet gotten an increase in income, or if you plan to stay a very long time.

Many would-be buyers, upon learning how much money it takes to get into a home, spend several months (if not years) focusing on saving and making arrangements to become champion borrowers. If you're mulling buying, or if you're wondering how people are financing their home purchases, bear in mind that they're not all making 20 percent down payments like Alex—although in surveys, many consumers say if they bought they'd make a big down payment. Despite the tough financing markets of recent years, 70 percent of all first-time buyers made a less-than-10 percent down payment to get into a new home, according to NAR. The median first-time buyer down payment is 4 percent.[8.1]

It seems that buyers are of two minds. They either strive to make as big a down payment as possible or, unable to save for a high down payment, they compensate by deciding they'll stay in their homes as long as possible and wait for their equity to slowly accrue. (Homeowners now expect to stay in their places for at least a decade, according to NAR consumer surveys.) The percentage of buyers using 0 percent down payments, however, is rapidly declining. In 2007, 45 percent of all first-time buyers made a 0 percent down payment,[8.2] whereas by 2010 only 17 percent used 0 percent down payments.[8.3]

There are exceptions to the notion that it always costs more to get into a purchased home than to rent. In some pricey cities renters pay such high broker fees to get into a rental that they could almost buy a place (though perhaps not as nice a place as they could rent) for the same price. And in some markets where home prices have dropped steeply, it's conceivable that consumers who opt to use low down payments can buy a home for not much more than what they pay to get into a rental.

EQUITY CUSHION CRUNCH TEST

1

Using current home price, **ADD 1 PERCENT** per year *(2 percent for price increase, minus 1 percent for repairs)*.

2

DEDUCT 10 PERCENT off your result, which represents the home's value minus the costs to sell it.

3

SUBTRACT YOUR MORTGAGE OUTSTANDING
(use an amortization calculator— www.amortization-calc.com is handy) from the result.

4

SUBTRACT YOUR DOWN PAYMENT from that result, since you're recouping it in the sale.

5

This is a ballpark of what you'll take away—or owe—at the end of your time period.

EXAMPLE

Sue and Jim and their 10 percent down payment

Sue and Jim buy a $175,000 house with a 10 percent ($17,500) down payment and a 5 percent interest rate on a thirty-year loan. If they stay five years, here's what could happen if there's a slight price appreciation:

1 175,000 + 5 percent (5 years × 1 percent) appreciation, or $8,750 = **$183,750**

2 $183,750 − $18,375 (10 percent) = **$165,375**

3 $165,375 − $144,600 = **$20,775**

4 $20,775 − $17,500 = **$3,275**

5 **$3,275**

The couple would make $3,275 over five years, or about $655 per year. If they stayed thirty years, though, they'd exit with $187,500, or $6,250 per year.

Here's what might happen if there are moderate price declines of 1 percent:

1 $175,000 − 10 percent (5 years × 1 percent price declines, 5 years × 1 percent repairs), or **$157,500**

2 $157,500 − $15,750 (10 percent) = **$141,750**

3 $141,750 − $144,600 = −**$2,850**

4 $2,850 − $17,500 = −**$14,650**

5 −**$14,650**

The couple would lose $14,650, despite living in their home for five years—or a loss of about $240 per month. They'd have to bring $2,850 to closing in order to move out.

DOWN PAYMENT AND EQUITY

In the short run, discovering that a rental deposit and down payment resemble one another price-wise can feel liberating to would-be buyers. But in the long run, the bigger issue with down payments is how much of an equity cushion you're building, and how much flexibility you'll have should you need to sell sooner than anticipated or want to eventually "move up" to a different sort of place.

Mark Hanson, a mortgage expert, told CNBC that owners need to be able to fetch home prices that pay off their current mortgage in full, pay a Realtor 6 percent of that sale price as commission, and then have anywhere from 3.5 percent to 20 percent left over to launch a down payment on a new home purchase.[8.4] This means that, while a homeowner might not have "negative equity," for purposes of selling he or she could find that, once they've paid commissions and fees, they're walking away with nothing or even less than what they've started with.

Being able to make a down payment that created sizable equity was a big factor in Alex's decision to buy—and lacking one is a big factor in Erin's decision to wait and work on her financial situation before even considering a purchase.

"Rent versus buy came up a lot while I was looking for a place, especially because my sister and her husband are losing money on a home they turned into a rental," Alex says. "But I have no regrets about how I went about buying."

THINGS TO CONSIDER: DEPOSITS AND DOWNS

1. **Inventory your assets**—savings, CDs, IRA, 401(k), big-ticket belongings you'd be willing to sell for cash—and their value. How much of this value do you feel should be invested in real estate? If you emptied out most of those assets to buy, how long would it take you to replenish those assets?

2. **If you're emptying out assets to make a down payment or deposit, could you replenish them faster by getting creative**—take on a roommate, host an overseas student for a stipend, get a part-time job pre- or post-move, or rent rooms out short-term?

3. **Inventory what others would give you to help you buy or move into a place.** Would they provide you with these funds whether you rent or buy, or only in one scenario? Are these funds an outright gift or a loan? Is someone agreeing to pay rent for you, or only act as a guarantor? If someone is helping you with a down payment, are you confident he or she can and will come through, and what is the maximum he or she will provide?

4. **Attend a first-time-buyer workshop in your market, offered by a non-profit—not a bank.** These workshops are designed to promote financial literacy and thus forestall foreclosures in communities and present neutral information about realistic monthly housing payments and, for those interested in buying, pointers on where to seek down payment assistance.

5. **Consider the matters of tenure and equity cushion if owning. How long do you plan to stay in your place?** If you're considering buying, ask yourself whether you could sell your home—assuming modest appreciation of 2 percent but subtracting a modest 1 percent back out for maintenance—for a profit at two, three, four, or five years, based on your down payment. Now model this by subtracting 2 percent of your home's price per year—what could happen in a bear market. Look at the results, and think about a 2 percent annual rent increase, no home repair costs, and a refundable deposit versus a down payment. What looks better to you?

CHAPTER 9

MONTHLY PAYMENTS

Rent Check vs. Mortgage Payment

When Ellen, a thirty-three-year-old who works in the financial industry in Houston, saw the rent on her two-bedroom apartment in the city's Galleria area jump from $1,075 to $1,175, she decided it was time to finally buy her own place. She already had savings set aside and had been tracking the for-sale market for a while. But something about the increase—even though it was the first she'd faced in four years—pushed her off the fence. The $100 monthly hike felt like a lot of money.

Before the rent change even had time to take effect, Ellen had made an offer and was scheduling closing on a $210,000 newly constructed home in a partially completed subdivision featuring an extensive trail system as well as a pool, clubhouse, and gym. While the monthly payment for her mortgage loan and interest together resembled her apartment's, on second look, the monthly costs to own her home are actually much pricier—$600 more, thus far, than the rent hike she fled.

But still, she perceives her new home as a good deal, a valuable investment that kept her from tossing more money at a landlord, even as evidence emerges that she's tossing money at other costs associated with owning. As an owner, she's now paying about $135 per month for a mix of landscaping work and homeowner association dues. These fees cover work previously included in her rent. She also has a high $5,900 tax bill, part of the territory with new construction in her region.

"I bought new construction because that's what's mostly available here, and because I thought maintaining it would be cheap at least for a few years. But where I live we're charged all these fees and taxes to pay for the infrastructure in our new subdivision," Ellen says. "It's hard to change your thinking from a renter's mentality to a homeowner's mentality."

COMPARING APPLES TO APPLES

Many buyers don't understand how much more owning costs than renting. For buyers who can make the necessary adjustments to their budget, learning what it truly costs to own a home—the trips to big-box stores, the midnight calls to plumbers—is mostly a test of patience. But for lower-income homeowners, or those who have little discretionary savings left for emergencies, the hidden costs to own a home can snap an already stretched budget.

Russell James, a professor at Texas Tech University, has studied flaws in the comparisons consumers are taught to make between renting and owning, noting that, both in their own analysis and in the analysis offered by rent versus own calculators, they tend to compare the price of rent and the price of a monthly mortgage payment (including mortgage principal and interest, taxes, and insurance) but not acknowledge several hidden factors such as higher utility costs in an owned home, the expense of furnishing and decorating a home that's likely larger than their rental, and, most important, not understanding what home maintenance costs or how expensive it can be to replace home appliances and systems.[9.1]

Experts estimate that annual maintenance costs for owners vary from 1 percent (optimistic) to 4 percent (cautious) of a home's purchase price. If you're comparing the monthly payments to rent and to own, you need to estimate repair costs on an owned home and then convert them (dividing by 12) to monthly costs, then add them to the monthly mortgage. Now you're comparing apples to apples.

For buyers with lower incomes, James says, what homes are available in affordable price ranges may be affordable because they require more work. Also, the amount spent on maintenance and repairs as a reflection of household income is much higher—about 7.5 percent of income—the less you earn than it is for wealthier owners, for whom this spending represents only 5.9 percent of income. The Urban Land Institute and other organizations concerned with urban development note that many buyers have to "drive till you qualify," meaning that reasonably priced housing payments may be accompanied by a pricey commute.[9.2]

Ads from lenders and builders frequently trumpet the possible low monthly payments available to buyers, suggesting that you can have a mortgage pay-ment resembling rent and get rid of that landlord. To Dr. James's point, these advertisements omit any sort of estimation of how home maintenance feeds into future housing payments that owners will make, so in that sense the cost to own is incomplete. Also, the mortgage types typically used in these promotions or in mortgage calculators often assume (or indicate in tiny-font footnotes) that you'll make a high down payment and have a top-notch credit score, both neces-sary to qualify for the rates that give you that payment.

By hooking you with a promise of a low payment or a "base price" similar to rent, you may tend to forgive or overlook the modifications to that price you'll ultimately pay, rationalizing that you still want to own and are still getting a good deal—paying, if not the equivalent of rent, then maybe just 10 percent more than rent per month to own. Renters' resentment at rent increases is, quite often, dis-proportionate to their resentment (or lack thereof) at the hidden costs they pay as owners to fund services included in their rent. Ellen's potential rent increase was a nearly 10 percent jump during the year it happened. Had her rent increased $25 per year for four years instead, it might not have felt so significant.

Once renters have withstood a few rent increases at lease renewal, they typically begin asking whether owning might make more sense, says Ron Johnsey, president of Axiometrics, a Dallas-based real estate research firm. When renters hit a tipping point with rent prices, Johnsey says, they're acting out the economic theory of substitution, which states that at a certain point a consumer becomes willing to replace one product with another—in this case, rented housing for owned. (Of course, this theory appears to have begun working both ways. Owners who've seen their home's value drop steeply—to where the home is worth less than its purchase price or the mortgage owed—are reconsidering renting.)

Nationally, annual rent increases in larger buildings have averaged less than 2 percent in recent years, according to Chris Brown, an executive at Apartments.com. He says that renters who commit to longer leases (twenty-four or thirty-six months) can lock in their rent at more favorable prices, as landlords are willing to concede a little bit of profit for the assurance that a particular unit won't need to go back on the market (and sit empty while a new renter is found) for a long period of time. Even in hot rental markets, Brown says, rents haven't risen more than 6 percent in any single year in recent history. However, the rental market, like the for-sale housing market, follows economic cycles: Rent increases in many markets are coming in part because of a mix of demographic factors and a slowdown in new apartment construction.[9.3]

○━

MONTHLY PAYMENTS

RENT

COST PREDICTABILITY FACTOR: High! The monthly payment to rent is very predictable for the duration of your lease. Your lease spells out the rent (and any other building services you elect to pay) for six, twelve, eighteen, or twenty-four months (or whatever your lease duration) at a time. Your only variation in monthly housing costs is likely to come at lease renewal, when you may get socked with a rent increase.

THE MAIN COST: Monthly rent. But it can go up with each lease renewal.

RENTER'S INSURANCE: Not a requirement, though some landlords are introducing it as one. It's cheap (typically $200 per year or less), according to the National Association of Insurance Commissioners.

PARKING SPOT: Often an option that's included, or available separately for an upcharge.

UTILITIES: Some rents include utilities (garbage and sewer, for instance), while others require that you set up your own utility accounts (phone, electric, gas, heat, cable).

STORAGE: Some buildings offer storage for free, others for an added fee.

MAINTENANCE: Included with the monthly rent.

RENT VS. OWN

OWN

PREDICTABILITY FACTOR: Semi-predictable. If you have a fixed-rate mortgage your monthly principal and interest payment is predictable, and generally your insurance rates won't rise precipitously year over year. But taxes, homeowner association dues, and maintenance are often out of your control.

THE MAIN COST: Monthly mortgage payments (including taxes and insurance), maintenance costs.

TAXES (either bundled into mortgage payments or paid separately): These can rise year over year based on your community's "assessment" of your property or if your community votes for increased property taxes to subsidize local government.

HOMEOWNER ASSOCIATION DUES:

These are usually stable, and set by you and other homeowners, but they can rise from one year to the next. You may face special assessments (read: expenses above and beyond the usual HOA dues, usually spread out over time) for major repairs.

UTILITIES: You're responsible for all your utilities, and if you're moving from an apartment to a house you may be surprised at how pricey they are.

INSURANCE (bundled into mortgage payments or paid separately): Homeowner's insurance is typically about $60 to $100 per month. You can lower the payments by making safety-related home upgrades or by using the same insurer for both home and auto. If you've made a less than 20 percent down payment, you may also be required to pay private mortgage insurance (PMI).

SUPPLEMENTAL INSURANCE: You can buy additional insurance if you live in a region with frequent Acts of God (hurricanes, a fire season, a fault line).

ADDITIONAL LOANS AGAINST YOUR PROPERTY: If you borrow against your property via a home equity loan or second mortgage, you are essentially increasing your mortgage balance and creating another monthly debt payment. It will be tax-deductible, though, and the interest rate will be far lower than conventional credit card rates. But depending on which funding type you choose, you will be required to make a set monthly payment (second mortgages are installment loans) or a varying monthly payment (home equity lines of credit are revolving loans).

MAINTENANCE: Not included. Assume 0.12 to 0.48 percent of your home's purchase price per month—or $83 to $332 per month per $100,000 worth of home value.

WHO'S GOT CONTROL OVER THEIR MONTHLY PAYMENT?

One of the most oversimplified arguments in the rent vs. own debate is that renters can't control their monthly housing payments, but owners can. It's correct that owners who choose a fixed-rate mortgage can rest assured that a portion of their monthly housing spending will be fixed—namely, the combined payment for principal plus interest on their loan. But that's not the whole story on the costs you'll pay as an owner.

Renters actually *can* control their monthly housing payments—but for a much shorter time period. They know exactly what they'll pay each month, but only for the number of months (six, twelve, twenty-four) represented by their lease. The price of rent includes the space where you live, building or community amenities, and repairs or maintenance. When you renew your existing lease or move and get a new one, the rent can rise.

Owners actually do see some components of their housing payment rise, if only slightly. Property taxes can rise as home values do or because of locally enacted tax levies expensed to citizens via their property taxes. Owners who live in condominiums, co-ops, or communities with a homeowner association can also see dues or collectively paid maintenance fees increase slightly from year to year. And for extraordinary repairs and big-ticket needs, these communities can add "special assessments"—added fees for pricey repairs—to your monthly bill.

Fortunately, Ellen can absorb the costs that accompanied her particular property. She bought a place priced far less than the $300,000 to $400,000 she'd been approved to purchase. In addition, she's gained a lot of space. Her 2,300-square-foot home is nearly three times as big as her old apartment and has four bedrooms and two bathrooms, meaning she has plenty of room for guests, a home office, and storage for materials related to a charity for teenage girls that she chairs.

She says she doesn't regret her purchase but acknowledges that she didn't incorporate all the expenses—which are not one-time fees, but recurring ones—associated with owning a home into her monthly payment estimates.

QUESTIONS TO CONSIDER

1. If you're a renter and your rent increase is making you think about buying, ask if the increase is justified by work the landlord has done to your unit or the building. Did you get new appliances that are lowering utility bills, new safety features, new amenities?

2. **Are you willing to forecast your future housing expenses?** If you're considering buying, and want to model how much more it might cost, take the expected mortgage payment and add 0.12 percent to 0.48 percent of your home's purchase price to it each month. If the total adds up to more than your current rent, then start setting aside the difference (owner's monthly payment minus rent) so you become accustomed to not having the same amount of disposable income due your new, more-expensive mortgage payments.

3. If you're considering buying, how much higher than your current monthly payment are you willing to go in order to write a mortgage versus rent check?

4. Would you be willing to eliminate some of your personal expenses (cable TV, some subscriptions, a little luxury like a monthly spa treatment) to become a homeowner?

5. If you're considering moving into a condominium or community with a homeowner association, did you ask to see board meeting minutes, a history of special assessments, or info on planned improvements that might necessitate dues increases or other special fees?

6. **Have you factored in the commute?** While moving farther from downtown or work may make for a cheaper housing payment, how much money and time will you spend commuting?

CHAPTER 10

HOW MORTGAGES WORK

Learn About Life's Biggest Loan

Caitlin, a twenty-four-year-old who works at an international adoption services company in Tulsa, bought an $86,500 house at the age of twenty-three. She's the youngest person among her single friends to buy, and she acknowledges that the $8,000 tax credit the government briefly dangled at buyers in 2009 propelled her into the market a bit sooner than she had expected.

But tax credits weren't the only motivating factor. After returning to Tulsa after college, Caitlin kept modeling the costs to own and coming up with numbers that made buying seem doable. Homes in Tulsa are much less expensive than in other parts of the country—the median home price there has toggled between $100,000 and $105,000 since mid-2007, according to data from Zillow.com. This means monthly payments, even factoring for hidden expenses, are closely comparable to the rents Caitlin had paid around town.

She had a small down payment on hand—about $5,000—and knew that FHA lenders were sympathetic to people like her with younger credit histories and scores. She also had a roommate at the ready (her brother) who would share her rent, helping her keep costs down after she bought.

"I had an idea of what my monthly payment should be, but not the home price or the financing options that would let me have that payment," she said.

Caitlin was also unsure, frankly, whether she could buy. She understood pieces of the mortgage process, but not the whole picture. Though she had money saved for a down payment, she didn't have funds for closing fees, which can run up to 6 percent of a home's price. She didn't know how much PMI cost. She didn't know how property taxes factored into a home payment.

She decided to research the buying process anyway just to double-check whether she had any options. Googling away, she stumbled upon a program administered through the City of Tulsa Housing Authority that offered first-time buyers assistance with purchase costs, with a few stipulations: Participants had to attend a first-time buyer workshop, then meet with a financial planner to discuss budgeting basics.

"The idea was to get people into houses but make sure they don't get foreclosed on in two or three years," she says. "In exchange I could get help with closing costs."

Caitlin qualified for the program, and when she closed on her three-bedroom house she paid only $4,000 (representing a 3.5 percent down payment and some fees for inspections), while the city paid $5,000 of her closing costs—or about 5.8 percent of her home's sale price. She has a thirty-year fixed-rate FHA loan with a 4.75 percent interest rate, and that includes private mortgage insurance. Her monthly mortgage payment, including homeowners insurance, PMI, and taxes, is $625—which she splits with her brother. She considers it a much better deal than the $475 she paid for a small one-bedroom apartment, even factoring in maintenance and higher utilities.

The only hitch for taking closing assistance? She has to stay at least five years in the home or else return a portion (prorated based on her tenure) of the closing fees given to her by the city.

MAKING SENSE OF MORTGAGE MECHANICS

Caitlin is like a lot of tire-kicking buyers. She understood pieces of the mortgage loan process—like that she had enough money available for a 3.5 percent down payment—but not the whole puzzle. Unfortunately, if you want to buy a home— or confirm your hunch that renting makes more sense based on your financial situation—you need to understand the lending industry's sea of acronyms and principles, and where you fit into the mortgage landscape as a borrower.

When you buy a home, you generally make a down payment for a percentage of the home's price and then finance (or mortgage) the rest. A mortgage is a secured loan—meaning it's a loan made against an asset (property), and if you default or fail to pay on that asset, the lender can repossess it. A mortgage includes principal (total amount you're borrowing) plus the interest rate you're paying on the debt. When a lender calculates your total permissible monthly housing payment, they'll refer to your housing payment as your PITI—which stands for principal, interest, taxes, and insurance (both homeowner's insurance and private mortgage insurance, if applicable).

Each month when you pay the mortgage you'll be paying for your principal and interest (and possibly PMI), but whether you spread the taxes and insurance out across twelve months and wrap them into that monthly payment or pay those separately depends on your loan type or personal preference. Generally, when you pay all expenses in one monthly bill, the portion of it that goes toward taxes and insurance is placed in an escrow account by your lender, which then pays these bills for you when they're due.

To determine how much you can borrow, lenders look at your finances. They generally don't want you to pay more than 28 percent of your total gross income for housing expenses—including the mortgage payment (principal plus interest), property taxes, insurance, and private mortgage insurance (if applicable). In addition, lenders generally don't want your housing payment and other debts combined to exceed 36 percent to 45 percent of your gross income (depending on the lending environment and loan type).

Lenders look at two other major variables aside from your debts and assets to determine how much and what type of mortgage you're eligible to use for a home purchase: Your down payment and your credit score. Based on these variables, they can determine the loan types and interest rates you're eligible to use, whether you need to pay private mortgage insurance (required on down payments below 20 percent), how much loan you can borrow, and what rate you'll have to pay for these options.

Mortgage Terms: How Long Will You Take to Pay Your Home-Related Debt?

The length of time you have to repay your loan is known as its term. Common terms are thirty-year or fifteen-year, but many terms are available. The shorter your term, the faster you'll pay your loan and the less you'll pay in interest during the life of the loan. The longer your term, the slower you'll pay your loan but the lower your monthly payment. Some buyers start out with a thirty-year mortgage and then refinance it to a shorter term later, when they've accumulated equity By waiting to gain more equity before refinancing to a fifteen-year mortgage, such owners are financing less principal in a new loan and thus—despite the shorter term—will pay less per month than if they'd started with a fifteen-year term at the outset. Another bonus: Fifteen-year interest rates are usually cheaper than thirty-year interest rates.

Mortgage Interest: How Will You Pay Interest on the Loan?

The interest rate you pay on your loan is determined primarily by your down payment size and your credit score. Interest rates are applied as "fixed" rates, meaning your loan has the same interest rate throughout its term, or "adjustable" (also "variable") rates, meaning your loan can start with one interest rate and then adjust or "reset" to another rate as frequently as from one month to the next. The rates on adjustable-rate mortgages (ARMs) are generally tied to benchmarks (certain indices whose rates you can find in larger newspapers' financial pages or Web sites) and rise and fall (or "float") in relation to the changes in them.

A hybrid ARM blends elements of a fixed-rate and adjustable-rate mortgage. This type of loan offers a fixed rate for a set time period, and then resets for the rest of the term. Hybrid ARMs are typically described with two numbers: A 10/1 ARM, for instance, is a loan with a fixed interest rate for its first ten years and rate adjustments annually throughout the remainder of the term. A 2/28 ARM would be fixed for two years, then adjustments over the next 28 years.

Fixed-rate loans with thirty-year terms typically carry slightly higher interest rates than ARMS, but borrowers who use them like the predictability of a rate they know won't change. In addition, if loan rates drop, borrowers with a fixed rate can always shop around and refinance to a better deal. ARMs typically start out with a markedly lower interest rate (say, 0.5 percent below fixed rates), so payments are lower than on a fixed rate. Buyers who have used ARMs during the current period of sustained low interest rates have found that, even with resets, their new rates are still quite affordable. Some ARM users, however, choose to refinance to a fixed rate eventually.

During the housing boom, many so-called subprime loans were built from adjustable-rate mortgages that offered initial low "teaser" rates followed, a few years later, by dramatic resets that many owners couldn't afford or hadn't understood, or both. Because these loans had expensive refinancing penalties, borrowers often became trapped between new, high mortgage payments and the costs to refinance to a saner mortgage.

A "balloon" mortgage lets the borrower make low regular payments for a set term, and then pay off the lion's share of the balance in a short period toward the end of the term—thus, the balance "balloons" toward the end of the loan's term. During the run-up to the housing crisis, you could even get an "interest-only" loan, meaning you only made payments on your loan's interest and never actually cut into principal, or a "pay option" loan, where you could pay interest, principal, both, or some other portion of your loan, but not necessarily the entire amount due.

You could also get what's known as a negative amortization loan, where you paid less than a full mortgage payment—meaning that the interest portion left unpaid is deferred or rolled over, allowing your amount owed to grow (or amortize negatively), rather than shrink over time. These loans have maximums at which point they're required to amortize—but essentially, they're recipes for negative equity if you never make full loan payments.

With the exception of fixed-rate loans and adjustable-rate loans that have caps on their reset rates, these other loan types have fallen out of favor with lenders and consumers alike. But that's not to say these loans won't return to the market or attract some borrowers.

HOW HOUSING TYPE IMPACTS MORTGAGE OPTIONS

The type of home you choose to buy can also influence your mortgage options. If you're debating between a single-family freestanding home versus a condominium or other type of attached housing, you may be surprised to learn that you can borrow slightly more to buy a house than a condo. The reason why is that lenders factor the amount of money you'll pay to a condominium's homeowner association into your total monthly housing payment, which reduces the principal you can borrow. These communities may also require that buyers use particular financing types.

Following the housing bust, lenders began adding additional stipulations to condo loans. Some request higher down payments on condos, since condos tend to appreciate at a more modest rate than houses. Others placed caps on how many condo properties can be investor-owned (i.e., operated as rentals). FHA loans began stipulating that buyers of condos could purchase homes only in buildings or developments where construction was complete, 90 percent of units were occupied, more than half of all units were owner-occupied (i.e., minimal investor/rental presence), and only a certain percentage of other units were already FHA-financed. These restrictions may ease moving forward, but if you're debating between a condo and single-family home, it's worth asking your lender as well as your agent questions about financing restrictions in condo buildings.

In addition, if you're buying a "fixer" or a distressed property, you may be ineligible for certain types of loans because they require that properties purchased fulfill certain standards with respect to habitability. If a fixer is sufficiently damaged (and the seller can't or won't update it) or if a home is sold "as is" (meaning the seller will make no fixes), you may hit roadblocks.

FHA offers an interesting loan called the 203k that serves as a workaround for people buying fixers: Using a 203k loan, buyers can borrow above the asking price of the home they're buying and finance the cost of home renovations within the mortgage. The process requires extra steps and slightly higher loan origination fees, and it includes multiple site visits, appraisals for the home's "before" and "after" value, a work repair plan that must be lender approved, and use of approved contractors who can fill out 203k paperwork. The overage borrowed by the buyer for repairs is held in escrow by the lender, who pays contractors as work is completed.

For Mark, a forty-nine-year-old president of an online marketing company in Seattle, the 203k loan was a godsend when he and his family were searching for homes in 2010. With moderate incomes but a need for plenty of space for two toddlers and frequent guests, Mark and his wife were hard-pressed to find a move-in ready home priced below $375,000 that suited their needs—even in the suburbs. With the 203k loan, they were able to borrow $32,000 above the $325,000 price of the 1950s fixer they bought in the city of Shoreline. With the extra funds, they paid for updates to the home—including two bathroom overhauls, replacement of the home's electrical system, and installation of new energy-efficient windows and doors.

CONFORMING LOAN VS. JUMBO LOAN

Mortgage loans are also classified by amount. This has less to do with you, the consumer, and more to do with what happens at a bank or lender after you've been given your loan. In the past, if you borrowed up to $417,000, you were making a "conventional" or "conforming" loan that adhered to Fannie and Freddie standards and was insured. If you borrowed more, you were seeking a "jumbo" or "nonconforming" loan. (Keep in mind: This number represents the part of your home's price you are borrowing, not the price of the home itself.)

In recent years, the Federal Housing Finance Agency overseeing Fannie and Freddie allowed the limits for conforming loans to exceed $417,000 in certain higher-priced markets, up to $729,750. This has since dropped to $625,500. So if you live in an area that's known for being expensive (think major cities on the coasts), and you're wondering about the line between conforming and nonconforming, search "loan limits" on Fannie Mae's site and investigate the numbers for your metropolitan area.

Jumbo loans require higher down payments, strong credit scores, and, even with them, will cost you more than a conforming loan. In the past, a jumbo loan would add on about 25 basis points (0.25) to an otherwise non-jumbo mortgage rate, but these loans can carry even higher interest rates, often adding another 150 basis points (1.5) to an otherwise conforming interest rate. Because these loans are typically overseen by the lender or bank that originated them with a borrower, rather than sold to investors on what's known as the secondary mortgage market, they are more risky for lenders to offer. Some companies that offer jumbo loans require down payments up to 40 percent, depending on whether the buyer is purchasing a house or condominium.

Loan limits for single-family homes or condos are adjusted annually. In recent years, they've been as follows:

$625,500 OR MORE	$625,500	$417,000 OR MORE	$417,000 OR LESS
The borrowing range for jumbo loans in high-priced markets.	The top limit for conforming loans in high-priced markets.	The borrowing range for jumbo loans in normal local markets.	The limit for conforming loans in normal local markets. *

*(FHA loans may have lower maximums in some markets.)

Mark advises anyone trying this type of loan to work with a local bank or lender—one that has offered the loans before and can recommend contractors who know the 203k guidelines.

"We tried this first with a large bank and it didn't work very well, but once we went to a small bank everything happened smoothly," he says. "The loan officer and underwriter knew all the contractors we were using, and so information flowed back and forth much faster."

SHOPPING FOR A LOAN AND DECODING THE RESULTS

Most home buyers approach the process by thinking about the monthly payment they can ultimately afford, and then working backward to find mortgage options permissible for their credit score and down payment size. If you go directly to a bank or lender, you'll learn about the products that particular organization can offer you. If you go to a mortgage broker—a professional who scans available loans from multiple banks and lenders—you'll be exposed to more choices, but you will also pay that broker a fee embedded within your financing. It always pays to shop around, online and off, for the best offers.

When you think of a mortgage, you probably think of how much down payment you're making. But lenders think of your loan from the other side—that is, how much of a home's price they're helping you finance. If you make a 10 percent down payment, lenders say you've got a loan-to-value, or LTV, of 90 (meaning the percent of your loan as a percentage of home value is 90 percent) or that you're doing 90 percent financing. If you make no down payment, that's 100 percent financing. It's possible to finance more than 100 percent of the home's value in some circumstances, such as financing closing costs and paying them back within your monthly payments instead of upfront with your purchase.

Depending on the balance you plan to borrow (jumbo or conventional/conforming), the down payment you want to make, and your credit score, you'll have access to different loans. Some borrowers confuse the "genre" of loan they have with who their lender actually is. For instance, if you have an FHA loan, FHA didn't actually lend you money. Instead, another lender loaned you money using FHA guidelines. When you seek preapproval, it's important to ask the lenders you're talking to what loan types they do and don't offer with respect to your situation.

If you need to make a low down payment, your credit score isn't very high, and you have a fairly high debt-to-income ratio, an FHA loan may be a strong option. These loans require a minimum 3.5 percent down payment (10 percent if your credit score is below 580), and will include private mortgage insurance. They're available to first-time buyers and those who haven't bought within the past three years, as well as to non-U.S. citizens with documentation.

Military alums who served a minimum number of days and were honorably discharged can tap Veterans Administration loans, which allow a 0 percent down payment. Lower-income households (50 percent to 80 percent of local median incomes) living in designated rural areas can also make 0 percent down payments to buy a home via the U.S. Department of Agriculture (USDA) loan program. Borrowers able to put anywhere from 5 percent to 20 percent down will be able to tap multiple loan types, some backed by Fannie Mae or Freddie Mac, depending on credit scores and down payment type. And borrowers making more than 20 percent down payments won't face private mortgage insurance.

Qualification vs. Approval

Many buyers get prequalified for a loan—a process in which you generally describe your debts and assets, income, financial position, and a guesstimate of your credit range, and in exchange you learn from a lender what your *borrowing potential* is. This helps you ballpark your borrowing power, and doesn't involve a credit check. It's not official, but it helps you set expectations and discuss potential problems and loan products with a lender (or a Web site)—however, it's important that you be honest with the company preapproving you, or else you'll come away with false expectations about your borrowing potential.

If you're ready to start shopping, you can get preapproved. Preapproval is more involved and more official: It is a binding commitment by a company to provide you with financing up to a certain limit, on certain conditions. You can seek preapproval with multiple lenders simultaneously to see who can offer you the best terms. During the preapproval process, a lender will ask for your identification, credit scores and reports, tax returns, pay stubs, bank statements, asset statements (paperwork connected to stocks and bonds or to retirement accounts), and more. Preapproval helps you prepare for the final loan application you'll make once you've identified a property. It isn't a guarantee of funding—it's more like a mock-up of conditions in which you'd get funding, once you've chosen a home and once you've jumped through a few more hoops.

Through the preapproval process, within three days of your application, the lender will be able to provide you with a "good faith estimate" of your borrowing limit, future mortgage terms, and a ballpark estimate of how much money you will need to place not only in a down payment but also bring to cover closing. A good faith estimate includes all the fees associated with your potential loan and will show you a close approximation of your ultimate monthly payment on a property based on the down payment you plan to supply, your credit score, and the maximum home price you can consider. Fees outlined on good faith estimates include lender-related fees (such as loan origination fees), fees charged by other parties required for you to complete your transaction (inspection, appraisal, title) and escrow, as well as the total you're expected to bring to closing. A good faith estimate is only an "estimate," which means some figures can change. As of 2010, the government made it illegal for some of those costs to rise and capped other costs' increases at 10 percent. Costs that cannot increase include points, loan origination fees, and transfer taxes, while costs that can rise up to 10 percent include lender-required services such as title services or government recording charges. It's up to you to shop for a home inspector and insurer.

When you are ready to buy a specific property, you begin the formal loan application process—and, if all goes well, you'll get what's called a commitment letter from a lender, which becomes part of your purchase offer paperwork.

MANIPULATING YOUR INTEREST RATES

Once you've identified a mortgage program for which you're qualified, you have the option—if you can afford it and are interested—to pay an extra fee to your lender in order to further lower the interest rate on your mortgage. Doing this is known as buying additional "points." You are already paying points—a certain percentage of your home loan amount—to secure your loan. These points are also known as origination fees, or expressed in mortgage interest rate charts alongside those rates (i.e., the points you pay at closing to get this rate). In some cases, you can ask a seller to finance them.

When you buy additional points to lower your loan rate, you pay 1 percent of your loan in exchange for an interest rate reduction. By paying upfront to lower your loan rate, you're betting that, over time, the lower loan rate will save you so much money that the upfront cost to get it is worth it. When considering buying points, you or your lender need to calculate how many months it will take for the points to pay off for you—in other words, how many months of points-related savings it will take before you're benefiting from them.

As we explored in chapter 6, homeowners can also manipulate their interest rates by refinancing their mortgage. Often, owners refinance a few years after buying to lower their interest rate to currently available market rates and thus

PLAYING WITH POINTS

CALCULATE the monthly payment at the interest rate you're approved to use.

CALCULATE the monthly payment if you buy points.

SUBTRACT the difference between these payments to find out your monthly savings using points.

DIVIDE the amount you're paying for points by the amount saved per month. The result is how many months it would take (i.e., how long you need to stay in your home) to break even for buying points.

get a lower monthly payment. They may refinance to exit an adjustable-rate mortgage and move into a fixed-rate loan. They may refinance to shorten the term of their loan—say, from a thirty-year loan to a fifteen-year loan—in order to pay it off faster or reduce what they pay during the life of the loan. And, finally, they may do a "cash-out" refinance—in effect, increasing their loan balance in exchange for cash to fund major expenses, such as remodeling, education, or a surprise expense.

To refinance successfully, you need two things: Good credit and equity. Normally, buyers who have stayed in their homes for several years and are paying bills responsibly should have both. However, if your market is sluggish or you take out a loan whose terms you dislike on the assumption you can refinance later, you need to be prepared for the possibility that your refinancing options may not be much better than the loan you already have. When you refinance your mortgage, you will have to pay for (or finance) the same closing fees and possibly an appraisal that were required when you first bought your home. You are, in essence, buying your home again—but using a different loan program or lender. Because you'll pay new fees to refinance, many lenders will model for clients how long they'll need to remain in their home in order to get a "payoff" for having paid those costs, much the way you can model whether points will save money.

Industry experts say that if your goal with a refinance is to get a lower rate on a loan with the same term, you generally need to get a rate that's at least 0.5 percent lower in order to justify the closing costs that will accompany the refinancing. If you're able to refinance with a lender or broker who won't charge closing costs, you may be able to justify the refinance to the same term if you're getting a 0.25 percent drop in rate. If you're considering refinancing to a shorter term, you need to consider whether your interest rate will improve so much that it justifies the closing costs of a refinance: In some cases, making higher payments on a loan can achieve the same impact as refinancing to a shorter-term loan, and without the fees.

LOANS FOR MODERN LIVING

The banking industry isn't traditionally known for flexibility. In an ideal world, banks like to lend to steadily employed, high-net-worth individuals who can pony up big, fat down payments. In the real world, middle-class half-employed student loan–indebted singles and unmarried couples and lots of fiscally reorganized divorcées are out scanning real estate sites, wondering how a household—and a life—like theirs fits under a lender's lens. But fear not, if you're self-employed, have low-income, a negative financial history, or are shacking up, you can still qualify for a loan if you're realistic and determined.

Unmarried buyers account for about 8 percent of the home-buying market, according to NAR. In some cases, these pairs are friends, siblings, or family members who co-purchase a home that they intend to share for several years before one or both parties makes an exit. In other cases, these pairs are romantic partners. Especially among platonic co-buyers, these types of shared buying situations are often structured as what's known as a joint tenancy (fifty-fifty ownership) or a "tenancy in common" deal, whereby you and your co-owner share the space disproportionately. Such deals are more common in expensive markets where it takes more than one income to make a purchase.

For lending purposes, your credit scores and collective debt and assets will be plugged into the same lending formulas used for individuals—but be forewarned that if you have two very different credit scores, your options may hew toward the lower-scoring borrower's. If the stronger-scoring borrower is capable, he or she can buy the home himself or herself and then, post-purchase, draw up paperwork outlining the intention to split that home with you. Often, this is as simple as drawing up what's called a "quit claim" deed, stating that a homeowner is giving another equal ownership or a particular ownership stake in the property. But there are other options, some of which vary by state law. It's worth talking to a lawyer if you plan to co-buy with a platonic partner and perhaps form a "property prenup."

Self-employment presents another sticky scenario for buyers. For a time, lenders made loans with little or no income verification to self-employed people. These loans were known as "stated income" loans, meaning you stated your income, and the lender took your word for it. (They later became known as "liar loans.") The days of the stated income loan are over. If you're self-employed, you need to have at least two full years of self-employment under your belt, because lenders will want two full years' worth of tax returns—pretty much the equivalent of a tally of your pay stubs. Second, you're going to need to bring a boatload of paperwork to your lender demonstrating your financial worthiness as a buyer and possibly even dummy up a "profit and loss statement." If you're self-employed but buying with a salaried partner, you may have an easier time qualifying, but you should expect extra scrutiny nonetheless.

The lending landscape has changed enormously in recent years, stretching from a lenient, creative environment where just about anyone could qualify to take out a mortgage to a conservative, tough-talking environment where high credit scores, extra paperwork, and even extra appraisals may be necessary. That's why finding out your financing options is a good first stop if you're considering renting versus buying. By finding out the borrowing options that make sense for you (if any), you can move on to your shopping options. But if you shop first and seek financing later, there's higher risk that you'll take a loan—any loan—because you've fallen in love with a home. Thinking financing first may help with the goal of sustainability.

CHAPTER 11

WHAT DOES AN AGENT DO?

Shop, Negotiate, Close

One day it just happens, a few of your friends buy, and the next thing you know you're hearing about their real estate agents, or maybe even meeting their agents at social gatherings. The more friends who buy, the more agents appear, sprouting like kudzu. Whether you're a die-hard renter or are mildly curious to find out what's out there, before you can say "Hi, my name is . . ." there's a chance you'll have an agent's business card and a friendly offer to help you house hunt, *whenever you're ready*.

○—

SHOPPING AND NEGOTIATING ON YOUR BEHALF

The majority of all buyers will hire an agent to help them acquire a home, according to the National Association of Realtors. Real estate agents play a huge role in the home-buying process; they not only help you shop for homes, but, more important, they help you negotiate your purchase. In between shopping and buying there are dozens of other tasks agents do that are integral to a successful real estate deal.

But for the purposes of the rent versus own debate, you need to know that traditional or full-service agents' most important tasks are helping you find and access homes that suit your criteria and fall within your budget, then negotiating your purchase for you. An agent is both a personal and financial partner in your transaction, and should serve your interests.

These two functions, shopping and negotiating a deal, represent the emotional versus the rational or practical part of buying. Ideally, your agent will be great at both, intuiting the properties that suit you as well as negotiating a deal that works for you. After all, if you find a great home but you overpay for it or cave in to a feisty seller, that will impact your living and financial experience of ownership for years to come. And an agent who cuts great deals but has the wrong bedside manner for you as a client may not ever get to show off their deal-making moxie. But find the right home, and strike the right deal? Then you'll be happy to refer friends to your agent one day.

In the past, information about homes for sale used to be firewalled in databases only accessible to agents. But advances in technology and the Internet's growing role in real estate during the past two decades have made the home shopping process much more transparent for buyers. There are still layers of data viewable only by agents, but, generally, you can get a pretty good idea before you tour a home in person about many of its details, its neighborhood, and its owner history.

While some buyers like an agent to field listings for them and help them sift through an abundance of data about individual homes, zip codes, and cities, or to help them process their responses to touring homes, some tech-savvy or more-independent buyers feel they can do much of that on their own and lean on their agent mainly for the negotiating. If you're the latter type of buyer, there are a few types of lower-fee brokerages such as Redfin (www.redfin.com) or ZipRealty (www.ziprealty.com), which will leave you with a little more autonomy and responsibility for the shopping process, but represent you fully during the offer and purchase negotiations, and then discount or rebate some of their commissions with you when the deal's done, in the form of a rebate.

NOT ALL AGENTS ARE CREATED EQUAL

Julie and Chris, a Seattle couple in their late thirties, hired a newly minted traditional real estate agent whom they knew via friends when they bought their first home seven years ago. They already knew her, they reasoned, so she could help them find a fitting home. After all, how hard could it be?

The couple knew they'd have to buy a fixer to get into their first-choice neighborhood. The two-bedroom, two-bathroom home they found for $339,000 needed extensive work, including a new sewer line, extensive structural work to support a failing basement wall, and electrical upgrades. There was evidence of rats in the unfinished basement, and in the finished portion of the house the couple wanted to restore a dining-room-turned-bedroom to its former function. They had a sense their work was cut out for them. But they didn't know that maybe they'd chosen the wrong agent.

"Back then, I didn't really understand the value of an agent other than their unlocking doors to show you around," says Julie. "Now I know better."

After living through an expensive remodel that consumed most of their weekends, Julie says she regrets that their agent didn't discourage them from buying the home. But what she regrets even more is that during negotiations their agent suggested they pay *more* so the couple could in essence finance the home's repairs rather than negotiating down so that the home's sale price better reflected its condition. The couple paid about $20,000 above asking in exchange for the seller tackling $20,000 worth of work. In retrospect, Julie feels they could've paid less—and still demanded that the seller do some of the work.

"She could've counseled us to bring the price down based on what we found in the inspection," Julie laments. "But she wanted the deal to get done. In the end, I think she would've sold us anything."

Fast forward several years, and the couple sold this home and bought another, using a different agent. Rather than "go with the flow" this time, the duo interviewed agents, eliminating the ones who sent underlings to show them houses, the ones who "talked up" homes for sale rather than pinpointing potential issues and red flags, and who were slow to respond to e-mails.

The agent they ultimately hired was responsive, involved, objective, and offered to cut them a deal on her commissions—lowering her commission to sell their original home to 1 percent (from 3 percent) if they also used her to buy their next home. They were happy with how she negotiated their new purchase deal. When they arrived at their new home, however, it was filled with junk the seller had abandoned. But their agent was on it.

INTERVIEWING AGENTS

EXPERIENCE

How many years have you been in business, and how many deals have you done? Where are you licensed? Have you represented more buyers or sellers?

RESPONSIVENESS

How many clients do you have at one time? How long does it take for you to get back to clients on e-mail, via phone, or text? How often can you take clients on home tours?

CLIENT PROFILE

Who is your typical client? Where are they shopping for a home and in what price range are they spending? Are you willing to work in other neighborhoods and at other price ranges?

HOME TYPES

Have you helped buyers mainly with single-family homes or condominium projects? Have you helped your clients buy distressed property?

LISTINGS DIVERSITY

Will you be an exclusive buyer's agent? Will you show me properties listed by others in your brokerage? Will you show me for-sale-by-owner homes? What about homes listed by discount brokers, where the seller's fee—and thus, yours—may be lower?

COMMISSIONS

What is your standard commission fee? Will you negotiate lowering it or sharing it?

LENDING REQUIREMENTS

Do you require clients to be prequalified or preapproved, or will you start working with clients while they're pursuing their financing?

PATIENCE

How patient are you? If a client wanted to look casually during a long period of time, would you lose patience?

"Both our agent and the seller's showed up with a truck to haul away junk," Julie says. "That was above and beyond. Our agent looked out for us even post-sale. Our first agent was just gone."

It's not hard to find an agent. But finding an agent you like and who can serve your needs may take some research. Don't be afraid to interview agents, like Chris and Julie did, asking them about personal style, typical clients, the typical price range or neighborhoods with which they're most experienced, and how they will represent your interests.

UNDERSTANDING CREDENTIALS

AGENT
A real estate agent represents consumers who are buying or selling a home. They are licensed according to state laws and are typically required to take continuing education courses to remain licensed. Some states require that agents be Realtors as well.

REALTOR
A Realtor is an agent who is not only state licensed but also a member of the National Association of Realtors (NAR), which requires an additional layer of education from its members—including ethics education. For more information, visit www.realtor.org.

BROKER
A broker is an agent who has sought additional education, as required by their state, to run a real estate business (or brokerage). Agents are affiliated with broker-run offices and pay various fees or fractions of their commissions to their broker.

BUYER'S AGENT

If you're buying, then in a transaction your agent is the buyer's agent, the person representing your interests. Buyer's agents are paid by the seller, typically getting half or a portion of the commission the seller pays. (Often, this translates to 3 percent of sale price.)

LISTING AGENT

The agent representing the seller is the listing agent. Listing agents are paid by the seller and get a portion of the commission the seller pays. Sellers typically pay 5 to 7 percent, so listing agents typically get half that amount (the rest goes to the buyer's agent).

REDUCED-FEE AGENT

These agents work for lower commissions, costing sellers less and/or refunding a portion of their standard commission. Some reduced-fee agents charge on a "fee-for-services" basis, while others may use a "team" approach to make the process efficient and then provide the most face time when you get to the offer process.

DUAL AGENT

This is an agent who may represent both buyer and seller in a transaction. While dual agency is less common now than in the past, some listing agents bring their buyer clients to properties they represent—meaning they'll get commissions on "two sides" (buyer and seller) of the deal. On the one hand, an agent who knows both parties' interests can forge a successful negotiation and will often reduce commissions. But on the other hand, there may be inherent conflicts concerning the agent's priorities—the seller's, or yours—in this setup. Additionally, if your agent and a different listing agent work in the same brokerage, some consider that a dual-agency situation, since it's possible the two agents could share information that would compromise your interests.

EXCLUSIVE BUYER'S AGENT

This is a buyer's agent who represents only buyers and won't take for-sale listings so as to avoid the conflicts that may arise in dual agency. Such an agent may belong to the National Association of Exclusive Buyer Agents. For more information, visit www.naeba.org.

SPECIAL DESIGNATIONS

Many agents seek special credentials from NAR or other organizations so they're trained to cater to specific buying populations (seniors, minorities) or buyers after a specific property type (distressed property, "green" homes, vacation homes, investment property, etc.).

WORKING WITH A LOWER-FEE AGENT?

Neha, a thirty-one-year-old attorney, and her husband, a software engineer, knew they were slowly outgrowing their first home, a two-bedroom condo. A work-from-home husband crossed with frequent guests meant their space was often cramped. They liked their area of northwest Washington, DC, and wanted to stay there, so Neha's husband began tracking listings in their area. They hit a few open houses but weren't impressed with their options.

Eventually, they saw a recently built five-bedroom townhouse hit the market. It was near their Metro stop, had room for guests and a home office, and parking for two. Since they were clear about the zip code where they wanted to buy and had a specific property in mind, the duo decided to work with Redfin, a lower-commission agency. They didn't need help shopping or vetting a neighborhood, Neha says. What they wanted help with, she says, was cutting a deal with the seller.

"Our generation's idea of the personal touch doesn't mean you have to see your agent in person all the time," Neha says. "We communicated a lot electronically."

Indeed, much of their offer moved along virtually. Neha's husband was traveling extensively, and the duo were able to sign many documents electronically and negotiate a "lease-back" deal so that the seller, after closing, could remain in the property and lease it back from them for several weeks.

The couple's home cost $1.3 million—a high price tag for a high-powered duo. But considering that their agent refunded half of the 3 percent fee a buyer's agent is paid—in this case half of $39,000, or $19,500—the couple was happy both with the efficient process and saving on fees.

There's more to say on agents, but for the sake of the rent versus own debate, you've got the basics nailed down. Agents aren't just there to push you into any old property—though occasionally, a bad one will try—but to help you solidify your own ideas of how you want to live in a space you'll commit to for many years. Generally, if you've gotten to where you're talking to agents, it's likely that for you there's no turning back—at least emotionally speaking—about your desire to buy.

But even if you've got conviction, a good agent will rein you in when your emotions get ahead of practical considerations—reminding you of budgets, commutes, or issues that you're willfully ignoring in the hazy fog of house lust. Reality checks are what Michelle, a forty-one-year-old tech contractor, liked about her agent. When shopping for a home with her boyfriend, the agent kept reminding them when a home that "almost" fit actually fell short of the duo's stated requirements.

"What I loved about my agent is that she wanted us to be happy, even if that meant talking us out of a place we thought we liked," Michelle says. "She'd say, 'I know you're in love with this kitchen, but remember how you both said you wanted separate office spaces and how, Michelle, your space had to be set apart from the TV area so it would be private and quiet? Well, this place doesn't have any of that.' "

WORKING WITH A BUYER'S AGENT

Once you've chosen an agent, the process of shopping and buying goes something like this:

SUMMIT MEETING

You meet with an agent and discuss your budget, ideal neighborhoods, and priorities (requirements versus preferences) in a home.

SHOPPING

The agent chooses appropriate homes and takes you to tour them. You're free to also find homes and nominate them to your agent for consideration, and to go to open houses as well. If you're working with a discount agent, your agent may not be the one who takes you to tour homes—sometimes that falls to a partner agent—but will ultimately represent you when you buy.

OFFER CONSIDERATION

When you're getting serious about a particular property and mulling an offer, your agent will develop a "comparative market analysis" (CMA) of similar homes on the market to make sure that the one that interests you is priced sensibly and to give you added perspective.

OFFER PROCESS AND ACCEPTANCE

Your agent guides you through the offer process and paperwork, refers you to third parties (escrow, inspector, insurers, contractors), and deals with contact from the seller's agent. Your agent makes sure various components of the transaction happen on time and represents any changes to your offer—such as further negotiation after an inspection.

COMMISSIONS

These are typically 5 percent to 7 percent of a home's price and paid by the seller. Your agent typically gets half these fees and the selling agent the other half. If you work with a discount broker, you may get anywhere from a portion to half of your agent's fees back as a rebate. At Redfin, for instance, an agent who gets 3 percent for helping a buyer get a $300,000 home would share half of their $9,000 commission with the buyer—giving them $4,500.

CHAPTER 12

RESEARCHING PROPERTIES

Wish Lists vs. Realities

Claudia, a forty-four-year-old IT manager who rents an apartment in Harlem, is looking to buy in the New Jersey suburbs. She's from Jersey, and she works on the New Jersey side of the Hudson River, too. In between New York taxes, her commute, and her desire for some sort of yard or garden space, going back to the old stomping grounds makes more sense than shopping for a home in Manhattan. Besides, she's lived in the city for ten years—above a Mexican restaurant.

Approved to pay up to $400,000, she's looking to spend far less—under $300,000. She's been shopping for four months with her agent, and after visiting at least twenty homes has narrowed her search down to a small community called Fair Lawn, a close commute to both work and social life in the city. Her search has been an iterative process: At first, she wanted her future home to have three bedrooms, two bathrooms, central air, a porch, a fireplace, and maybe a pool. Now, she laughs at her initial must-have list.

"Along the way, you drop those goals," she says. "Now I'm thinking more about the structure's condition, ceiling height, the potential resale value. I don't have a fireplace now, and I'm doing just fine. But I might stick with the three-bedroom goal, because that's important for resale where I'm looking in New Jersey."

Searching for a place to live is fun, but also complicated. Claudia, who is single and can foresee living in her new home for at least five years, has waited until now to buy because she wants to pay a mortgage resembling her rent. She's prepared to make a 20 percent down payment using a mix of savings and a loan from her 401(k).

And she has also just started making offers. The first home is a two-bedroom house built in 1940. It has hardwood floors, a small backyard, and an unfinished basement—where she'd likely have to build storage space to compensate for the upstairs area's lack of storage. Listed at $269,000, she's offered $250,000—and the sellers have countered at $262,000. Her attorney and agent are looking at her paperwork for a counteroffer at $254,000.

Meanwhile, closer to the heart of Fair Lawn, she's also put in an offer on a $269,000 three-bedroom row house in the Radburn neighborhood. If she lives there, she'll pay dues for access to neighborhood facilities such as a swimming pool and parks. She'll also get the three bedrooms she wants. The owners had listed it for $369,000 a year ago, then rented it out for a year before relisting at their new price. Since she made an offer during the home's first week on the market, she's not sure whether she'll succeed.

O——

WORKS NOW; WHAT ABOUT LATER? THINKING ABOUT A HOME'S FUTURE RESALE VALUE.

"I'm nervous about buying the two-bedroom house because there's no room to add or make a third bedroom, and two bedrooms are hard to resell," Claudia says. "But now I have to step up my decision making, because I need to give notice to my landlord within three months."

If she doesn't get a workable seller response to either home offer, her backup plan is to move to the Fair Lawn area and rent, then continue looking.

THINGS TO CONSIDER

RENT

BUDGET: Can you afford to live here? Are rent increases expected in this building or neighborhood? Can you lock in your rent? Is the place a deal for a reason?

MOVE-IN TO-DO LIST: Do existing furnishings fit into this space, or do you need to buy special furniture or storage items to make it workable?

LOCATION: Do you feel safe? How's the commute and public transit? Are there resources for kids (schools, playgrounds, other kids)? Are services (groceries, bank, shopping) and houses of worship nearby? Is the area walk friendly? Pet friendly? What can you do for fun (parks, nightlife, dining)?

AMENITIES: What's inside your living space versus available in your building? Do you have twenty-four-hour access to laundry, a workout room, storage?

SINGLE FAMILY OR MULTIFAMILY: Do you want to live in a building, or in a discrete dwelling space?

ACCESS: Are there safety features to the property? Are you on the ground floor or above? If in a multiunit complex, is there a front gate, buzzer-based access, a front desk, or a doorman? Is it easy for you to receive packages, takeout, and deliveries, or to leave a key for a visiting friend?

CONDITION OF THE PROPERTY: Will the landlord make repairs or upgrades, if needed, before you move in?

THE MANAGEMENT: Is the landlord local? Does he or she live in the building or employ an onsite manager? Is your building or home corporately managed, through a property management company, or via an individual landlord? Can you call or report problems 24/7, or only within certain working hours? What's your preference?

TURNOVER OPTIONS: Can you get a flexible lease, a long lease in exchange for low rent, and/or permission to add roommates or sublet?

RENT VS. OWN

BUDGET: Can you afford the monthly payment? Does the seller want to get offers from buyers using your type of loan?

MOVE-IN TO-DO LIST: What needs repair and maintenance? What aesthetic changes would you make?

LOCATION: Do you feel safe? How's the commute and public transit? Are there resources for kids (schools, playgrounds, other kids)? Are services (groceries, bank, shopping) and houses of worship nearby? Is the area walk friendly? Pet friendly? What can you do for fun (parks, nightlife, dining)?

AMENITIES: What are your must-have home features (a certain number of bedrooms or parking spot/garage?) versus your like-to-have features (a fireplace, brick patio)? If the home doesn't offer these amenities now, would they be easy to add later? Could you live without them?

HOUSE OR MULTIFAMILY: Does it matter to you if you're in a single-family home versus a multifamily building? Why do you prefer the choice you've made?

NEW CONSTRUCTION OR OLD CONSTRUCTION: Do you like the idea of a home that's newly built with the latest and greatest technologies, a low-maintenance, turnkey place? Or do you prefer an older home you can customize yourself?

IS THERE A HOMEOWNER ASSOCIATION OR DUES: How much are they, what do they include, and who's managing the funds? Are meeting minutes available?

CONDITION OF THE PROPERTY: Is it move-in ready? Does it need aesthetic work? Is it obviously a fixer? What types of problems would make you walk versus leave you unfazed and ready to negotiate?

SUSTAINABILITY: Will this home suit your lifestyle in one, two, five years? Will your commute or family status likely change? Is its current configuration suitable for these changes?

RESALE PROSPECTS AND ISSUES: Does your home offer conventionally sought-after features (a certain bed/bath count, a garage) or are its charms extremely unique in other ways? In the latter instance, will its custom look or unusual attributes (a houseboat, yurt, or converted loft) appeal to future markets?

Renters don't necessarily face momentous financial consequences each time they sign a new lease—although if you move frequently enough, or within expensive markets, your moving and (if applicable) broker costs can begin to resemble fees buyers pay. Indeed, some smaller markets don't offer much rental choice at all—which, paired with affordable for-sale home pricing, is why some people who might be better suited to renting tend to buy a little sooner than they'd planned.

While the Great Recession was prefaced with lots of new for-sale home construction, builders didn't necessarily add a lot of new rental housing to the market—although the market downturn may mean more unsold condo buildings and single-family homes are on offer as rentals than before. If you're looking to rent, there's good news: Between now and 2014, larger apartment building operators, developers, and builders are going on a spree of buying, building, and renovating buildings. Rent prices may slowly start rising again, but what you get for the money may be more attractive than before. Landlords of larger buildings are also interested in "retention"—not just getting new renters, but keeping them. Many see younger adults "unbundling," with roommates moving out and getting their own places, and then having the opportunity to keep the ones who stayed behind living under the same roof.

Claudia enjoyed some aspects of her rental—her $1,600 rent was cheap for New York, and her home had a rare in-city patio area. However, the Mexican restaurant downstairs was very noisy on weekends. With her money saved, her employment secure, and her conviction set, her decision to buy is as much about life stage as about choosing a property that suits a need for space that's been slowly accumulating as she's progressed through adulthood.

You've heard a lot about taking a sustainable approach to living in your home in this book. But as you shop for property, consider location's role in sustainability. Have you "gone undercover" in your prospective neighborhood? If you've found a rental or for-sale home that suits, spend time in the neighborhood the way you would if you already lived there. Try out the commute at rush hour. Go shopping after work and check store prices. Talk to small-business owners and call the local PTA. Read the neighborhood blogs, attend public meetings or events, and drive by at night. Do people, prices, and logistics fall in line with a lifestyle you could afford and enjoy?

WHAT'S THE INVENTORY LIKE?

Claudia's search took her to New Jersey for a handful of reasons, and it took her to Fair Lawn because it's a town with a small village core and where she can afford a home with a yard. As she narrowed her search down based on her budget—she'd originally started out looking in some more-expensive areas—she also began to see that not all homes priced alike offer the same benefits. The older two-bedroom home has charms, but the resale value of two-bedroom homes isn't that compelling. The row home has a lower-maintenance yard, offers access to community amenities such as a pool, and is within walking distance to the town core.

Depending on where you live, or are looking to live, what's for rent and what's for sale can often differ widely. If you're making the leap from renter to owner, or vice versa, you may find yourself looking at new construction (conventional and "green") in a gated community for the first time, or mulling a townhouse, or evaluating moving from an apartment to a single-family rancher with a deep backyard. What's the inventory like in your area, and are you comfortable with the options? Is your agent open to showing you all of them?

Buying a Single-Family Home

Most recent real estate transactions have involved single-family homes. A stand-alone house has been the American ideal. But in modern society, it takes work to maintain. Ask yourself if you're buying a home that's the right size for you, or if it's more home than you need. Are you prepared for yard work and maintenance? Are you happy with the home's layout and features, or are you already remodeling it in your head? Will you use the yard? Are the basics in working order? Can the home be made more energy efficient? Can you get a look at the utility bills?

Buying in a Multifamily Building

Who's the typical owner in this building? Is the building well maintained, and is your prospective unit well maintained? Do you want to serve on the homeowner association board? Is the building or community's reserve well funded? Have you read the minutes? Are you allowed to rent out your space? Have foreclosures happened in the building, and are any units investor-owned? Is a certain type of financing recommended?

Buying in a New-Construction Community

Who's the builder, and do they have a good national and local reputation? Does the builder try to force you to work with their financing partners? How much of the overall development has sold, and how long have units taken to sell? Are other neighbors using the amenities provided by the community? Do you face any special assessments as an owner for the new construction? If the home isn't built yet, will you be able to hold inspections before, during, and after it's built? Can you customize your interiors? What's the resale potential? If you're buying in a community of similar-looking homes, will you be able to distinguish yours sufficiently for resale?

Buying a For-Sale-by-Owner Home

In any market there's a fair amount of FSBO activity. These owners want to save on listing-agent commissions or feel they have the know-how to list their own home. Additionally, if underwater, they may be sidestepping using an agent because they *have to* save on commissions to stop their losses. This means such sellers may be stubborn on price. If the seller won't even pay a discount broker-age's fee (which can be as low as 1.5 percent of sale price), consider whether he or she will negotiate price with you. Still, just because an owner is underwater on a home doesn't mean that home isn't desirable for you. Just be prepared for tough negotiations, and make sure to rely on your inspection, agent, and all the traditional steps when buying. Better FSBO sellers order inspections and appraisals in advance to set the stage for successful negotiation.

Buying a Co-op

In some markets, especially Manhattan, many multifamily buildings are "co-operatives," which means that the building has a single mortgage and that owners of units pay what amounts to a "share" of that mortgage. While condo owners own what's within their four walls, and pay dues for other community features, co-op owners own a sliver of the whole. This may sound like semantics, but it means that in a co-op the co-op board may exert as strong an influence on who's allowed to buy a home as does the individual seller. Co-op boards may require extremely high down payments, which can make them seem exclusive or daunting but also fiscally responsible.

Buying Cohousing

Cohousing communities are a form of multifamily housing where you have your own home unit but where "common areas" are more extensive than in a typical condo or homeowner association–managed community. This is because residents in cohousing, while owners of discrete living spaces, are expected to participate in community activities and also share in maintenance and other community duties. Most of these communities have shared dining rooms, gardens, and public rooms with flexible features. These homes are sold as FSBOs or via agents, but may also require a community "interview."

Buying Rent-to-Own

Some renters wind up buying places they've leased. A landlord might mention that he wants to sell and you as renter might decide you're interested. Or, you might ask the landlord and learn that a sale was on the agenda. Often, investors buy homes and use "lease to own" to sell them. Some charge a slightly higher rent, but set aside a portion of that rent as a down payment if, at lease renewal, he or she wants to buy. (Otherwise, the renter gets the money back.) If you're considering lease-to-own options, seek the advice of a real estate attorney or a local real estate agent (hopefully for a reduced commission since you have a single property in mind). These deals, like FSBOs, may need tire-kicking.

CHAPTER 13

CUTTING A DEAL

Loan vs. Lease

If you agree to a lease, it's typically pretty clear what you're getting. You've got a contract that's a few pages long, regulated by local or state laws, and good for a year or two's worth of renting. What actually happens when you make an offer on a home is a lot more complicated. If you're considering buying, and you have a time frame in mind by which you'd like to be in a new home or haven't quite nailed down your financing, you need to take a look at how the process works before you start making offers you can't close.

Generally, you shouldn't start making offers until you've looked at a lot of homes and have been prequalified for a loan. Even if you've decided you want to make an offer on a home, if it's the first you've seen you need to comparison shop—only to get a sense of what else is available in your price range. Also, your offer may get accepted. Some buyers throw out lowball or curveball offers just to see if sellers will accept them, and wind up surprised.

Another warning about making offers on homes: Your offer will involve negotiation—and negotiation is a game of brinksmanship, in which you and a seller may go back and forth via your agents about what you will and won't do in order to make a deal happen. In case this needs saying, the offer and purchase process will expose you to many opportunities to make bad decisions you later regret. For instance, if there's a bidding war, you'll have to decide how high you'll raise your offer before walking. If the home inspection turns up an expensive fix that the seller won't repair or subsidize via a price drop, you'll have to decide if you're willing to pay the sticker price *plus* the costs of the repair yourself. If the home's sold "as is," you'll have to guesstimate what a remodel costs.

Just as you'll have to set priorities—as well as personal limits and boundaries—during the home shopping process, you'll have to adjust them much more quickly during the heat of an offer. Often, you have just a few days to digest new details and contingencies that accompany your purchase of a particular property, or a short window of time within which to respond to a seller's counteroffer (or response) to your price offer. It's tempting, especially if you've already paid fees for your loan application or inspections on a particular property, to continue down the path or accept terms that you'll later regret rather than walk or start anew.

MAKING AN OFFER

No two offers are alike, and you'll generally need the assistance of your real estate agent or attorney (in some markets) to write one. Your offer will typically contain the following:

- **Personal letter:** This isn't really part of your offer, but more an occasional accompaniment to an offer. In a (perceived) competitive bidding situation, some buyers will write sellers personal notes about their desire to buy a home, with promises to never ruin it, raze it, or rent it but instead honor, love, and cherish it. Sometimes, this can sway sellers. It's not necessary though, and, done wrong, it may tip negotiating power in the seller's direction.

- **Earnest money:** To show a seller that you're serious, you typically write a check for a portion of your down payment. The money is set into escrow— meaning it's cashed, but not in the seller's actual hands—and returned if your deal doesn't proceed. If your deal does proceed, however, the earnest money is kept aside and becomes a portion of your down. If you are putting earnest money into an offer, it shows the seller you're serious. (After all, assuming you have a finite amount of money for your home buy, it'd be hard to put earnest money into a lot of simultaneous offers.)

- **Home price:** You tell the seller what you're willing to pay. Keep in mind that you don't have to offer full price. You can offer substantially below full price, if you want, to set a floor for negotiation. Your agent can advise you on this. You want to negotiate but not insult the seller.

- **Proof of financing:** Your lender provides a letter indicating you're pre-approved and seeking full approval for a loan sufficient to fund your offer.

- **Deal timeline:** You'll let the seller know how long the offer is good (i.e., how long they have to respond) and when you'd like to close (thirty days is common, but longer closes are possible).

- **Contingencies:** Contingencies are the buyer's "easy outs." It's common for buyers to ask for contingencies such as financing (since you can't buy if your loan doesn't come through, or if an appraisal indicates the property is overpriced and you're thus overborrowing) and a general home inspection. You can also ask for extra inspections that go beyond the scope of a normal home inspection (a sewer or pest inspection, for instance), or make your sale of a home a contingency. By stating your contingencies, you set the stage for negotiation. You'll be able to provide new qualifications to your offer once the contingencies are satisfied, but will need to give the seller the opportunity to respond within a reasonable time frame. For instance, if an inspection turns up problems, you can ask the seller to respond with a price reduction or an offer to fix the problems, and walk if the seller doesn't agree to your adjusted terms.

- **Counteroffers:** Generally, a buyer and seller may go back and forth a few times via their agents in any transaction. Sometimes a buyer needs the seller to subsidize part of the closing. Or sometimes a seller would rather offer the buyer a price drop than withstand the headache of a repair before closing. If two parties want to make a deal happen, lots of adjustments are possible.

ASSESSING THE LOCAL MARKET

The way real estate is sold can vary widely by local market. In a seller's market, sometimes a seller will specify in a listing that he or she wants to "review all offers" by a certain date, presuming multiple offers and a position of power. In a buyer's market, you might be able to get away with an offer much lower than what the seller is asking—especially if the home has been listed for a long time. Remember, though, whether you rent or own, your market will typically be trending in one direction or another. And all sellers are individuals: Some are stubborn, some get offended by what your inspector finds, some just want to get the deal done, and some are underwater.

HOME INSPECTIONS

A home inspection is a lot like a first date. It's the little things that indicate what the other person's character is like, and where they might be strong and weak over time. Same goes with homes. In most markets, a home inspection

WHAT'S NEGOTIABLE

RENT

NEGOTIATING IS STANDARD AND SOMETIMES WORKS

Most landlords and management companies use boilerplate lease forms when they rent apartments or houses to tenants, and these are easily amended. It never hurts to try and negotiate the following with property managers.

FINANCIAL DETAILS: Want to see if you can knock $20 off the monthly rent? See what the landlord says. Can't pay a deposit and first month all at once? Ask to pay first month now, and make three or four installment payments toward the deposit.

LEASE LENGTH: Do you want a longer or shorter lease? Month-to-month starting after six months? No penalty to end the lease before twelve months, with notice?

CONCESSIONS: "Concessions" is landlord-speak for incentives, like free parking, one month free on a twelve-month lease, etc. Let the landlord know you're comparing places, but need a sweetener.

BROKER FEES AND COMMISSIONS: These one-time fees don't apply in all markets, but when they do they're expensive. Ask a broker to lower them. Or avoid them by going directly to management companies to ask about vacancies.

RENT VS. OWN

NEGOTIATING IS STANDARD ON THE HOME'S PRICE AND ON OTHER FEES

"Buy low, sell high," the saying goes. It applies to stocks—but here, also to making money from your home. Here's what's negotiable, in order of impact on your bottom line:

SELLER'S PRICE: Negotiating the "list price" of the home is the most common area to negotiate. Getting the seller to drop the home price saves you the most money, typically because you need less loan (and thus less mortgage interest) to fund the purchase. Keep in mind that if you are buying "distressed" property (a foreclosure, a bank-owned home, a "short sale"), you may face an uphill battle in offering a lower-than-asked price. It never hurts to try, though.

REPAIR WORK: You can make your offer conditional on repairs the seller completes before you move in, or in instances when repairs are required for your insurance or loan to go through. But many people opt instead to use needed repairs as an excuse for a lower offer price, then they use the money saved to fund and oversee repairs themselves.

TRANSACTION TIMING: You can negotiate closing dates on the purchase—for instance, asking for a "long close" can let you lock up a deal and also gain more time before the first payment is due.

CLOSING COSTS: The various costs tied to your purchase are known as closing costs, and they can run anywhere from 3 percent to 5 percent of your purchase price. Negotiate that the seller will pay some or all of them. This is a common tactic with first-time buys. If the seller won't pay them, but you really want the home and can't pay them either, negotiate paying slightly more for the home in exchange for the seller handling closing costs. You may be able to finance these costs in your loan.

FEES FOR PARTIES INVOLVED IN THE TRANSACTION: You pay a variety of one-time fees as a subset of closing costs, ranging from your mortgage lender's origination fee to title company fees and fees to a home inspector. Other fees are ongoing, such as what you pay for insurance.

is used as a way for the potential buyer to see how flawed (and expensive) a property will be and if its asking price is worth it. Renters don't need to worry about an "apartment inspection," because when you rent the landlord is responsible for the place's condition—although how well and how fast maintenance happens can vary.

Your real estate agent likely has several inspectors on speed dial. If you want to find one on your own, you can go through the American Society of Home Inspectors (www.ashi.org), National Association of Home Inspectors (www.nahi.org), or a state-level home inspector organization. If you're buying an existing home (versus buying a home that will be built), you typically get an inspection after you've made an offer and use its findings to provide you with a reality check about the home's condition, major repair issues, and to give you negotiating power with a seller. Typically, you and your agent meet the inspector at the home under consideration and spend two to four hours trailing the inspector, who reviews the exterior, foundation, overall structure, basement/crawl space, interior and exterior walls, siding, heating and cooling system, electrical, plumbing systems and fixtures, porches and decks, attic, roof, gutters, fireplace, and chimney.

After the inspection, you'll get a report with remarks about the home's condition, which becomes part of the documentation of your offer. Sometimes the inspector may find hints of problems that further, supplementary inspections can pinpoint, or you may have particular concerns and want to hire supplementary inspectors to examine a home for pests, radon gas leaks, mold, carbon monoxide links, or the sewer system. In addition, if a home is advertised as energy efficient, or you're concerned whether it is, you can also ask for access so an energy auditor can review the home using special tools to assess whether the home is airtight, well-insulated, and built from environmentally friendly materials.

Inspection is no joke. If you buy a home without an inspection, you can always hire an after-the-fact inspection, which some buyers will do if they buy homes "as is" in a distressed transaction. While an after-the-fact inspection won't help you negotiate, it will help you set home-repair priorities and give you a realistic sense of the home's condition.

How Does an Inspection Impact an Offer?

Nancy and James, a thirtysomething couple, thought the three-bedroom 1930s bungalow they'd found was awesome. They felt lucky the seller had accepted their offer, considering there had been more than one made on the home, and their agent had them schedule an inspection within three days—a time frame within which they could renegotiate based on the inspection's findings.

Initially, the inspection went well. But as the couple and their inspector were heading from the upper to the lower floor, Nancy saw a knee-height door leading to an attic crawl space and asked the inspector to take a look behind it. What he found was scary: The insulation had been chewed and clawed by rodents.

"I definitely would've never known that," Nancy said. "What's worse is that when he looked around a bit more, he noticed a hole in the wall where it appeared that the rats had chewed through, meaning they were likely in the walls of the house."

The inspector looked in another trapdoor (in the top of a bedroom closet) connected to another part of the attic, and sure enough found rat feces. The couple, though fond of the house, weren't sure if they could move into a place that was rat infested. They called a pest company who told them, without even visiting the home site, that they should run like the wind. With the high likelihood of rats inside the walls, the couple would have to rip walls out as part of the process of ridding the place of rats. Suddenly, Nancy says, the potpourri the sellers were using in the house—allegedly to mask their dog's scent—made a lot more sense.

The couple's agent notified the sellers that the couple wanted to back out of the deal, but the owners said they'd call an exterminator.

"Since it sounded like such a bad problem, we said no thanks. But the sellers got uppity and threatened to sue us, saying we had to by law give them the chance to fix it," Nancy said. "We had two good arguments. One was we said we would require them to take down all the walls to make sure there were no dead rats left. And the second was that we were still within the three-day waiting period that lets you back out of the deal. So that was that!"

CHAPTER 14

DISTRESSED PROPERTIES

Damaged Goods . . . or Good Deals?

Grace, a thirty-one-year-old who works for a San Francisco online media company, began looking to buy in April 2009, encouraged by down payment help offered by her family and the $8,000 first-time buyer tax credit the government was then offering to spur the housing market. She was looking for a two-bedroom home priced in the low $400,000 range—which, in metro San Francisco, constitutes the lower-priced end of the market—and knew she'd face competition.

Considering the daily headlines about the recession, the competition to buy surprised her. Between April and June, she hit twenty-five open houses and made two offers on homes in Berkeley, both of which she lost to rival buyers who could pay cash. Finally, she found another prospect, a 1920s stucco bungalow in Oakland in need of an aesthetic reboot. She could see its promise in period details like built-in bookcases and charming moldings, and it had a workable layout with a living room, dining room, fireplace, and backyard. More important, it had two bedrooms—crucial, since she'd need a roommate to help with the mortgage.

She bid on the home, along with twenty-one other buyers. The seller told her she'd be the winning bidder if she raised her price slightly, to $428,000. She agreed. But then began a long wait—a five-month-long wait—for final approval to close on the home. Unlike a regular home, this house was a so-called short sale—a home whose seller owes more on their loan than the home can fetch at current market value, meaning the seller's deal will come up "short" of the money needed to pay off the mortgage. In a short sale, sellers must get their lender's approval to sell for less than is owed. The seller chose Grace because she seemed patient, the buyer least likely to bolt in frustration.

"The seller had to shop my offer to their bank, and we all had to wait while the bank decided," Grace says. "I didn't have any other good options, though."

While Grace succeeded in closing on her home, she acknowledges that she had already grown attached to it before she fully understood the implications of buying a short sale. The home retained a lot of its original character and had room for her to make equity-bumping improvements, and, more important, its layout was conducive for sharing space with a roommate. After losing out to buyers who obviously were either wealthy or investors, and could trump her financing by dangling cash—always appealing to a lender expecting a loss on a mortgage—she felt lucky her bid to buy was chosen. Fortunately, she could offer the price that the sellers needed to bring to their lender and she had a flexible landlord who let her rent month-to-month while she waited out the process.

"I was told it could take this long," she says.

But she was surprised that it did. What, exactly, was the lender pondering? Indeed, many short sale deals fall apart. Buyers with jobs to accept or school district enrollments to complete can't wait forever, sellers can't get their lender to approve offers fast enough, or the seller falls behind on the mortgage and winds up in foreclosure before a short sale wraps up.

HALF THE MARKET IS "DISTRESSED" (FOR NOW)

Welcome to the world of distressed properties—a world that includes short sales, homes where a seller is behind on payments and is in preforeclosure, and properties already repossessed by a lender, some with claims against them from other creditors. No longer a niche corner of the market, distressed homes accounted for about 45 percent of all U.S. home sales in 2010 and are expected to represent nearly half of all home sales in 2012, according to Guy Cecala, CEO of Inside Mortgage Finance Publications, a Bethesda, Maryland–based research firm.

Rick Sharga, senior vice president of RealtyTrac, an Irvine, California–based property research firm, estimated in 2010, that between late 2010 and early 2012, some $300 billion worth of adjustable-rate mortgages will reset, adding on average an extra $1,000 per month to impacted owners' loan payments. As if that's not tough enough, he says, owners facing these resets will experience them at a moment in history when their homes' values are worth 30 percent to 50 percent less than their purchase prices. This sets a stage for further short sales or foreclosures: Who wants to pay ever-higher prices for assets worth increasingly less? A Harris Interactive poll conducted for RealtyTrac and Trulia, a for-sale and rentals listing site, found in late 2010 that nearly half (48 percent) of homeowners, if faced with negative equity, would consider a "strategic default," deliberately stopping mortgage payments. This represented a leap from prior levels of 41 percent, and what executives from the companies described as conditions ripe to produce more foreclosure activity.[14.1]

Distressed properties are concentrated in states such as Nevada, California, and Arizona—where more than 40 percent of sales in recent quarters were foreclosures and preforeclosures—according to RealtyTrac. But distressed properties are present in every state—and they come in all shapes, sizes, and price ranges. If you're considering buying, keep in mind that some of the "good deals" you see may be distressed properties containing hidden hitches, ranging from buyer competition from cash-toting investors to interminable delays from large lending institutions to complexities that arise when a buyer's lender-required appraisal shows a

A property becomes "distressed" when its owner's loan is in jeopardy. Typically, distressed properties fall into two categories—homes where the seller lacks equity and won't be able to repay the home loan entirely after selling, and homes where the seller has fallen behind on mortgage payments. Sometimes a home for sale can fall into both categories, such as a home where the seller has negative equity and also cannot pay their mortgage. Some owners who sell in a short sale or undergo foreclosure can be held liable under their state's law for the amount of the mortgage loan they've left unpaid. The average discount on distressed property is 32 percent below the price of a nondistressed comparable property, according to RealtyTrac.

home value worth less than the price sought by the seller. Agents often have to work harder on these transactions—but do so for less money, since some institutions behind distressed sales can't or won't pay full agent commissions.

Renters' Distress

Renters aren't immune to issues connected to distressed property. Landlords, just like primary owners, have also suffered from difficult real estate market conditions in recent years. Novice investors swarmed the real estate market during the mid-2000s, accounting for more than 20 percent of home purchases, according to NAR and other sources. Typically, these buyers sought out single units or houses, or multiplexes with less than five units. (Larger multiunit rentals require more complex financing.) They'd then make money by charging rents higher than their monthly mortgage payment, or by investing more money to remodel them and then sell them for a profit.

These weekend investors in some cases used the same tricky adjustable-rate loans primary buyers did, made low down payments, and used leverage (pulling money out of the homes) to acquire additional rentals. They may have also modeled their investment "portfolio" around the expectation of continued rent increases, which they'd need to cover their expensive mortgage payments, and wound up watching their cash flow go negative as rent prices dropped below the cost of their mortgage and other property-related expenses. Or wound up stuck with unsellable flip projects they had to rent for a loss.

Many renters in recent years have been unpleasantly surprised when a foreclosure notice arrives. The *Herald News* of Joliet, Illinois, reported on three families on the same block who found out that their rental houses—all owned by the same husband-wife landlord duo—had fallen in foreclosure. The renters had paid two months' security deposit and feared they'd never see it again, since the couple had also begun bankruptcy proceedings.[14.2] Unfortunately, the renters are in a tough spot: If they stop paying rent, they can be evicted. But if their landlords' foreclosure moves swiftly—and it may, since those renters found out about the foreclosure when process servers knocked on the door of one home looking for its owner and were surprised to meet tenants instead—they'll also, in effect, be evicted.

It's not just small-time landlords who have been caught short during the housing correction and, in some cases, left renters scrambling for alternative housing. In some cases, new owners of large apartment complexes who bought at the height of the market can't (or won't) pay for proper maintenance of new buildings.

In other cases, changes in ownership have led to changes in building strategy. Rental buildings became condo conversions (meaning renters weren't renewed and the building was remodeled to sell), and then the condo conversions reverted to rentals (meaning the condo market began slowing and the developers couldn't recoup their remodeling spending), for instance.

New York City's well-known rent-regulated communities Peter Cooper Village and Stuyvesant Town sold at the height of the real estate market in 2006 for $5.4 billion in what the *New York Times* called the largest deal in real estate history. However, the buildings' new owners defaulted, and the lenders inherited the two communities where 25,000 residents live. Several parties wound up in litigation over possibly illegal rent increases administered to tenants, and the buildings' fate is, at best, uncertain.[14.3] Will the new owners attempt to push rents beyond the normal 2.25 percent (one year) or 4.5 percent (two year) price increases? Will the whole community convert to a co-op, with renters able to buy in at reduced rates? Four years after the deal, renters in the community remain in limbo as these questions are batted around in boardrooms and courts.

Many condominium projects financed during rosier economic times have been completed in a market where sales are sluggish and sale prices can't fulfill projections set with construction financiers. Rather than let the units sit empty while sales trickle in, or sell at a loss just to spur transactions, builders and developers will instead rent them to bring in enough income to keep lenders at bay. While some renters enjoyed condo-grade finishes like granite countertops, high-end carpeting, or designer paint on the walls instead of "landlord white," as the market improves they may get notice that the next time their lease renews they'll have to either move or buy in—often at a discount to the unit's future for-sale price. Renters can benefit from what some refer to as "shadow inventory," homes constructed for primary occupants. If these homes can't sell due to market conditions, renters might be able to enjoy a better type of rental unit. However, in some cases—such as condo buildings that are treated as rentals—the property doesn't offer as many amenities as a designated rental building and may not have as professional a management company.

Short Sales

A short sale happens when the seller owes more on their mortgage than he or she can reasonably gain from the home's sale. In an ideal world, an underwater owner could continue making home payments and wait for the market to rebound. But in the real world, sometimes owners don't get to time their exits. They need to relocate for a job, or they've experienced an income drop or major expense (medical bills, divorce) and know that in the near future they won't be able to make mortgage payments. These owners try to sell even in a bad market or at a loss rather than foreclose.

In a normal home sale, the price you pay as a buyer more than covers the seller's outstanding mortgage and sale-related expenses. In a short sale, the seller must negotiate with his or her lender to accept a price that's "short" of the amount owed. In some cases, sellers will notify their lender in advance of the need to sell and the lender will provide them with a minimum price—what's often called a "prenegotiated" or "lender-approved" short sale, because the lender actually sets what's an acceptable sale price.

But in many cases, the lender won't commit to a price floor, waits to see what offers the seller gets, and takes a long time to decide a deal's fate—or says no. Depending on the lender and state laws, the seller may wind up on the hook for the amount owed on the home post-sale—a balance known as a "deficiency judgment," which must be repaid under a loan agreement between the seller and his or her outgoing lender.

Since short sales are often a good deal, offers may appear soon after these homes hit the market. But considering that short sales take anywhere from sixteen to twenty months from hitting the market to closing, according to Guy Cecala, CEO of Inside Mortgage Finance Publications, this may indicate that lenders are dragging their heels so slowly that buyers may come and go with offers as they lose heart or patience with the process. Short sales fail to close at a higher rate than regular home sales.

Auctions and Bulk Sales

Often builders or developers finance major building projects in a rosy economy, only to see the construction complete during a downturn. These companies, however, have construction loans to pay. So they may resort to renting out units and waiting until the for-sale market improves. Or they may hold an auction. Auctions can provide good values for buyers—but you'll need to understand down payment requirements, how the homeowner association is funded and structured, and dozens of other variables before you consider bidding.

In addition, rather than create the pressure associated with an auction, building owners will also sometimes hold a "bulk sale"—whereby homes are priced at discounts for a limited window—to bring in a large chunk of income at one time and solve financial headaches. While these homes (or the building containing them) aren't necessarily distressed, the market conditions surrounding them and the sales methods used to promote them are the product of a distressed real estate market.

In some cases, condo marketing specialists have said that a bulk sale can function well in a down market because it helps establish a viable price for homes in a new building that's been completed in a market where home valuations are uncertain. These sales may also fill a building sufficiently to where occupancy begins approaching the level required by FHA loans popular with first-time buyers. (FHA borrowers can buy condos only if a building fulfills certain occupancy requirements.)

From Preforeclosure to Foreclosure

When a homeowner falls behind on his or her mortgage payments, he or she technically enters preforeclosure—an unfortunate, credit-staining world where, after ninety days, a lender can begin proceedings to repossess your home or set an auction date to sell it for cash. This doesn't happen on the ninetieth day your loan is past due, but within the next ninety days—or, in the recent foreclosure market, heaven knows when, since many lenders are overwhelmed dealing with distressed real estate of all types.

In the past, loss of income, divorce, and unexpected medical expenses were among some of the major reasons people fall behind on their mortgage payments. Currently, this mix of variables is compounded by onerous loan resets that owners can't afford to pay—or choose not to pay—to demonstrate to a lender that they need a loan modification to more-affordable terms. In other cases, owners anticipate that a foreclosure is inevitable, so they stop making payments despite the financial capability to make them—a choice known as "strategic default" or "walking away." These owners may send the keys back to their lender—in "jingle mail."

Buyers considering preforeclosures need to try and find out several key details about the property in order to handicap their potential success in purchasing it:

- **Has the lender actually served any notices or paperwork yet? How long before the property is repossessed or auctioned?**

- **How far behind is the owner on making payments? Less than ninety days?**

- **Is the seller both marketing the home and pursuing a loan modification concurrently?**

- **Would the seller keep the home if offered a modification? Is he or she marketing it as a short sale so that the credit impacts are better than foreclosure, but interested in staying?**

To make matters more complicated, because the distressed property market represents so much business for many lenders, the traditional time frame to foreclose on a delinquent owner has stretched and stretched—so an owner who is way behind on his or her mortgage could get a viable-seeming home offer, only to see it fail to close before the lender pops up and completes the foreclosure. In recent years many homeowners have squatted in their homes for much longer time periods than the norm (one or even two years) after ceasing to make payments, letting their credit plummet in the process and remaining in preforeclosure simply because their lender hasn't started sending them notices or serving them papers.

When a home is repossessed by a lender, it has undergone (or is) a foreclosure. Sometimes the lender doesn't keep the property for long—only long enough to auction it on the courthouse steps. But lenders often reclaim the homes, board them up (for safety reasons), and then reason that they'll figure out what to do with the home later. Most major banks and lenders now have large portfolios of foreclosed residential properties, obtusely called "nonperforming assets," on their financial statements—meaning the loans aren't "performing" by bringing in expected loan revenue. REO (real estate owned) properties used to be a tiny and slightly embarrassing business for lenders—proof that a loan failed and is losing the company money—but now some banks and lenders proactively market these homes on their Web sites.

Problems with Foreclosures

Owners who are behind on their mortgage payments may also wind up behind on other key bills, such as a second loan against the home (home equity line of credit or a second mortgage), or property taxes. These other creditors can place what's known as a lien against the property, meaning that, after the mortgage debt is resolved, other parties with liens are not in line to be repaid.

One down side to foreclosures is that these homes are typically sold "as is," meaning that regardless of the property's condition, the seller will neither make nor negotiate funding for repairs. Foreclosures are often—but not always—left in terrible condition. Well-meaning owners who couldn't pay the mortgage may not have been able to maintain the home or keep it aesthetically updated. Angry owners trash the place on the way out, vandals and squatters break in, thieves rip out copper wiring, and sometimes these homes become illegal dumping grounds.

In other cases, the absence of occupants means easy-to-solve problems can swiftly mushroom into expensive, structurally damaging issues that lessen a home's safety and value. For instance, a windowpane cracked in a fall storm might turn into a broken window. That broken window, paired with a rainy season, could lead to water damage, which could lead to mold, which could ruin walls and floors, maybe eventually the foundation.

These sorts of foreclosures are often sold without the buyer getting to enter the property, although you're welcome to drive by or bring a contractor or inspector to do a visual inspection. That's why they typically appeal to more-sophisticated purchasers, such as investors who aren't looking to move into a new primary home right away, or buyers with a trusted general contractor at the ready—and a whole lot of faith.

REOs: The Tidy Foreclosures

Some foreclosures are tidied up and put on the market, represented by a real estate agent as a normal listing. These foreclosed homes are often known as REO (Real Estate Owned) properties, meaning they're owned by a bank or lending institution in the real estate business rather than an individual; some regional banks even have property listings on their Web sites, so if you find a listing that links back to a lender's site, you can generally surmise it's an REO. As distressed properties go, REO properties listed for sale will come with prices preset by the lender (no rushing to auctions, and no waiting around as in a short sale). Since the last owners have already moved, quick closes may be possible. In addition, since these properties are traditionally listed, you'll be able to tour and inspect them.

Remember though, that even REO homes are "as is" properties. This can cause headaches if the loan type you're using requires that the home you purchase meet certain minimum criteria with respect to habitability or up-to-date home systems; occasionally, it may be hard to inspect the home if it has been "winterized" by the seller—a process involving lowering the heat and turning off water to prevent problems from changes in weather or vacancy.

Sometimes, the price markdown that comes with a foreclosure may be directly proportional to the amount of repair work the property needs to resemble its non-REO peers. So if you're stretching to buy a foreclosure, but can't fund or don't understand the costs associated with bringing it up to livable standards, you may be setting yourself up to repeat the home's history—or, at the very least, foreclosing on common sense.

One thing's for sure: the market's roller coaster has left both the renting and owning population reeling. Some buyers feel nervous—karmically challenged, even—by stepping in and buying where another buyer suffered from the market about-face, misjudgment, or unfortunate personal circumstances.

"I benefited from the housing crisis," Grace says. "I feel a little weird about it."

One year after her purchase, though, and she's in good company. Much of the market is in some state of distress. Weird, it seems, is a big part of the new normal.

QUESTIONS TO CONSIDER

1. **Renters, is distressed property common in your market?** Consider
    running searches on your current or future address from a service like
    Rental Foreclosure (www.rentalforeclosure.com) so you're not caught in a
    foreclosure-related eviction. If renting from an individual landlord, look
    up his or her property via a local tax assessor's office to see if there are
    any liens (claims) on the property. If your property is owned by a large or
    publicly traded real estate investment trust, look up the company and read
    about its financial condition and planned rent increases or building sales.
    Use sites like Daily Finance (www.dailyfinance.com) or Yahoo's business
    portal (finance.yahoo.com) to find the companies' information.

2. **Are you specifically interested in buying distressed property, and are
    you planning to deliberately search for it?** What's your motive: Getting
    a deal, or perhaps finding a fixer to which you can add value? Make sure
    to ask your lender if your particular loan will work on a foreclosure or
    distressed property, or if there are special requirements.

3. **If distressed property is a large part of your market, does your agent
    have the skills to help you succeed in negotiating the purchase?** If you
    already have an agent and he or she isn't experienced with distressed
    property, can they get up to speed quickly or draw on the expertise of
    someone else in their brokerage? Can you part ways amicably and find an
    agent skilled in handling such transactions?

4. **Are you prepared to wait a long time for your transaction to close?**
    Can you preserve your credit score and sustain your financial profile while
    awaiting a seller's decision?

5. **Are you prepared to renegotiate if there are appraisal problems?**

6. **Are you capable of paying cash for your property?** All-cash buyers may
    be your competition, so the larger your down or more "bulletproof" your
    financing, the better.

PART 3

OPERATING INSTRUCTIONS

REALITY CHECKS, REALITY BITES

CHAPTER 15

CONTROLLING YOUR SPACE

Four Walls

Stephanie, a thirty-five-year-old mother of two in Los Angeles, has to be picky about where she and her family live. As Orthodox Jews, the family needs to live within walking distance of a synagogue to adhere to Sabbath practices, which limits their options to two major neighborhoods in the city. With an asthmatic in the home, they also need to live in a building that's well maintained and clean. And with toddlers, they need to live in a safe area and intersection.

The rap on renting is that you can't control your space and are dependent on a landlord's temperament and whim when it comes to the general living environment and maintenance issues. Sometimes, as Stephanie will attest, this is true. Initially, she and her husband rented a unit in a fourplex that was owned by a cranky landlord who lived two hours away in San Diego. The experience was difficult, to put it mildly.

"He made it wrenching to get repairs done. He'd get angry if we even called about a problem," she said. "When we had termites he told us we were being hysterical."

Still, she and her husband put up with him, stayed in the rental, and started their family. The final straw, though, came when the landlord hired an illegal day laborer to make repairs in their home. Stephanie was there alone with the children, who were napping in the other room, when the handyman approached her and tried to caress her leg, making her very uncomfortable. Stephanie and her husband learned the handyman drove a stolen van. Moving plans ensued.

Their next landlord relationship—and living situation—is a major improvement. In 2009, the family moved into a duplex owned by a psychologist who grew up in the building. He let them negotiate on rent, lowering it below the $2,900 per month he originally sought as a reward for a long lease—they started out at $2,100 per month, which increases by $200 each year till they hit $2,900. When it comes to maintenance, he's authorized them to go ahead and make appointments from among a list of contractors he provided them not long after they arrived.

"He just handed us the list. He knows we're not going to call a plumber unless we really need a plumber," Stephanie says. "A day or two later he'll e-mail to double-check that the repair person came and to verify what work is on the bill."

When a duct cleaning revealed asbestos in the building, the landlord agreed to Stephanie's request for asbestos removal—an expensive process, but one which she convinced him was important for her family's health.

O——

WHAT CAN YOU CONTROL?

Clearly, you can't control what kind of landlord you get. But you can control your decor and how you personalize your space. Of course, personalizing your space will cost you, whether you rent or own. If you own, you have several layers of nesting-related expenses: Furnishing, maintenance and repair, and the option to remodel. When you rent, it's pretty much all about furnishing since maintenance is included in your lease. There's no denying that the maintenance costs of owning far outstrip how much a renter *needs* to spend on furniture or decor.

Still, renters can spend a lot on furnishings and items unique to each space they live in, and at the end of several moves may realize these expenses add up to down payment proportions.

Laura, a media entrepreneur in New York, fell in love with her ground-floor studio rental in the Village when she first saw it. While the place was small even by New York standards, essentially a 12-by-17-foot rectangle, it offered the bonus of a courtyard patio that served as an extra "outdoor room" at least part of the year.

Because of her home's small dimensions, however, she bought a new couch ($650) that fit into the space as well as a table with a folding leaf that could serve as both dining space and desk ($200). The biggest expense, though, was the $2,000 Murphy bed—a bed that folds up against the wall when not in use—so that during waking hours she could move around in her space freely.

"In the tiny studio, my extra expenses were due to my needing a Murphy bed," she says. "It was *essential* to living in such a small space."

Laura took a few additional steps to make the space habitable, lucking into a free budget remodel (valued at $325) from a company that does what's called "interior space redesign"—in which a designer works with a client's existing belongings and improves their placement in a given space, minimizing additional purchases. Some interior space designers borrow from feng shui principles, while others just eyeball a room, interview clients about how the space is used, and take it from there. Laura's new furniture arrangement and a few touches of color made the place cozier.

She moved less than two years afterward and got rid of the bed in the process. In total, she spent about $2,850 on furniture specific to that unit—and that's atop her $2,250 monthly rent, and not including the $325 normally charged for an interior redesign. She sold these custom belongings on Craigslist—just as she had sold her furniture from another apartment when she moved from Brooklyn to the Village.

Like owners, renters spend money on their homes—and when they move, sometimes they don't fully recoup those costs. Rent a house with a deck? You'll need patio furniture. Lease a loft-style apartment? You may need freestanding storage units or room divider screens or extra-long window coverings that won't work in a conventional space. If you spend heavily on just-for-this-place furnishings and move often or within a short window of time, you may wind up selling these belongings at a loss, paying to store them, or giving them away if they don't fit in your next rental.

WHAT CAN'T YOU CONTROL

Owners in theory have more control over their living experience because there's no landlord in their life, no person authorized to enter the home when they're away and make repairs or, well, get nosy about that extra cat or cigarette habit you might be hiding. Owners also have aesthetic control over their space. Many buyers get a tremendous amount of pleasure from customizing a space and making it their own with wallpaper and boutique paint colors and new countertop textures. But even if you own your property, you can't control the neighborhood.

Matt, a thirty-eight-year-old software engineer in Portland, Oregon, learned the hard way that he'd stumbled upon bum neighbors after he bought a 1915 Craftsman bungalow in the Southeast section of the city. It was 2005 and the height of the market, meaning it was a seller's market where bidding wars among buyers and quick sales were the norm. Matt, who was raised in and had previously lived in rental-heavy San Francisco, said that after he moved to Portland he was stunned at how affordable it was to buy there—and, with friends his age snapping up property and the sense that prices would get away if he didn't pounce, he decided to join in.

Matt wanted a home that was in generally solid condition because he is, admittedly, "not handy." He was preapproved to pay up to $300,000, and he also wanted to live close to downtown.

But as he home-shopped, he realized that he'd have to make compromises. He didn't need a big home or have a huge list of requirements: He wanted one bedroom to sleep in, another for a home office, and off-street parking. However, all the homes he liked in close-in neighborhoods near the city's downtown cost at least $350,000.

"Even though Portland is cheap compared to other major cities, you add $10,000 or $20,000 every few blocks as you get closer to downtown," he says. "If I was going to shop within my budget, I wasn't necessarily going to live in a location I loved."

Finally, as he drove farther east, he found a home for $289,000 and bought it. Before he made his offer, he'd cased the joint day and night, making sure that the services and nightlife and the safety level were up to snuff. But only after he moved in did he realize that his neighbors, with whom he shared a driveway, were a little off.

It became swiftly apparent, especially given his bedroom's location facing the neighbors' home, that just a few yards away his numerous neighbors were running a drug operation. Occasionally, someone would knock on his door with a fistful of cash, then realize they'd rang the wrong house. He'd often wake up to find a man from next door trespassing in his yard. It was awkward to complain, though, because the neighbor was often doing neighborly favors for Matt like rolling his trash bin to the curb or cleaning up the minor leftovers from some small gathering Matt had hosted the night before. Matt felt creepy about the intrusion.

"He was clearly in my business," he says. "About six months in, I said to myself, 'I absolutely have to sell the house. Nothing will stop me.'"

Fortunately, he had a friend who adored his house, had flippantly remarked she'd have bought it if she'd seen it first, and was willing to tolerate the offbeat neighbors. Matt sold to her in 2006, one year after he bought, and was able to exit financially unscathed because the home's value had risen by about 10 percent during his twelve months living there and he sold directly to his friend, without real estate agent commissions.

Maintenance issues, it turns out, were the least of his troubles. He estimates he spent $1,000 total on home-related expenses, which included his purchase of a lawn mower and gutter repairs. In fact, if he had to do it over again, he'd willingly trade an expensive repair year for an emotionally exhausting year rubbing elbows with criminal neighbors.

So where's Matt now? He's renting an apartment with his girlfriend in another part of town. He says he'd like to buy again, but this time he'd like to do it with a partner so that the experience is one he shares both emotionally and financially, meaning two incomes provide more home-buying power. Ironically, for all the renters who reportedly have little control over their environment, Matt has this to say: "As a renter, I never have to live again in a neighborhood I don't like."

CHAPTER 16

NEST IN PEACE

Do You Have an Inner Martha Stewart?

There's nothing wrong with spending to feather your nest and create your own unique environment. However, if you thought saving for a deposit or down payment was the expensive part of your move, it turns out you've only begun. Renters obviously don't have to set aside money for maintenance, but then, most renters don't have as much creative license with their use of a space. If you rent, the fact that you don't own the place may curb how far you can go with customizing it. So if you're a renter mulling buying, ask yourself this: To what extent is your interest in buying driven by an interest in having creative license within and beyond your four walls? And if you're an owner mulling a return to renting, ask: How much will you miss that creative freedom?

PRESERVING THE VALUE AND CHARACTER OF YOUR SPACE WITHOUT GOING BROKE

Owners have endless possibilities for decorating and personalizing not only within their walls but also with respect to moving the walls themselves in a remodel. However, the fact that you own the place and have to maintain and repair it may mean it can take a while to actually get around to funding expensive aesthetic work like an amazing kitchen redesign or a new spa-like master bathroom. It also means that if you blow your budget on aesthetic or remodeling work upfront, you'll wind up financially overextended when the inevitable emergency or system failure erupts.

Repairing and Maintaining Your Home

While many would-be or current owners daydream about custom renovations, reality often forces them to put repairs and maintenance first and put off the "fun" work and personalization until later. One of the tougher aspects of a homeowner's job is prioritizing repairs—and confronting the reality of how expensive some of them are. And that's assuming you can get out in front of your repairs, choosing which to tackle first versus facing emergencies that force open your wallet.

Freddie Mac, the government mortgage giant, advises owners to budget anywhere from 1 percent to 3 percent of their purchase price annually for repairs. Other experts say you should plan to spend up to 4 percent of your purchase price per year for repairs. Many owners scoff at how high that sounds. In a good year, home maintenance expenses might be nominal, maybe just a few hundred bucks total for a new window screen here, some deck stain there, maybe shelling out for a major appliance repair or chimney or duct cleaning. But when a big system goes, it offsets all the "cheap years" combined.

The median age of a home in the United States is thirty-six years, according to the U.S. Department of Housing and Urban Development's and Census Bureau's most recent American Housing Survey.[16.1] Considering that many home systems aren't built to last that long—a typical roof lasts fifteen to twenty years, a furnace lasts about twenty years, and appliance shelf life can vary—it's likely that if

NESTING EXPENSES

RENT ▸ *POST-LEASE*

MAINTENANCE: Maintenance is included in your rent, unless otherwise negotiated with a landlord. However, if you go beyond "normal" wear and tear the landlord expects, you can fund light repairs yourself before move-out or otherwise expect the landlord to withhold a portion of your deposit.

CUSTOM FURNISHINGS: Everyone needs furniture. But how nice it is, and what dimensions and proportions it should occupy, are up to you and the configuration of your rental home. Sometimes this furniture won't physically or aesthetically translate from one home to the next, so if you invest heavily each time you move, you may wind up spending more on furniture than on a down payment.

CUSTOM FIXTURES OR HARDWARE: Sometimes a rental doesn't offer quite enough storage or needs extra hardware for you to mount, hang, install, or otherwise incorporate your belongings into its dimensions. If you plan to stay awhile, maybe that pricey closet system is worth it. If you leave in a year, that $1,000 collection of rods and shelves might be your priciest craft project yet.

RENTER'S INSURANCE: Renter's insurance typically costs about $200 per year, and it protects your belongings in the event of theft or disaster. It's not required, but it can help preserve your assets.

RENT VS. OWN

POST-PURCHASE   OWN

FURNISHINGS: If you're moving from a small square footage to a large one, you'll need more furniture. If moving from one architectural style of home to another, you may consider changing your look for "when in Rome" reasons. After making it through the hurdles of financing and moving into your place, you'll probably want to reward yourself. But how far should you go?

HOME-REPAIR TOOLS AND HARDWARE: Not only do you need to furnish your home for daily living, but you're also going to need to decide whether to buy, rent, or share everything from a lawn mower to an electric screwdriver. Most owners start a tool collection on an as-needed basis post–move-in. But you'll have to decide whether you need (or just want) to buy some occasional (but kind of cool) gear— say, a pressure washer. Sure, most everyone ought to own a Philips-head screwdriver, but not everyone needs a circular saw. Neighbors will often loan tools. And in some communities, neighborhoods offer a "tool library"—a share-and-borrow system.

EMERGENCIES: Fire, flood, earthquakes, landslides, and extreme storms can rip off roofs, crack windows, damage foundations, and leave homeowners emotionally devastated. Insurance ought to cover damage from these problems, but not always.

MAINTENANCE: Maintenance is the preventive medicine of home operation. You can put it off for a time, but eventually lack of maintenance can lead to a need for more expensive repairs.

REPAIR: Depending on how old a home system or appliance is, and how expensive or fundamental its problems are, you can often repair rather than replace it to extend its life. Repairs are sometimes covered by a home or system-specific warranty.

REPLACEMENT: If the home appliance or system is deep into its lifespan and repairing it is expensive, you may need to replace it outright. Replacement isn't cheap, but is necessary to uphold—or sometimes increase—your home's value.

REMODELING: If you want to make major, elective changes to your home—expanding a room, building an addition, knocking down walls, replacing an old bathroom— you'll pay. You'll also need to talk to experts to develop realistic expectations about how much the remodel contributes to personal enjoyment versus your home's equity.

you buy an older home some of its systems have already been replaced a few times, while others may be teetering on the verge of expiration or entering their golden years. This means that if you buy a home with a twelve-year-old roof, depending on its condition and prior owner's attention to its maintenance, you can expect to replace it within three to eight years. And if you buy a neglected distressed property, you can bet some of its "discount" price stems from deferred maintenance.

Four Degrees of Maintenance and Repair

If you're considering buying, keep in mind that no home is structurally or aesthetically perfect and that no matter what, you're going to recognize a few red flags in any property you visit. If you've already done your own homework, have heard from homeowner friends about their own home-repair headaches and projects, or are home-shopping with an experienced real estate agent with a good eye for trouble, you can make a mental note about how soon you'd have to address a home's issues—and how much they'd cost to address—in any home you're considering.

Some problems are deceiving. For instance, are hairline cracks in an older home's walls due to the fact that they're made of lathe and plaster, a wall material that predates the drywall more commonly used today? Or are those cracks signs that the home was damaged in an earthquake or is beginning to develop foundation issues? In the first case, lathe and plaster walls can be left as is or you can hire out or DIY a "skim-coating" procedure to treat them, essentially painting a thick "mud" over them and sanding it down to make smooth-looking surfaces. But if a home's foundation is compromised or it needs shoring up against a future earthquake, that's a very different proposition—an engineering problem.

Because it can be hard to distinguish major from minor problems, you typically work with a home inspector when making a purchase so you fully understand the condition of the property you're buying and whether you're willing to take on the property's mix of strengths and weaknesses. If you buy a home without an inspection, it's wise to hire an inspector after the fact so your home can get a proper "physical" and you can learn vital details from a professional about the systems you'll be tasked with maintaining and replacing. While a real estate agent or fellow homeowner who's suffered through some expensive fixes can also give you pointers on any home you're eyeing, an inspector is your one-stop-shop for figuring out what's wrong with a property—and how wrong.

1. BIGGIES: PROBLEMS THAT MAKE YOUR HOME UNINHABITABLE

A home isn't a home if it's not habitable. Does your home have a problem that's so risky or potentially dangerous, or a system so unreliable, that it'd be unsafe or unhealthy to live there? For instance, if your electrical system is dated, that's a fire hazard. If you've got evidence of a toxic carbon monoxide or radon gas leak; the presence of poisonous building materials such as lead paint or asbestos; or severe mold or pest/rodent infestation, which can cause illness, your home isn't healthy.

If the home's "outer envelope" is compromised, meaning the foundation is weak or the roof or walls are damaged or rotting, you're already physically vulnerable; a storm could make it worse, taking the place down completely. These fixes are all about your personal safety. Separately from your home's condition at move-in, accidents and natural disasters can crop up and compromise your home. Severe rain or snow storms, floods, landslides, and fires can all damage property. Typically, these issues are covered by insurance because they're due to Mother Nature or accidental causes.

2. MAINTENANCE AND MINOR REPAIRS

Ongoing maintenance is the preventive medicine of homeownership. Cleaning furnace or air-conditioning air filters and ducts can maximize energy efficiency, keep utility bills down, and keep home residents healthy. Unclogging gutters and downspouts or replacing broken or missing roof shingles can prevent roof damage and water leaks in the attic or around a home's foundation. Caulking and patching cracks in a home's siding or around windows can prevent water damage and rot. Landscaping your yard so that trees don't brush rooftops and watching that tree roots don't upend sidewalks, driveways, or the foundation are also important. These and dozens of other seemingly minor gestures go a long way toward preventing more expensive problems later. ServiceMagic, an appliance and home-repair services referral company, offers a handy online tool called "My Home Maintenance Plan" that reminds you which home upkeep tasks need doing monthly, seasonally, and annually via ServiceMagic.com. Your home inspection company may also provide guidance.

3. ENERGY ENHANCEMENTS

Many homeowners whose home appliances and systems are in good working order replace them with energy-efficient models or augment their older machines with energy-saving accessories on the assumption that doing so will save on utility bills. Some home energy enhancements are relatively low-cost, such as swapping out regular light bulbs for compact fluorescents, installing a programmable thermostat and setting it to cool temperatures while you're at work, or buying a floating toilet-tank device that conserves water when you flush. Others cost more but may offer high impact, such as replacing windows and doors, incorporating solar power, or opting for a tankless water heater (which heats water on demand, versus keeping water hot all day so it's sitting there prewarmed when "demanded"). If you're interested in making your home more energy efficient, consider hiring a professional energy auditor via your local city government or one of your local utilities. Look for an auditor that uses infrared technology (to detect air leaks in your home) and/or "blower door" air-pressure testing, versus a visual-only inspection. Consider your investment costs versus energy returns, and research whether your purchases qualify for local or federal tax credits or deductions. The U.S. Department of Energy's Energy Efficiency and Renewable Energy's Energy Savers Web site (www.energysavers.gov) and Energy Star (www.energy star.gov) offer resources and tips.

4. SYSTEM REPLACEMENTS

So you've maintained your appliances and various home systems throughout the years, repaired them a few times, and noticed the signs of age. As with a car, eventually you'll hit the point where the scope of repairs or lingering life on the system just aren't worth further investment, and it's time to replace the whole works. To predict how soon your systems may go, ask a home inspector before you

FUNDING YOUR FIXES IN A CONDO

When it comes to maintenance, renters are covered, owners of single-family houses are on their own, and condo owners are somewhere in the middle. For condo owners, homeowner dues typically cover the broader building-wide issues and "common areas," but they're on their own for repairs and maintenance inside their units. In addition, while condo owners can expect that their monthly dues will cover the big issues—new roofing, building-wide siding, elevator repair—occasionally a condo board decides to charge what's known as a "special assessment," or dues upcharge, atop the monthly homeowner association fees.

Clare, a fifty-eight-year-old technology contractor, was surprised when her thirty-two-unit condo development in Austin, Texas, began charging residents an extra $100 per month to subsidize replacement of a fence that ran along a slope at the edge of the condo property. She and the other residents had to pay the extra charge each month for an entire year. For Clare, the extra $100 was a lot of money each month atop her $1,000 mortgage payment, $250 in homeowner association dues, and $250 in real estate taxes.

"It was quite a struggle for some of us. The condo was at the very limit of what I could afford," she says. "I didn't understand why they couldn't just pay for this fence repair out of the regular building fund."

When a new condo board president—an accountant—took charge, the building restocked its reserves and hasn't slapped another "special assessment" on residents. Clare suspects she won't face another one at all, or at least not for a long time. But the assessment stands as a reminder that even in a "lower-maintenance" residency, such as a condo, you still face surprise costs.

buy about the remaining shelf life of various appliances and systems—or ask a repair professional you've hired for a fix. If you know when you move in that the dishwasher, disposal, and washer/dryer are all more than halfway through their typical twelve-year lifespan and that each costs about $500 to replace (depending on model), you can make a mental note about how soon you'll need to replace them and how much it will cost. Freddie Mac offers guidelines and a worksheet for estimating how long various home systems last and how much they cost to replace at www.freddiemac.com.

Financing Choices for Home-Maintenance Fixes

Ideally, if you've bought a home you have some funds set aside for repairs and maintenance. But sooner or later, homeowners will need to decide how to finance major home repairs. Your choices include the following options.

COLD, HARD CASH

Ideally, you've got enough money on hand to fund home fixes without depleting your rainy-day fund. However, if you can tap low-interest debt to fund repairs, you may be tempted to sit on your cash instead.

PROS *You don't go into debt for home repair, or mess with your home equity.*

CONS *If you deplete your cash reserves, you may be financially vulnerable the next time you face an expensive home repair or fiscal emergency (medical, work loss, auto repair, etc.).*

BIG-BOX HOME-STORE FINANCING

The big-box stores run nearly perpetual financing specials, offering 0 percent financing for up to six or twelve months when you use a store charge card to pay for supplies and services. The length of the grace period typically depends on the dollar size of the purchase, and if you don't have a store card you can typically get swift same-day approval for one.

PROS *If you can reasonably pay off the debt within the allotted time, this is not a bad way to finance the purchase. You conserve cash, and you don't tamper with home equity.*

CONS *These cards have very high interest rates, and if you don't pay the balance in time you can expect to pay a lot for the privilege of the financing. In addition, if you use the big-box stores for services in addition to materials, you won't have much say over the contractors who do your work. (You can always finance store materials and hire other contractors—albeit with out-of-pocket money.)*

MAJOR CREDIT CARDS

If you have no other options, you may have to use a major credit card to pay for materials or services. Your major credit card will carry a high interest rate and won't typically offer any grace periods on interest charges (unless it's a new card) for home services and repairs.

PROS   *If you don't have the cash or don't want to use what cash you have, a major credit card is an option—albeit, not a great one unless you expect lo pay the balance down quickly.*

CONS   *These cards' interest rates are so high you might be better off using whatever cash you have. If you have to use a credit card for major repairs, you may need credit counseling.*

HOME EQUITY LINE OF CREDIT

A home equity line of credit (HELOC) is a revolving, secured line of credit against your home's value. A revolving line of credit is one with a set limit and interest rate, and which you can repay at your own pace (provided you make minimum payments) and run up and down according to your needs. It's secured against your home, meaning if you stop paying the line the lender or bank that offered you the HELOC can place a lien (or claim) against your home— or even foreclose on it. Because the line is secured against your property (versus "unsecured," like a credit card) it will carry much lower interest than a store or general-use charge card.

PROS   *Home equity lines of credit carry low interest rates—typically just above prevailing mortgage rates. The interest on these lines of credit is tax deductible, just like your mortgage interest. You can close down this line of credit when you sell the home, or beforehand. You can use the line of credit for purchases of any sort, although it's secured against your home.*

CONS *Home equity lines of credit require a detailed mortgage-like application process. If your home's value drops, the lender may reduce or even recall your line of credit—after all, the loan is against the equity you have in your home, so if a price drops and your equity does too, you may lose access to the line. If you max out your HELOC, you reduce your home equity. And if you use the HELOC for non-home expenses, and never repair the home, you may be in double trouble if and when you need to sell.*

SECOND MORTGAGE

A second mortgage, like a HELOC, is extended against the equity you have in your home. However, unlike a HELOC whose balance can be run up and down and paid as you like, a second mortgage is typically an installment loan with set terms and a set monthly payment.

PROS *Unlike a HELOC, you can't run your second mortgage balance up and down. A second mortgage will most often carry interest rates just higher than prevailing mortgage rates, and its interest is tax deductible. Prepayment may come with a penalty.*

CONS *Funds from a second mortgage are extended to you the minute you get approved for them, even if you don't need the money yet, and you typically must begin repaying the set monthly immediately.*

CASH-OUT REFINANCE

If you'd rather not apply for a HELOC or second mortgage, and you've got decent equity in your home and good credit, it is possible to do what's known as a cash-out refinance of your home. This is a refinancing where you get a new mortgage for a new outstanding balance that is higher, because you're borrowing some cash (taking "cash out") and repaying that cash borrowed in the form of a higher home loan balance.

PROS *Since interest rates on primary loans are lower than those on second loans, HELOCs, and credit cards, withdrawing cash from your home and paying it back at a low rate may make more sense from an interest-paid perspective than the other options.*

CONS *If you just moved into your home within the past few years, paying closing costs and related financing fees to in effect re-buy it for more money just a few years after your purchase can be an expensive proposition, and your monthly payment will rise. If your credit scores aren't top shelf, your terms may not be very favorable—and these are terms, remember, that impact the giant loan balance on your mortgage, not just a few tens of thousands of dollars typical on a HELOC or second mortgage. As with a regular mortgage application, it can take weeks (or well over a month) to get approval for your refinance.*

DIY

Otherwise known as "sweat equity," doing your own repairs and maintenance can help you save a lot of money. However, if you don't know what you're doing, it can cost you more in terms of time and dollars than just going straight to the pros. Depending on the nature of your repairs, if you feel competent or have friends or family who can oversee or assist you with your particular task, doing the labor yourself can help you save.

PROS *Cutting out the labor costs on a major project can save thousands. You'll still need to buy materials and in some cases secure permits, though.*

CONS *Saving thousands on DIY labor may mean you need pros to come undo the damage. Professionals can source materials, permits, and other must-do tasks more quickly than you.*

QUESTIONS TO CONSIDER

1. **Do you have an emergency fund for home-repair expenses?** Or if you have an emergency fund in general, how much is on hand for home-repair expenses?

2. **What do you *need* to do to your new home versus want to do to your new home?** If you're a renter and plan to stay awhile, would a landlord let you make a semipermanent change to the space (installing carpeting, changing flooring, mounting shelving), and, if so, is it worth the expense to you?

3. **What's the financial—or personal—payoff for your project?** If you're making an energy efficiency–related upgrade, are you eligible for tax credits and are you anticipating a reduction in utility bills as a result? If you're remodeling a kitchen and expect you'll eat out less now that you've got a great dining spot, can you mock up the savings? If you're improving the home's safety level, will you get a discount on home insurance?

4. **If you're in the market to buy, do you have sense of the costs associated with issues common to homes in your price range?** For instance, if you're looking at older homes from the 1920s that need upgrades such as new windows and roofs, call a window vendor or big-box home or hardware store or ask a homeowning friend what those costs might look like.

5. **If you're in the market to buy, will (or can) the seller transfer warranties they have on appliances or home systems to you?**

6. **How's your credit?** If you don't have a significant cash cushion when you move in to a new home, and you have poor credit, you'll have fewer financing options for repairs. Consider improving your credit or securing small lines of credit at a retailer that sells home-related products and services, before you secure your new home, just as a cushion.

CHAPTER 17

PRESERVING PROPERTY VALUE IN A DYNAMIC MARKET

Preventive Medicine and Preservation

Tracie and John, a forty-something couple, found out during the inspection of their 1930s house that the cedar shingles on its south-facing side needed replacement immediately, and that the rest of the home's siding was well on its way to obsolescence. The windows were aging, too. Not long after they bought, one of them fell from its casing due to wood rot in its frame.

The couple bought the house knowing it needed work. But they knew there was no way they could fund a whole-house re-siding and window replacement at once. Contractors quoted them $18,000 total for re-siding, and adding nicer wooden windows on the home's front alone would run $12,000. Tracie discussed the dilemma with John and her father, an experienced handyman, and they decided to do the work themselves, tackling the problem window first and then doing siding during summers, one side at a time.

She and John bought siding materials, insulation, and paint. Then they rented scaffolding, borrowed power tools, and got help from Tracie's father each summer. The siding project's total costs as a DIY effort were $4,000. On the front of the house, they bought less-expensive look-alike windows and also self-installed them, for a total of $4,000. So far, the duo has saved $20,000 (not counting their considerable labor hours) by doing the work solo.

"We chose to DIY these projects because the costs saved by doing it ourselves seemed so big compared to what we'd get in return if contactors did the work," Tracie said. "Also, siding and windows are kind of idiot-proof. When we get around to the kitchen? There's no way we're doing that ourselves."

There's another reason the couple tackled their projects the way they did: By doing the work themselves, and spreading it out over a few years, they haven't had to go into any debt to make the fixes. Tracie, a controller of a coffee accessories business, puts it this way, "We're 'cash-flowing' the work."

DON'T SCREW UP YOUR INVESTMENT

Welcome to the world of home maintenance. Renters, you already know that the more you want in a home, the more you'll have to pay for it via the monthly rent. If you want a one-bedroom that has a modern kitchen with granite counter-tops in a downtown building with indoor parking, it'll likely cost more than a more-suburban unit in a fourplex with dated laminate counters, 1970s light fixtures, and street parking.

Owners face a more confusing residential landscape, since once they've acquired a home they're tasked not only with maintaining it but making their own choices about upgrades. Owner's choices about how to preserve and expand their home's footprint and look play heavily into a home's future value and the owner's equity—and yet, there are few hard-and-fast rules for where and how (and how much) an owner should spend after move-in. Every home is different, and all scenarios relative.

If you own, there are factors you can and should try to control regarding your property's value, like fixing your home (if it's a fixer), maintaining it, and making careful choices if you remodel so that the aesthetic changes you fund also stand a chance of providing returns in a resale. But you need to remember that you're doing this work against a backdrop you can't predict: Sometimes the local (or national) real estate market suffers and drags down the value of well-maintained homes, and sometimes the remodeling choices you made that suit you don't fall in line with what future home shoppers in your market prefer. If you want to do your part for equity preservation and enhancement, without making yourself vulnerable in the process, consider the following factors.

Know Your Budget

Does it add value? Indirectly.

After you move into your home, you need to keep your credit as clean as you did when you were seeking mortgage financing. That's because if you face a home-related (or, frankly, other) emergency, you'll want to have some financial options regarding how to deal with it.

If you've got no savings or no access to credit or financing at good rates, you're going to have trouble addressing an emergency. And if you've got some savings but deploy it all on elective remodeling, you may find that when a major system blows you're caught short when you most need those funds. If you decide to work on a project, ask yourself (or your contractors) if it can be done in phases. Some projects don't lend themselves to this approach, but others may.

Fix Your Fixer, Address Emergencies

Does it add price value? Typically.

If you buy a fixer and don't fix it or you don't address home emergencies, you can't expect your home value to sustain itself. Your home will become or remain a fixer, and the next buyer will perceive it thus. Also, the types of repairs fixers most often need—new roofs, new electrical or plumbing systems—are fundamentals. If these systems aren't working, and you get them working again, that's a fast value-add, depending on the home's purchase price.

One benefit: You get to oversee all the fixes, customizing or remodeling along the way. As you address key systems, you'll have the opportunity to introduce aesthetic changes that range in price and impact. For instance, if you have to upgrade plumbing, you may want to remodel one or more bathrooms while you have plumbing labor on-site. Or once the electrical is upgraded, you might want to rethink the kitchen layout, where outlets are, and your major appliance mix.

Some of the biggest home improvements that fetch the best "return on investment," according to Freddie Mac, include kitchen and bathroom remodels, two-story additions, and garage additions. Freddie Mac also cites the following projects, which can be done less expensively or incrementally, as high-return improvement projects: Deck addition, window and siding replacement, basement upgrades and remodels, and attic bedroom additions.[17.1]

If you've bought a fixer, it's a good idea to photograph its condition before, during, and after renovations. This creates a record of the work that you may want to use in order to negotiate lower home insurance rates or for future marketing purposes when and if you eventually sell.

Preserve Your Property

Does it add value? Yes, by postponing system breakdowns and major repairs.

Property maintenance and repairs come in many flavors—some elective, some out of the blue—and you'll have choices about how soon to address problems and how to fund them. Think of property maintenance like car maintenance: Your car is a depreciating object, which starts losing value the minute it leaves the seller's lot. However, if you keep its systems in good working order, you'll get lots of mileage out of it.

How do you preserve property? Clean it, service it, fix or replace broken stuff, and landscape it. Sounds easy enough, but consider the consequences of *not* doing them. If you don't clear leaves and debris from gutters in the fall, water drainage, frozen material in gutters, and roof problems can result, or water could pool near your foundation leading to basement leaks, or gutters could tear off, necessitating pricey repairs. If you don't clean or treat floors and carpets periodically, with appropriate products suited to their fibers or surfaces, you may need to pull and replace them sooner rather than later. If you don't service your fireplace periodically before enjoying it in winter, you might not find out that buildup or other structural issues are compromising your indoor air quality and the home's fire safety. The list goes on and on.

Remodel Your Property

Does it add value? Yes, usually, but it's hard to predict how much.

Most people who remodel a home that's already in good working order aren't doing it to "make money." After all, remodeling is expensive, and it can be a dusty, disruptive, painful exercise in introducing a new look—or new wing. Generally, you remodel for lifestyle reasons. You need more or reconfigured space to accommodate new family members or lifestyle needs.

However, one justification owners make when they look at the high price tag for a remodel is the potential to recoup much of the remodeling spending when the home sells. If you're staring at the blueprint for a $70,000 kitchen remodel, wondering if you should put an entire year's salary into granite countertops, a farmhouse sink, a Viking six-burner stove, and reclaimed hardwoods, guesstimating that you'd get 80 percent of that back makes digesting the price easier.

Generally, remodeling pros tell homeowners that if they're staying five or more years post-remodel, then they should prioritize their own needs over what flies in "the market." If you're staying awhile, they say, the remodel is about customizing a home for your needs, versus making it pretty for a future buyer. Also, over time trends change. That claw-foot tub in your Restoration Hardware–styled dream bathroom might be totally out of vogue by the time you sell. But if you wanted it, could afford it, and enjoyed it for a decade, should that matter?

Remodeling magazine (www.remodeling.hw.net) publishes a "Cost Versus Value" report each year to help owners see how much different types of remodeling gestures—ranging from replacing siding to redoing a bathroom—tend to return at resale time. These numbers provide a gauge for how well remodeling performs. Returns were high during the boom that predated the Great Recession and have since trended lower. But in general, you can use these figures to get a relative sense of which projects get the most bang for your buck as both personal and financial decisions.

SIX KEY REMODELING QUESTIONS

If you're very concerned about how work will impact future value, discuss your plans with a local real estate agent. An agent will offer a frank opinion on which remodeling gestures will add sentimental versus financial value, or can offer input that may help you adjust ideas about how to prioritize projects. Agents know what else is on the market in your area or home category—and trends among homes that have sold for a premium—and can give you an idea of your home's condition relative to its peers. Here are some questions to discuss.

- **Are you adding new space, or upgrading unfinished space within the home?** Additions add value. But finishing existing "raw" areas can help, too. If you add insulation, drywall, and new flooring to an unfinished basement so it is now a den, that's an improvement from its prior condition. If you've punched up the roof and turned the former attic into a bedroom/bathroom combo, that's also a plus.

- **Is the aesthetic improving—or just changing?** If your home has a recently installed kitchen and you decide to swap out its cottage look for a sleeker green one, you're not necessarily upgrading its condition. You're simply swapping like value for like value to satisfy your own aesthetics. While you might like the new look better—which is its own reward—if you're not actually *improving* upon prior finishes or features of the space then you may not improve much on your home's value.

- **Are you upping bedroom or bathroom count?** Depending on your home's size and local home inventory, this can have positive impact: Adding a third bedroom to your two-bedroom cottage will widen its appeal to families. Adding a sixth bedroom may be necessary for you but overkill to others. Keep proportion in mind for bathrooms: Going from one and a half to two and a half bathrooms is nice, but a fourth may be excessive.

- **Are you adding square footage?** Appraisers and your county tax assessor judge a home's value partially on square footage. However, square footage in spaces such as basements and attics or transition areas (say, a semi-enclosed area between garage and a home's interior) may not count 100 percent, especially if finish levels aren't consistent with the rest of the home or up to newer standards.

- **Are you up to code?** If you're replacing major systems (plumbing, electrical, HVAC) your contractor probably needed permits or licenses to do the work. If you use an off-price contractor or skip permits, you may be subject to fines, city inspections, or questions from a future buyer's inspector. In addition, if you think you've added a bedroom but it doesn't include "code" features like a window for emergency escapes and a closet, you may learn it won't count as a bedroom in a future listing.

- **Are you pursuing an "overrated" remodel?** According to Freddie Mac, the projects with the least return on investment include remodeled home office areas and master suite, family room, or sun room additions. By all means, if you want and need these additions, do them, but consider the future. For instance, rather than use built-ins in the home office, consider regular furniture so the room offers future "flex space."

REMAIN AWARE OF YOUR LOCAL MARKET

Many owners who hunker down for a while lose sight of their own market's dynamics. After all, if you've moved in a decade ago, and the place works for you, your kids, your pets, and your partner, and you're not in the market to move, it's possible you might not realize that the newer construction in your neighborhood is making your old charmer either a hot rarity or oh-so-yesterday's news.

While you should enjoy your home, keep in mind that as the demographic changes around you and trends in home design and amenities shift, your home may be perceived differently than you see it by a future buyer. That's not to say you should try to run out and make crazy changes to appeal to public opinion, or festoon your home with the latest gadgets or color palettes when they offer neither functionality nor aesthetic pleasure for your lifestyle. But retain realism about where your place fits into the local property ecosystem.

"It's hard to judge whether our changes have increased our home's value, since we don't have the home on the market and won't any time soon," Tracie says. "But I'm guessing it would have a higher value than, say, the place that's across the street from us, which is the same size, but has worn siding and doors."

QUESTIONS TO CONSIDER

1. **Renters, how much premium would you be willing to pay for a well-maintained, attractive atmosphere, versus a functional but not necessarily cutting-edge home?**

2. **Owners, how long are you staying in your home?** If you left in two, four, or six years, would you feel the work you did was worth it?

3. **What's the most pressing repair issue in your home?** What does it cost to address, and how soon before it could become an emergency?

4. **What's the biggest aesthetic change you'd like to make in your home?** What does it cost to address, and how would you finance it?

5. **What's your DIY capability and temperament?** Do you like doing things yourself, or would you rather hire out work to a professional?

CHAPTER 18

EXITING GRACEFULLY

Nailing It on the Dismount

Ben, a thirty-nine-year-old human resources professional in Anchorage, Alaska, regretted extensive home remodeling when it came time to sell the 1956 Cape he and his family had owned. That's because customizing the suburban Chicago home they bought for $255,000 in 2002 came to bite him in the wallet at sale time. He and his wife planned to raise their kids and eventually retire there, so with longevity in mind, they spent $150,000 on renovations. But when Ben unexpectedly lost his job in 2009, they realized they'd have to move. They chose Alaska both because he could find work there and because his wife's family lived there.

"My job loss changed everything," Ben says. "If I have any regrets it's that we put so much of our resources and ourselves into our home. We still think of those hardwood floors, the creaking radiators. We wanted to make that home *ours*."

But the timing of their sale in late 2009 accompanied the Great Recession. They listed the home for $450,000, lowered the price to $415,000, and found a buyer. The buyer's lender required an appraisal, and the appraisal came in at $415,000, and so the sale progressed. But two days before closing, the buyer's lender asked for a second appraisal: This time, the price came in at $365,000, meaning the buyer's loan was jeopardized. With moving trucks on the way, Ben and his wife huddled; they could sell at a loss, or keep the home. If they held on, they'd either have to become remote landlords or put the home back on the market and possibly suffer through another scuttled deal in a tough lending environment. The buyer was also over a barrel and willing to negotiate. So Ben's family sold to the buyer for $390,000—the halfway point between the original list price and appraisal price—and they split the difference.

"Market-timing anything is always difficult," Ben says, in retrospect. "We didn't ever count on needing to leave so soon. But when you own a home, you need an exit strategy ahead of time."

HOME AS INVESTMENT: UPSIDE, DOWNSIDE

Ben's story highlights a truth about owning real estate that many buyers and homeowners, distracted with the complex process of just getting into a new home or focused mainly on the sentimental pleasures of ownership, never consider: This whole thing about a home as investment or forced savings plan hinges on what happens at sale time. And what happens at sale time hinges on the market conditions in which you sell, how you've treated your home equity along the way, and how well or how much you've invested to maintain or remodel the property during your time there. In other words, when it comes to the investment case for real estate, it's all about nailing it on the dismount—into an unforeseeable marketplace.

Yes, generally speaking, home values rise over time and many owners exit with a profit. Prior to the Great Recession of 2007 to 2009, stories of sellers losing on a sale were rare. But one of the great lessons from the housing reset in America is that it's quite possible to exit empty-handed or even indebted to your former home—especially if you don't stay for very long. If you're going to become an owner, you need to think of your home as an investment that has both potential upside and downside, and develop a sense of how much you'd be willing to *lose* in order to own. And once you own, you also need to remain aware of market values so you have a relative sense of your equity's strength in the event that, like Ben and his family, you have to sell sooner than predicted.

"I used to think of a home as something that does a little bit better than a savings account. But after this experience I've downgraded that to a little bit better than a checking account. Or maybe better than a cookie jar," Ben says of his family's losses. "It was a timing thing."

RENTAL EXITS: LESS UPSIDE, LESS DOWNSIDE

Elizabeth, a fifty-something college instructor, moved into a beachfront apartment a year and a half after she was widowed. After twenty-seven years of homeowner-ship and with a sizable profit on the sale of her former home, she was ready and willing to pay in the $1,800 to $2,000 ballpark to enjoy a lower-maintenance living experience along a quiet boardwalk.

She put down an $1,800 deposit—$500 of which was nonrefundable—on her unit. But a few years in, she came to regret telling her landlord she was mulling a move, because it became apparent the landlord wanted to refurbish her unit and increase its rent. However, when two other units opened in the building, she pounced on the opportunity to get out of the one her landlord had been eyeing. Her landlord rolled over her prior deposit and she moved, essentially, for free.

"Now I'm paying $100 less per month, and I have more privacy, a lower heat bill, and better security since I'm not on the ground floor anymore," she says. "The best part is that now the landlord isn't bugging me."

If you're a renter, you don't stand to make money when you move out. But at the same time, you also don't stand to lose much, either, because renting isn't a leveraged financial situation. If you want to move out of a rented home, you generally notify your landlord in advance that you don't want to renew your lease. Or, if you suspect but aren't sure that you might soon move, you can ask to renew your lease to a month-to-month format, meaning that at any point you can leave with a month's notice. If you play by these rules, and don't leave the property damaged, your deposit is typically returned within thirty days of move-out. (Rules on this may vary by lease or by state laws governing rental property.)

It is, however, possible to lose money on a move-out. Some landlords do charge nonrefundable fees—although these must be disclosed upfront. If you break your lease, you're technically responsible for the remaining months' rent, but it's possible that if you or your landlord can locate a replacement tenant who passes an application screening you can avoid the lost months' rent. Alternatively, you might be able to sublet your place to another renter, but only with landlord permission. Whether you move out at the end or in the middle of a lease, you can lose a portion of your deposit for beyond-normal wear and tear. What constitutes too much wear and tear can vary by market or by rental contract, or by landlord temperament, but the big items are carpet stains, dinged-up windows and drywall, smoking in a nonsmoking building, etc.

Finally, if you live in a market where real estate agents or brokers charge fees to help you gain introductions to the right buildings, those nonrefundable fees aren't recouped at move-out. They become a portion of your housing spending on the particular property you acquired with their help. And these fees can add up if you move frequently.

Also, how particular a landlord is at move-out can vary widely depending on individual landlords, management companies, and the economy. Sometimes a landlord is simply looking for expenses to charge to you. Other times, landlords are accommodating to long-time tenants who have paid on time and behaved well.

MOVING ON

ENDING A LEASE

FINANCIAL PREDICTABILITY FACTOR:
HIGH

MOST YOU CAN GAIN: Your entire deposit back plus a minor amount of interest.

MOST YOU CAN LOSE: Your entire deposit and/or the remaining months left on your lease; nonrefundable broker or agent fees (in some markets).

THE FORMULA (for those not breaking their lease): Deposit − cost of your own cleanup efforts − any deductions landlord makes = cash back.

MOVE-OUT COSTS: Move-out prep expenses are generally nominal, unless you've made the place sufficiently dirty or damaged to where you need to embark on a major fix-up spree.

DEPOSIT: You should get this back, plus interest. While the interest you get on your deposit will likely be minor, landlords are legally required to put your deposit into a separate, interest-bearing account. If you're not getting all your deposit back, the landlord has to indicate why in writing. Photograph your place before and after cleanup and move-out if you distrust your landlord.

DAMAGES: Damages that lead to withheld deposits include dents or holes in walls; stains, tears or burns in carpets; broken windows; or owing a balance for back-rent or the last month of rent.

BEST-CASE SCENARIO: You give notice, your landlord reviews how you left the space, and your deposit is returned within a few weeks—or as promised per local law or your rental contract. You've got a good reference for the next rental you need.

WORST-CASE SCENARIO: You give notice, but your landlord makes it difficult for you to move out. Your landlord doesn't like how you leave the space, nitpicks about light wear and tear as if you've upended the place, and threatens to withhold your entire security deposit. It's hard to communicate—difficult to get calls and e-mails returned—and your landlord makes you fight to get a written statement about why your deposit was withheld or to get a portion of it back. If you pay a nanosecond late, the landlord reports you to credit bureaus. You don't have a good reference for the next rental.

SELLING A HOME

OWN

FINANCIAL PREDICTABILITY FACTOR: LOW, much is beyond your control.

MOST YOU CAN GAIN: This varies by how much equity you have in the home and market conditions.

MOST YOU CAN LOSE: The home's entire value—or more—in a foreclosure scenario or down market.

MAINTENANCE COSTS: Repairs, replacement, and maintenance fees paid during homeownership.

SALE-RELATED REMODELING OR REPAIRS: Repairs that will likely attract notice during inspection, possible pre-inspection, and fees aside from agent fees (like a stager or other contractors).

AGENT FEES: Typically, if you're using a real estate agent and selling to an agented buyer, you will pay fees of approximately 6 percent of your home's sale price—half of which go to the listing agent, and half of which go to the buyer's agent. If you don't use an agent and go the discount agent route, you can pay as little as 1 to 2 percent of the home's sale price in related fees, but you may be responsible for à la carte expenses for marketing the home (staging, open houses, signs) that a full-fee agent sometimes pays.

CAPITAL GAINS: If you make more than $250,000 profit as a single person, or more than $500,000 as a couple, the amount over this profit is subject to capital gains tax. (So if you make $265,000 as a single, you will pay taxes on the $15,000 above the $250,000 you made.)

BEST-CASE SCENARIO: In a seller's market, you may find that a bidding war ensues and buyers start bidding up the sale price, thus upping your profit. Another best-case scenario is that you have substantial equity in the home, meaning you're more likely to exit in the black than the red—though how profitable your exit may be is harder to predict.

WORST-CASE SCENARIO: In a buyer's market, you may find that buyers will pay less than you thought. If the home sits, you may have to lower the price. If you did a low down payment, you may find that you're going to get less than what you owe on the home—a situation in which you either have to pay to exit the home or in which you need bank permission to sell for less than what you owe and in which you may exit the home owing your bank the difference.

EYES ON THE EXIT: THE PERILS OF PREPARING FOR A SALE

Kathy, a fifty-something Internet executive in Seattle, began thinking about selling her 3,000-square-foot lake-view home in 2008 but was advised by agents and friends that to get top dollar she'd need to take care of cosmetic repairs and replace her twenty-one large windows. So she refinanced her home with a loan that let her pull cash out of her equity to fund the work. The loan came with the stipulation that if she sold in less than two years she'd pay a penalty fee, but Kathy assumed that the market would remain relatively stable and reasoned she could wait the two years.

At the time she refinanced, her home was appraised as having a $716,000 market value and she owed $495,000 on her mortgage. Since she had what seemed like a large spread of equity—more than $200,000 worth—she did a cash-out refinance, borrowing $45,000 in cash and bumping her mortgage balance to $540,000. She paid $25,000 to install energy-efficient windows, replace major appliances, paint the exterior, tackle landscaping, and pay off a few bills.

But fast-forward to 2010, and the market had deteriorated in Seattle and "move-up" homes like hers weren't selling at their former, high prices. She hired an agent who listed her home at $725,000, but as the home sat they wound up lowering the price several times. After letting it sit on the market for several weeks at $625,000, she pulled the listing and decided to stay.

"It became painfully clear that it wouldn't even sell for $625,000," she said. "I was living under the belief that it was worth it to make the investments I did back in 2008 because I thought I'd make the money back when I sold. I thought I'd be making at least $100,000."

Kathy's frustration mirrors that of many owners whose expectations of a home as an investment outpace the realities of how modest that investment may be. While she says she loved her home and has fond memories of her life in it, she also acknowledges that the investment case for ownership motivated her to stay in the home longer than she wanted to and also to spend money on remodeling on the assumption she'd recoup that spending—and how—at sale time.

"I didn't sell the home after I got divorced because I thought it'd be an investment," she says. "I was caught in between the brainwashing that a home is an investment and the belief that my home's value was greater than it is. The only silver lining to my story and to other people's is that we're learning the hard way how to look at our homes. People are becoming more realistic."

Had Kathy sold her home for $716,000 in 2008, she'd have exited with about $149,000—assuming she'd pay about 10 percent of her sale price in sale-related fees and had $495,000 outstanding on her mortgage. But in 2010, with about $525,000 outstanding on her mortgage, and the possibility that she'd have to sell the house for as low as $600,000, she was looking at making $15,000—or less, if the price inched farther south during negotiations with a buyer, the buyer required closing help, or an inspection turned up repairs she'd have to fund in order to make a deal go through.

As you mull your exit, you'll need to think about the mathematics involved in a move-out. If you're renting, be prepared to navigate your landlord. If you own, you'll need to decide whether and how much to spend on your home in the weeks or months leading up to a sale. And even if you're not considering selling, you'll never know when your circumstances might change. You need an exit plan more sophisticated than *when I sell I'll pay everything off*.

What Do You Make When You Sell a Home?

To understand how much money you'd make selling your home, use the formula on page 220. It's useful to model this formula if you're considering buying and wondering what would happen if you sold at various exit points in the coming years. It's also useful to play with this formula if you already own a home and plan to take on a second mortgage or home equity line of credit and are concerned about how this might impact your equity position. Use an amortization calculator (www.amortization-calc.com is handy) to predict where you'll be with equity at your point of departure.

To determine the profit you could make when selling your home, take your home's sale price and subtract the following:

- **Mortgage outstanding**

- **Second mortgage or HELOC outstanding**

- **Money spent on maintenance, remodeling, and repairs**

- **6–10 percent of home's sale price for sale-related fees to agents, taxes**

- **Money spent to prepare the home for sale**

- **Money spent to help the buyers with closing**

The amount you end up with is the proceeds from the sale of the home. Many people mistake the proceeds from the sale of their home as their profit. Technically, it's the proceeds that matter to you personally—you want to know how much money you'll have post-sale. But if you want to determine your profit, you'll need to subtract the down payment and closing costs you paid at purchase from your sale proceeds. Now, did you make a profit? Do you have more or less money than what you put into the home?

QUESTIONS TO CONSIDER

1. **If you had to move in six, nine, or twelve months, would you lose money on your lease?** What about in a home sale, if your home were priced for the current market?

2. **If selling, what's the market like for your type of property?** Remember that each type of property—first-time, move-up, luxury, single-family, condo, or other—may have entirely different dynamics within your market. For example, if you own a single-story property in a warm climate, chances are that property might appeal to an aging Baby Boomer household that plans to "age in place." Understand the inventory for your type of property and how you compete.

3. **How likely are you to lose money on a home sale due to the following issues:** the fact of a buyer's market, continued home declines, the need to sell swiftly (possibly at a lowball price), an inability to fund renovations that would make the home more marketable, or a lack of knowledge, how much to renovate to make the home marketable? Can you afford to "merchandise" the home?

4. **If you're considering buying, and aren't that concerned about your home as an investment, how much money would you be willing to lose at sale time?** $5,000? $10,000? $15,000? Nothing? Do you have that money on hand in savings? Will you by the time you sell?

5. **What's more important to you, owning a home that you really love or owning a home that is an investment?** If you had to choose between the two priorities, how would you make your decision? Keep in mind that your answer may produce different results when it comes time for a home search.

6. **If renting, are you moving often?** Have you researched your potential landlord or management company's history with local housing agencies regulating renting? Have you proposed signing a longer lease (twenty-four months, thirty-six months) in exchange for a capped rental rate?

CHAPTER 19

LIFE CHANGE: THE RENT/OWN LIFECYCLE

Rent, Own, Repeat

Joanne and Mark, a fifty-something couple with grown kids, bought their first home in the early 1980s, a starter condo in the Chicago suburbs. They sold it, for a profit, and rolled the proceeds from that sale into a Victorian-style duplex, and then they repeated the process twice, moving to a bungalow-style home outside Chicago and then to a 3,000-square-foot Arts & Crafts bungalow in Milwaukee. Owning gave them both a secure base from which to raise a family and an investment. Each time they sold, they bought a nicer property using proceeds from their prior place.

But in 2010, when the couple decided to sell their Milwaukee bungalow, the investment case for owning changed. Their timing couldn't have been worse. They'd bought the home in 2004 for $290,000, as the market was rising, and spent $165,000 on extensive renovations to add functionality and bring out its historic charm. However, in spring of 2010 they could only get $280,000 for the property.

The combination of renovation spending, 6 percent agent fees, other sale-related fees, and a sale price $10,000 less than their purchase six years prior left them speechless—and financially far behind where they thought they'd be at this point in their lives. They were fortunate to exit with part of their investment, but far less than they'd anticipated.

The couple moved into a tower apartment in Chicago and have been renters ever since. They're typical of an emerging subset of the rental market: The former owner. An Apartments.com survey indicated that 43 percent of its respondents are former owners who are either returning to renting or renting for the first time. It's not that the prior owners are permanently turning their backs on owning. Indeed, it's more that they recognize that their personal situations and market conditions may make renting more sensible than owning for the time being. Most surveyed still think that owning is a wise investment (though 20 percent disagree) and most consider renting to be more affordable since maintenance costs, home price shifts, and trouble selling in recent years have undercut the appeal of owning.[19.1]

Joanne and Mark admit that they overspent on remodeling in Milwaukee on the assumption they'd recoup much of their investment at resale. But their sale was difficult, time-consuming, and financially underwhelming. They'd grown accustomed to all their homes rising in value. Both acknowledge that they're the type of people who always equated owning with middle-class success, in part because they both grew up in families that mostly rented. In light of their recent losses, however, they're happy to pause, rent, and regroup. With their kids grown, they're also thinking about where and how they want to live out the rest of their lives—and whether to rent or own.

Though their rent is about $200 more per month in Chicago than the mortgage payment in Milwaukee, they no longer have maintenance expenses—like a $20,000 porch repair or busted snow blower—and don't have to worry about the direct impact of home-price fluctuations. Their building offers indoor parking, a gym with a pool, and free bagels on Fridays. Joanne can walk to work. And they have a stunning view of Lake Michigan from their forty-fifth-floor unit. Yet as they head toward their final years of the workforce and start mulling retirement, owning appeals—but this time, only under certain conditions.

RENTING AS AN OPPORTUNITY TO RETHINK OWNING

"We can finally move wherever we want," Joanne says. "But there are two issues. If we buy again, what do we get for our money? Prices here, in the area of Chicago we like, are still expensive. So we're thinking why not save and pay cash for another place somewhere else in five or six years? Then we'd have the money to build exactly what we want."

Because the duo is mulling moving to smaller communities near family in either Michigan or Tennessee, the money they save working in Chicago will go further when they take it elsewhere. Joanne estimates that in the communities that interest them, they could pay $300,000 to build a two-level home with a daylight-entry basement unit. By choosing a flexible architectural plan with an accessory unit, they could help house one of their aging parents or, when they are older, they could offer semiprivate quarters to live-in help or their adult kids, or get income from a paying renter.

The point, with this next-stage-of-life property, would be to build a home they can own outright and that has low monthly expenses—a goal they'd have pursued in Milwaukee had the job prospects there been better for them both. Joanne's interested in home designs offering solar panels or "net-zero" energy-efficient architecture that would minimize utility fees.

"I'm less concerned about what we spend to build than with low carrying costs once it's built," she says. "We're absolutely not going to go into retirement with a mortgage payment or lots of monthly expenses."

For Joanne and Mark, moving to a home where they could have 100 percent equity is a retirement goal. While they didn't expect to hop off the ownership train to regroup, their new strategy lets them take advantage of owning the way many lifelong owners do: They want to live mortgage-free in their senior years. Only because of their financial setbacks in Milwaukee, they're renting while they research the communities where they could work for another five or ten years and also afford to construct a comfortable retreat.

"We're cool with it," Joanne says of their status as owners turned renters. "We're curious about owning again, and this time we'll take a different approach."

RELOCATION AND RENTING

When Lisa and her husband sold their home in Santa Monica in the mid-2000s, they made a pretty penny. They'd lived there fifteen years and had the chance to move to another West Coast city. With kids in tow, they relocated, ready for the next adventure. Despite their considerable resources from a successful home sale, they decided not to buy another home immediately. After all, they didn't know if they'd like their new community or work situations. So, though they could afford to buy, they rented.

"We rented initially because we didn't know how long we'd be here," Lisa says. "Renting is good for parts of your life when you can't make a long commitment. It also gave us a chance to try out a new neighborhood."

After five years, though, the couple bought. It had become apparent that their new city was working out, their kids were in school, and they could even buy more home than before due to price drops. Also, with a daughter nearing ten and in a solid school district, the couple could predict that they weren't going anywhere anytime soon.

"Renting isn't free," Lisa notes. "Also, as parents, much of our real estate choice is dictated by schools."

Lisa and her husband had to carefully weigh the costs and commitment that buying upon arrival to a new city would've placed on their family. While

Lisa thinks owning is important, she also recognizes that during periods of life change you need to be careful before you commit to a big decision. (She's a life coach, incidentally.)

While she and her husband didn't squander the payoff they made from their prior home sale, and could deploy it for a new home purchase, they didn't feel the need to instantaneously transport home equity from one property directly to another. Indeed, many seniors are also selling and renting for a period before moving to retirement communities, so that their equity is liquefied in advance of their needing it for retirement facility entrance fees or medical expenses.

Bottom line: Once an owner, not always an owner. Once a renter, you're not always a renter. Don't lock your philosophy into one point of view.

QUESTIONS TO CONSIDER

1. **Are you living in an area where you can find a rental or for-sale home you like?** If you're an artist who needs a big garage or a loft space, can you rent that or is for-sale property the best bet? If you're a small family and mulling another child, can you find rentals large enough for the whole family? If you want to rent and need to live in a small community where most homes are owned, should you buy or try to find that needle-in-a-haystack rental that suits you—or move to the next community where there are more options?

2. **How many years from a "milestone" are you?** Are you nearing retirement? How soon? Planning a family? How soon? Can the property you're in—or considering acquiring—satisfy the financial and personal demands of this next life stage?

3. **Do you need to move often to move up, professionally speaking?** If you buy, and you want to move elsewhere, can you profitably rent out your former home? Can you afford to buy a home in a new market if your prior home is unsold? Do employers in your field routinely assist with home sales or financial support for key employees' unsold homes—a minor by-product of the recession that may apply mainly to the higher-ups? If you couldn't sell your home, would you be forced to turn down a job offer—or commute long-distance?

4. **Are you considering moving across the country or to an altogether different market?** Do you want to lease initially to get your bearings on the market or a new job? Or do you want to pounce to buy the minute you arrive, making the full-on commitment to the relocation? What would happen if your professional life changed after the move? Could you afford to stay or find similar work? Or would you be stuck because of a real estate choice?

5. **What are your financial expectations—if any—from your decision?** If you're buying and may move within a few years, do you expect to rent out the property? Do you expect a certain return if you hold on to your property for a certain number of years? Can you afford the fees you'd have to pay to a management company to oversee the rental in your absence?

6. **Financial tie-ups: What would you do with the money if you didn't rent/own?** If you and a romantic partner decide to move in together, and you both own properties, do you both sell? Does one of you sell? Do you both rent out your places and choose a third, new place as your nest?

CHAPTER 20

THE FUTURE

Where Do We Go from Here?

If you're looking for an objective answer to the question of whether homeownership—as practiced in the twenty-first century—is good for society, it's probably best not to ask the National Association of Realtors. In late 2010, NAR launched a public relations campaign called "Home Ownership Matters"[20.1] to promote what it called "responsible homeownership." The big idea? Tout homeownership's virtues and beat back what one NAR executive called a "war on housing" in a blog post, a battle waged by an "ill-informed" media willing to question ownership's relevance as a tool for personal satisfaction and financial security.

For several weeks, a flurry of opinion pieces—many penned by real estate brokers as guest columnists—popped up on blogs or in local papers. Some critiqued a provocative *Time* cover on the rethinking of homeownership.[20.2] One NAR leader blogged that articles he'd seen (like the *Boston Globe*'s "Rethinking Rent"[20.3]) questioning ownership were just the work of "chicken littles." The organization also announced a multicity bus tour promoting homeownership, and promoted the sale of pro-homeownership literature and pins to its members, who could buy these items in the organization's online store for distribution to consumers.

If a pro-ownership campaign sounds like history repeating itself, it is: In between World War I and World War II, the U.S. government and real estate trade groups both encouraged citizens to buy homes through a public awareness campaign encouraging ownership and the availability of new financing methods— low down payments, the thirty-year mortgage. Back then, the homeownership rate was in the mid-40 percent range. Politicians and industry were working together, encouraging ownership both for the sake of families and to create jobs for builders. Today, homeownership is still about two-thirds of households, and now government seems to be withdrawing some of its prior support—which, some say, has turned to life support—for homeownership.

But many in the real estate industry—and some politicians—want the government to remain heavily involved. NAR's modern-day ownership campaign is about reinforcing and keeping the very same mortgage products and government supports that made America into an owner-dominated society. Do Americans really need access to government support for ownership, in the form of government-insured loans, tax breaks, and so forth? Walt Molony, NAR's spokesperson, says that a government reduction of supports for ownership is the "throwing the baby out with the bathwater" of mortgage reform. Indeed, if people have to return to the days of the 20 percent down payment, roughly 80 percent of first-time buyers won't be able to buy for lack of down payment funds, he says.

Stephanie Singer, spokeswoman for the "Home Ownership Matters" campaign, says that the organization doesn't have a goal rate for ownership and doesn't suggest that everyone should own. "Our position is that when people are ready, they should have access to the tools that have always been available," she says, referring to Fannie Mae and Freddie Mac's roles with loans, to tax breaks that make owning beneficial, and to the option of low down payments and lengthy loan terms.

NAR represents Realtors who make commissions from home sales. That's the cynical take about the group's interest in sustaining consumers' access to low-interest and government-backed housing loans. But the key word they've mentioned is "responsible" homeownership—whereby consumers understand the risks, the financial pros and cons, and the effects of shifting markets or a sudden job change necessitating a sooner-than-planned sale. There's nothing wrong with advocating for responsible homeownership—or, as one NAR leader put it, "sustainable" ownership. It's just that making sustainable decisions is left entirely up to the consumer.

Fannie Mae and Freddie Mac, the government-sponsored entities created in the early twentieth century to spur easy access to homeownership, toppled in 2008 under the weight of loan defaults and were taken into conservatorship (finance-speak for emergency ownership) by the government. Banks and lenders, on the verge of failure, took government bailout money to remain in business. The government cobbled together emergency loan modification and foreclosure prevention programs to aid owners trapped in risky loans or in underwater situations, but these programs met with mixed success.

As of this writing, about 28 percent of all mortgaged homes have negative or "near negative" equity, according to CoreLogic data. The homeownership rate is on the way down. Home prices aren't expected to rebound until the middle of this decade, and when they do their future appreciation is hardly guaranteed to ascend in a steep slope. (This means owners who bought at market peaks and then lost equity won't necessarily see it return overnight.)

And while many people still see buying as a goal or a good thing, for all the old sentimental reasons owners have always wanted to own, they're also expressing an acceptance that walking away from a home with plummeting value may be more important than paying on a sinking investment. You hear about the "renter by choice" these days, the person who can afford to buy but doesn't. Or "delayed household formation"—policy-speak for young adults hesitating to move out of their folks' places or exit a roommate situation and rent on their own, much less own. Is this an overreaction by a collectively bruised psyche, or a needed correction in our attitudes to housing? *The Economist* asks whether the gestalt is really changing, or if post-bust Americans will display a form of "post-traumatic amnesia" and return to their faith in owning.[20.4]

WHAT NEXT?

The economy and housing market won't remain depressed forever, and, yes, home-ownership still offers benefits to buyers who choose to join the game. One of those benefits may be continued, affordable pricing. Renting isn't pain-free: Many urban areas are expecting rent price hikes as vacancies drop, a result of slowed multifamily construction during the recession. As those vacancies drop, renters with lower credit scores may have fewer appealing choices available and renters who can afford to own may begin crunching the numbers in light of price increases.

Just about every party with a stake in the future of the housing market—including you—now must consider a laundry list of issues that will blanket the news in the coming years as a result of efforts to rethink the government's role in the housing market and the resulting personal economics of renting versus owning. Here are themes you may read, discuss, or debate.

REINFORCEMENT FOR RENTERS

"There's going to be a continued cultural shift that says, 'Renting's okay,' " says John McIlwain, a fellow with the Urban Land Institute.

While the government won't likely start handing out incentives and tax perks for renters, it is slowly acknowledging that it may have expended more energy encouraging owning—at the expense of considering support for other housing—than was prudent. Rather than add incentives for renters, policymakers may subtly shift the emphasis to renting by subtracting incentives for owners.

Political sentiment toward support of ownership and the substantial payout the government has historically made to enable it—which runs into the trillions of dollars—is shifting. The Department of the Treasury and the U.S. Department of Housing and Urban Development put it this way in a report to Congress about the government's future role around housing: "The government must also help ensure that all Americans have access to quality housing that they can afford. This does not mean our goal is for all Americans to be homeowners."[20.5]

But many observers say the bad rap on renting stems from evidence that not enough rental housing—and not enough diversity in rental options for larger households—has been introduced to the nation's housing inventory in recent years. Others argue that the government has unfairly tipped the scales toward ownership—a *Congressional Quarterly Weekly*[20.6] report noted that owners get $230 billion worth of direct and indirect government support, while renters get about one-fourth that, or $60 billion—and is losing money doing it.

In any case, demand for rental housing is rising. Commercial investors, developers, and builders are gearing up for a wave of new apartment construction, anticipating high demand not just from recovering former homeowners but Gen Y and Echo Boomers. With tougher lending standards, would-be buyers may rent longer. Separately, a large population of young adults will be striking out at a time when rental vacancy is shrinking due to a dearth of new construction. The biggest under-twenty population is now entering the housing market, and most will be childless, unmarried, would-be renters. They'll join several other populations already living in rental housing: Prior owners who have undergone foreclosure or chosen to rent and wait out the market, empty nesters pausing before choosing where to move for retirement, and immigrants who typically rent while establishing credit and residency.

During the decade from 2010 to 2020, between 3.5 million and 4.5 million new renters are expected to hit the market, says Christopher Herbert, research director at Harvard University's Joint Center for Housing Studies. And this population comes on the heels of the 3.2 million renters who appeared between 2005 and 2010, many of them middle-aged adults fleeing the ravages of the housing market. The short take on these trends, he says, is that more multifamily housing construction is on the way to satisfy these renters—which Stephen Melman, director of economic services at the National Association of Home Builders, confirms.

This means that when construction finally picks up, you may see more cranes at future apartment building sites than hovering over shells of McMansions in tract subdivisions. One expert projects that, though currently one-third of American households are renters, half of all new housing construction built between now and 2030 will need to provide rental housing.[20.7] Building managers are focusing on "retention," looking to cultivate a longer-term tenant, by increasing community features—and even customizing apartment buildings to have their own "culture" and tone, a cue from the hotel industry whereby decor helps define brand image.

O—

RETHINKING GOVERNMENT SUPPORT FOR THE LENDING INDUSTRY

The debate about where and how the government should support housing has just begun. Treasury Secretary Timothy Geithner told the press that it could take until 2016 or later to wind down Fannie Mae and Freddie Mac, paring down their role in the housing markets.[20.8] In the meantime, the FHA may wind up as what Robert Edelstein, cochair of the Fisher Center for Real Estate and Urban Economics at University of California, Berkeley, calls the "ultimate lender," remaining in place but to serve a smaller universe of consumers—middle-class people buying inexpensive or moderately priced homes.

What exactly does a wind-down of Fannie Mae and Freddie Mac mean for you? Banks and lending companies are now expected to retain more of the risk associated with home loans they provide. Less able to securitize loans and sell them to giant offstage investors, banks won't likely offer money as readily as before. They'll ask for higher down payments from borrowers. (For instance, some large investors who buy mortgage loans off banks' books have indicated that they only want loans with a 30 percent or more down payment, meaning buyers better start saving.) And with less government support, mortgage interest rates could rise from recent historical lows in the 4 to 6 percent range.

O—

RETHINKING TAX BREAKS FOR OWNERSHIP

Aside from Fannie Mae and Freddie Mac, the government is also debating how to reduce the expenses associated with offering consumers tax deductions for housing-related costs such as mortgage interest. While rarely the sole reason buyers choose to own, deductions are often a tipping point that shifts the decision-making pendulum toward owning. Some say that the deductions encourage the wealthy to overborrow, and don't help the middle class, for whom the deduction could provide the most benefit, because to take advantage of it they'd need to change their tax-filing behavior, using more complex forms that allow listing (itemizing) deductions.

Some say the mortgage interest tax deduction (MID) should be eliminated altogether, while others advocate phasing it out the higher a household's income or larger a household's mortgage is. As of February 2011, the Obama administration floated ideas such as reducing the deduction rate for those earning $250,000 and up and restricting its applicability to mortgages of $500,000 or less.[20.9] The Urban Land Institute's John McIlwain says he assumes that eventually households earning less than $100,000 will be able to use it, those earning $100,000 to $250,000 may see a reduced deduction from present levels, and those earning more than $250,000 can bet they'll lose the deduction.

Others—builders, Realtors, some politicians—claim that if the deduction is eliminated then buyers will suffer in dozens of ways. But the government seems to be moving toward a reduction of some sort, even if the decision is politically unpopular or the change must occur incrementally.

WHITHER THE LOW DOWN PAYMENT AND THIRTY-YEAR MORTGAGE?

If you're a first-time home buyer, chances are you'll need to make a low down payment to get into a home and that you'll need to borrow on a thirty-year mortgage. But if thirty-year mortgages become more expensive—or even extinct—and if the low down payment goes the way of the horse and buggy, the real estate landscape could change quite dramatically. Lots of first-time buyers might not manage to get mortgages, or, if they do, they might have to save for much longer. According to NAR, only one out of five first-time buyers can make a 20 percent down to buy a home.

"Elimination of the thirty-year mortgage and requiring 20 percent down payments would turn us back into a nation of renters," says Walt Molony, NAR's spokesperson. "We believe proposals to reduce or eliminate the mortgage interest deduction and remove government support of the housing finance market could have disastrous consequences for the economy, not to mention making it harder or nearly impossible for millions of hard-working families to own their own homes."

While FHA is expected to continue offering low-down-payment-based mortgage products, those offerings could be reduced in the future, some say. And while NAR claims that making mortgages harder to qualify for by requiring buyers to put more equity into the home at the time of purchase will be "disastrous," you have to also wonder if a nation where four out of five first-time buyers can't make a 20 percent down payment *should* be owners or wait till they're more secure to buy.

It all goes back to the "investment" argument: Does owning a home make you financially secure (ergo it's worth a lot of leverage to acquire), or should you attain your security elsewhere and only buy a home when it's solidified? Which is the "responsible" and "sustainable" route for consumers?

"The plain vanilla thirty-year mortgage appears to be the preferred vehicle to buy for consumers," says Dr. Edelstein, Fisher Center executive. "But lenders are in a mixed situation. If they don't offer it, they could lose a lot of business. So they may offer it, but the rate may go up."

The thirty-year fixed-rate mortgage is a product most widely used by the American home buyer and the rates that borrowers pay to tap this type of mortgage are lower than rates paid by other owners around the globe. While consumers like these mortgages because it gives them a nice long time to pay off their debt, finance journalist Bethany McLean, writing in the *New York Times*, notes that they're tough on lenders. The thirty-year fixed-rate mortgage is locked for a very long period of time, meaning that if "going" market rates on such loans increase then the lender is stuck with borrowers locked into lower-priced loans and thus loses money. This, plus tougher rules for lenders and banks, may mean that the thirty-year mortgage will cost consumers more down the line.[20.10]

Edelstein estimates that the background roles of Fannie Mae and Freddie Mac may have lowered the rates on these loans throughout the years by as much as 50 basis points (0.5 percent), meaning a thirty-year fixed-rate mortgage available at 5 percent would, with a restructured or reduced Fannie and Freddie, really need to be 5.5 percent. This could lower consumer borrowing power.

LETTING GO OF LIVING LARGE

Americans have grown accustomed to a high standard of living, from a global perspective. In fact, compared to other countries, the square footage of housing per capita classifies us as some of the most "overhoused" around the globe, says McIlwain, Urban Land Institute fellow. In the future, we may learn to lower our expectations for home size and amenities, swapping out space and swagger for green bragging rights, energy efficiency, and access to urban amenities. Edelstein says that, just demographically, this makes sense; adults are marrying and partnering later, having children later, and focusing on living near expensive city centers during the career-building years. But the shift is psychological, too. The big, newly constructed McMansions of yesteryear seem a by-product of a bygone approach to real estate, suburbia, and security.

The National Association of Home Builders estimates that the size of new home construction will continue shrinking, falling to 2,152 square feet by 2015, down from a peak of 2,300 square feet in 2007. During the next decade, NAHB also predicts that in new construction formal living rooms will shrink or merge with other rooms, and that homes with more than three bedrooms and more than two-car garage spaces will wane. Lots will shrink, and fewer features will be included in the builder's standard package—though if you want to pay an upcharge, you can still have that his-and-hers sink or walk-in closet.

○—

TOTAL "COST OF OWNERSHIP" COUNTS

Those in the market to buy a home may pay more attention to "operating costs" of that home during their consideration of the purchase and also after they complete it. More than two-thirds of home builders plan to include energy-efficient or "green" features in future homes, according to NAHB research.

Builders of new construction, especially those that do "green construction," are increasingly explaining cost savings associated with energy-efficient utilities in a home in an effort to make a practical and financial case to would-be buyers about what, exactly, they'll spend beyond the monthly mortgage payment to live in a given property. Those who remodel are doing so with an eye toward paying upfront now for energy savings later.

Even the National Association of Realtors has launched its own home-maintenance site, HouseLogic.com, to provide guidance on home-related financial management and prioritizing maintenance. Everyone, it seems, is focusing on total cost of ownership and managing the expenses that follow home acquisition, not just those incurred during the purchase process.

REDEFINING OWNERSHIP AND COMMUNITY

Americans have become increasingly conscious about curbing excess consumption and are showing a new willingness to rent or "collaboratively" own various products and experiences, ranging from cars to textbooks to lawn tools. They're also enacting more of their personal and social life online, meaning their virtual address and community may be as important—if not more so—than their physical address.

This raises the question of whether owning a physical home is the wisest choice for some adults, says David Sleeth-Keppler, a senior consultant at Strategic Business Insights, a California-based consumer research firm. He expects that as the economy continues to recover, Americans may adopt a more friendly, slightly utopian approach to how owning objects defines them—and a rethink of to what extent we're actually owned by our objects, instead of the reverse. By 2020, he thinks new ways of bartering and sharing will proliferate in consumer culture.

"The value of owning things outright is changing. What people think you *should* own is shifting now," he says. "Will social networking, for instance, replace the need to feel that physical space defines us?"

While it's hard to tell which consumer behavior reflects a permanent change in attitude versus a reaction to a tightened economy, Sleeth-Keppler says that affluent and tech-savvy early adopters are embracing voluntary simplicity and frugality, taking a different and less-materialistic view on what creates happiness. Others, who are concerned with maintaining the status quo, are struggling.

○━

REDEFINING OWNERSHIP AS VIEWED BY MORTGAGE LENDERS

Moving forward, banks and other financial institutions will be required to hold more capital to withstand future recessions or significant declines in home prices, and follow stricter lending standards. This means homeowners may need to hold more equity in their homes at the time they purchase or refinance. It will be harder to acquire homes, and so those who buy them may hold on to them longer. Some economists and housing experts suggest that new models for ownership may emerge, most designed to offset the risks associated with owning.

Robert Shiller, Yale economist, says that there are several alternatives to owning worth considering. Aside from renting, of course, there are options such as "shared appreciation" or "equity sharing" whereby an owner and lender share both the upside—and, if the market falls, the downside—of shifting valuation. While this option has been criticized for its complexity and potentially difficult implementation, it's an interesting idea: It's a little bit like buying with a guarantor who has your back in the event of economic upheaval.

"If there was a simple national program, equity-sharing might make sense," McIlwain says. "But once there are multiple programs, you can imagine the potential for fraud."

A Cornell academic has launched a business called Home Equity Share to pair buyers with investors. The California-based business's site makes it clear to prospective investors and buyers that there would be risk involved in the equity-sharing arrangement—and does so in much starker terms than would, say, a traditional mortgage lender's literature.

Shiller outlines yet another potential option: A "continuous-workout mortgage" he described in the *New York Times* in 2008, essentially offering consumers a mortgage with a continually adjusting balance and payment schedule linked to housing cost indices and housing futures pricing, reducing the risk of the owner winding up underwater, in default, or in foreclosure.

These mortgage concepts are the creations of economists and theorists, but as Wall Street and Washington, DC, puzzle over how to help regular folks like you get into a home that you can afford, in a mortgage that makes sense for you, these and similar ideas may wend their way through the headlines. Risk mitigation isn't hot, but then, neither is a continued foreclosure crisis.

ADVANCING THE AMERICAN DREAM?

So will you rent, or will you own? Ownership has long been a part of the American Dream. Some say it *is* the American Dream. But if the American Dream is about upward mobility, the potential for innovation, freedom, the pursuit of novelty, perhaps housing's role—and all the values assigned to it—is ripe for a reboot. Maybe owning a home isn't so much an answer as an option, a nice option, for some people, in some circumstances, and an investment, occasionally.

When you opened this book, you met Janna, a young woman in Sacramento who just wanted to rent a nice place downtown after she came home from college, but wound up instead financially overstretched, her name on three mortgages at age twenty-six, under the assumption that the more you borrowed to own the richer you could be. This is true—in some circumstances, such as during the upward trajectory of a housing bubble—but not always so.

After a default and a humiliating personal bankruptcy, she's quietly looking at the housing landscape from the other side of her journey through an economic bubble. She's thirty-one, the average age of the first-time buyer, and home prices have dropped substantially. There's a little part of her that might not mind buying again, and her fiancé is kind of interested. But this time, definitely, she'd go about it differently, with a little more caution and a different set of expectations. She'll have to; the landscape in which she'll make this choice continues changing before her eyes.

RESOURCES

What next? That's the million-dollar question for most people facing the rent versus own debate. Whether you're thinking big picture or ready to get tactical, you can find resources and up-to-date information at the Rent vs. Own Web site (www.rentvsown.net). Here are some additional resources to address different concerns.

WHERE CAN I READ MORE ABOUT RENTING OR OWNING?

The **National Association of Realtors** (www.realtor.org) and its real estate site (www.realtor.com) are both valuable sources of consumer information about buying. The **National Association of Home Builders** (www.nahb.org) offers guidance about buying new construction. The **National Multi Housing Council** (www.nmhc.org), a trade organization for rental-property owners and operators, provides consumer advice on renting.

WHO'S WRITING MEMOIRS AND CULTURAL PIECES ABOUT CONTEMPORARY HOMEOWNERSHIP?

Meghan Daum's *Life Would Be Perfect If I Lived in That House* (New York: Alfred A. Knopf, 2010) traces her relationship to her many addresses over several decades. Mary Elizabeth Williams's *Gimme Shelter* (New York: Simon & Schuster, 2009) follows a three-year house hunt at the height of a boom, while Edmund L. Andrews's *Busted: Life Inside the Great Mortgage Meltdown* (New York: W. W. Norton, 2009) investigates a couple's transition from ordinary homeowners to overleveraged consumers. Daniel McGinn's *House Lust: America's Obsession with Our Homes* (New York: Crown Business, 2008) examines Americans' obsession with housing. Bill Bryson's *At Home: A Short History of Private Life* (New York: Doubleday, 2010) navigates the meaning assigned to home, using the example of a British property.

WHERE CAN I LEARN ABOUT THE HISTORY AND FUTURE OF HOUSING, THE ECONOMY, AND CONSUMERISM?

From an economic standpoint, *The Economist* (www.economist.com) and *Barron's* (www.barrons.com) both offer interesting coverage of housing, focused less on housing as a consumer purchase and more on how housing markets function within or impact the economy. On the blog front, NPR's **Planet Money** (www.npr.org/blogs/money), the *New York Times'* **Economix** (Economix.blogs.nytimes.com), the *Wall Street Journal's* **Real Time Economics** (Blogs.wsj.com/economics), and the independently run **Calculated Risk** (www.calculatedriskblog.com) all do a good job of unpacking the latest economic news nuggets.

Several books debate cities versus suburbs. Richard Florida argues on behalf of cities in *The Great Reset: How New Ways of Living and Working Drive Post-Crash Prosperity* (New York: HarperCollins, 2010) and *Who's Your City? How the Creative Economy Is Making Where to Live the Most Important Decision of Your Life* (New York: Basic Books, 2008). Meanwhile, Joel Kotkin sees the future in the suburbs in *The Next Hundred Million: America in 2050* (New York: Penguin Press, 2010). For an excellent history of the suburbs in America, read Kenneth T. Jackson's *Crabgrass Frontier: The Suburbanization of the United States* (New York: Oxford University Press, 1987). For a critique of suburbs and their role and situation in the American housing market, read John F. Wasik's *The Cul-de-Sac Syndrome: Turning Around the Unsustainable American Dream* (New York: Bloomberg Press, 2009).

To understand consumerism and debt markets, read Douglas Rushkoff's *Life Inc.: How the World Became a Corporation and How to Take It Back* (New York: Random House, 2009), in which he takes aim at the dysfunctional undertones of American consumerism. And Dambisa Moyo takes a look at where and how American culture may lose in stature within the global economy in *How the West Was Lost: Fifty Years of Economic Folly—and the Stark Choices Ahead* (New York: Farrar, Straus and Giroux, 2011).

The following books explore the subprime crisis—its origins and aftermath. *All The Devils Are Here: The Hidden History of the Financial Crisis* (New York: Portfolio/Penguin, 2010), by Bethany McLean and Joe Nocera, deftly explains how a mix of public-policy concerns, Wall Street banks, regulations, greed, mortgage products, and consumer confusion melded together to form the sub-prime crisis. Alyssa Katz's *Our Lot: How Real Estate Came to Own Us* (New York: Bloomsbury USA, 2009) traces how buying real estate became a yoke for many consumers. Also check out Shari B. Olefson's *Foreclosure Nation: Mortgaging the American Dream* (Amherst, NY: Prometheus Books, 2009) and Robert J. Shiller's *The Subprime Solution: How the Global Financial Crisis Happened and What to Do about It* (Princeton, NJ: Princeton University Press, 2008).

WHERE CAN I LEARN MORE ABOUT PERSONAL FINANCE?

If you want to stay on top of personal-finance news, the **Wall Street Journal** (www.wsj.com) and **New York Times** (www.nytimes.com) offer excellent personal-finance coverage, as do magazines including **Money** (money.cnn.com), **Smart Money** (www.smartmoney.com) and **Kiplinger's Personal Finance** (www.kiplinger.com).

Online, you can turn to **WalletPop** (www.walletpop.com) and **Bankrate** (www.bankrate.com) to keep abreast of personal-finance news, tips, and strategies.

Suze Orman's *The Money Class: Learn to Create Your New American Dream* (New York: Spiegel & Grau, 2011) lays out many new realities of real estate and other financial decisions.

If you're just starting out, you could read *Get a Financial Life: Personal Finance in Your Twenties and Thirties* by Beth Kobliner (New York: Simon & Schuster, 2009); *Generation Earn: The Young Professional's Guide to Spending, Investing, and Giving Back* by Kimberly Palmer (New York: Ten Speed Press, 2010); or *The 10 Commandments of Money: Survive and Thrive in the New Economy* (New York: Hudson Street Press, 2011) by Liz Weston.

If you're combining resources with a partner, Jeff D. Opdyke's *Financially Ever After: The Couples' Guide to Managing Money* (New York: HarperCollins, 2009) can be helpful. If you're not married and co-own, you may find guidance in *Money Without Matrimony: The Unmarried Couples' Guide to Financial Security* (New York: Kaplan Business, 2005) by Sheryll Garrett and Debra Neiman; *Legal Affairs: Essential Advice for Same-Sex Couples* (New York: Henry Holt & Co./Owl Books, 1998) by Frederick Hertz; or *A Legal Guide for Lesbian & Gay Couples* (Berkeley, CA: Nolo Press, 2010) by Denis Clifford, Frederick Hertz, and Emily Doskow.

If you're trying to understand how housing fits within your overall financial landscape, take a look at Carmen Wong Ulrich's *The Real Cost of Living: Making the Best Choices for You, Your Life, and Your Money* (New York: Penguin/Perigee, 2010); Charles Farrell's *Your Money Ratios: 8 Simple Tools for Financial Security* (New York: Avery, 2009); or Gary N. Smith and Margaret H. Smith's *Houseonomics: Why Owning a Home Is Still a Great Investment* (Saddle River, NJ: FT Press, 2008).

WHERE CAN I LEARN ABOUT CREDIT SCORES AND REPAIR?

TransUnion (www.transunion.com), **Equifax** (www.equifax.com), and **Experian** (www.experian.com) provide scores. Get all three for free once annually at **Annual CreditReport.com** (www.annualcreditreport.com). You can also visit **Fair Isaac Corporation**, the scoring methodology company, at myFICO (www.myfico.com).

The **U.S. Department of Justice** provides links to approved credit counseling agencies at www.justice.gov/ust/eo/bapcpa/ccde/cc_approved.htm. The **National Foundation for Credit Counseling** (www.nfcc.org, 800-388-2227), which is also called the **Consumer Credit Counseling Service**, has offices around the country. The still-evolving **Consumer Financial Protection Bureau** (www. consumerfinance.gov) may offer guidance on credit products and consumer rights and protections from credit card issuers.

WHERE CAN I GET EDUCATED ABOUT THE HOME BUYING PROCESS?

See **Freddie Mac**'s guide to buying and owning a home at www.freddiemac. com/corporate/buying_and_owning.html. The **U.S. Department of Housing and Urban Development** offers a guide to buying a home at Portal.hud.gov/ hudportal/HUD?src=/topics/buying_a_home.

Fannie Mae provides guidance on the home-buying process at www
.fanniemae.com/kb/index?page=home&c=homebuyers.

Check for state resources for home-buyer education and down-payment
assistance programs at www.hud.gov/buying/localbuying.cfm.

Real estate columnist Ilyce R. Glink offers exhaustive information for first-
time buyers in her books *Buy, Close, Move In!* (New York: HarperCollins, 2010)
and *100 Questions Every First-Time Home Buyer Should Ask* (New York: Three Rivers
Press, 2005). Other smart reads include Robert Irwin's *Tips & Traps for Negotiating
Real Estate* (New York: McGraw-Hill, 2010); Ilona Bray, Alayna Schroeder, and
Marcia Stewart's *Nolo's Essential Guide to Buying Your First Home* (Berkeley, CA:
Nolo Press, 2011); and Eric Tyson and Ray Brown's *Home Buying for Dummies*
(Hoboken, NJ: Wiley, 2009).

WHERE CAN I FIDDLE AROUND WITH
RENT VS. BUY CALCULATORS?

Calculators are instructive, especially if you're comparing different inputs
and assumptions—modeling what would happen if your credit score rose or
fell; interest rates changed; you shopped for homes with varying prices; or,
with the more sophisticated calculators, if you shifted tax brackets. Most real
estate brokerages, banks, and mortgage lenders, as well as many agents, offer
rent versus buy calculators. **Trulia** offers an interesting Rent vs. Buy Index,
updated quarterly at http://trulia.movity.com/rentvsbuy/. There are dozens
available. Just keep in mind that many calculators will differ in their analysis of
your situation, and the results may depend on assumptions you're making about
your future financials or the market's future behavior.

The *New York Times* offers one of the more respected but also complex rent
versus buy tools at www.nytimes.com/interactive/business/buy-rent-calculator.html.

Other calculators are found at the following sites.

Bankrate: www.bankrate.com/calculators/mortgages/rent-or-buy-home.aspx

Freddie Mac: www.freddiemac.com/corporate/buyown/english/calcs_tools

Ginnie Mae: www.ginniemae.gov/rent_vs_buy/rent_vs_buy_calc.asp?Section=YPTH

HSH: www.hsh.com/calc-wwrvb.html

MSN Money: Money.msn.com/home-loans/rent-or-buy-calculator.aspx

Realtor.com: www.realtor.com/home-finance/financial-calculators/rent-vs-buy-calculator.aspx?source=web

Smart Money: www.smartmoney.com/personal-finance/real-estate/to-rent-or-to-buy-9687

Yahoo: Realestate.yahoo.com/calculators/rent_vs_own.html

WHERE CAN I FIND A RENTAL HOME?

Check your local newspapers and alternative weeklies, **Craigslist** (www.craigslist.org), and listings sites such as **Apartments.com** (www.apartments.com), **ForRent.com** (www.forrent.com), **Rentals.com** (www.rentals.com), and **Home.com** (www.home.com). Need a rental home that allows Fido? In addition to searching within regular rental sites for pet-friendly landlords, try **Doghouse Properties** (www.doghouseproperties.com) or **PetsWelcome.com** (www.petswelcome.com).

WHERE CAN I LEARN ABOUT TENANTS' RIGHTS?

The **U.S. Department of Housing and Urban Development** (HUD) offers links to state tenant laws and organizations that help provide assistance to tenants with landlord disputes at Portal.hud.gov/hudportal/HUD?src=/topics/rental_assistance/tenantrights.

You can also read up on tenants' rights in Janet Portman and Marcia Stewart's *Every Tenant's Legal Guide* (Berkeley, CA: Nolo Press, 2009).

WHERE CAN I FIND HOMES FOR SALE?

Many people use their city's or region's local **multiple listing service** (**MLS**), a sort of massive search engine of all agented homes available in a given area. At MLS.com (www.mls.com) you can find links to local MLS organizations around the country. The **National Association of Realtors** listing portal is called Realtor.com (www.realtor.com). Rent versus buy–based searches are possible on **HotPads** (www.hotpads.com), **Zillow.com** (www.zillow.com), and **Trulia** (www.trulia.com). Want new construction? Try **Move.com** (www.move.com). Wondering about distressed property in a particular city or community? Try **RealtyTrac** (www.realtytrac.com).

WHERE CAN I FIND A TEMPORARY OR PERMANENT ROOMMATE?

Word of mouth helps you find a six-degrees roommate. Try friends, family, social networking sites like Facebook or Twitter, your school alumni network, your employer intranet, your church, even Listservs of like-minded hobbyists or professionals.

Also check **Craigslist** (www.craigslist.org), **Rentals.com** (www.rentals.com), **Roomster** (www.roomster.com), **Roommates.com** (www.roommates.com), **Roomie Match** (www.roomiematch.com), **RoommateClick.com** (www.roommateclick.com), and **RoommatesUSA** (www.roommatesusa.com).

Renting a room to travelers for occasional income? Try **Airbnb** (www.airbnb.com) or **Roomarama** (www.roomarama.com).

WHERE CAN I RESEARCH MORTGAGES AND MORTGAGE INTEREST RATES?

For mortgage basics, visit some of these resources: the **Mortgage Bankers Association's Home Loan Learning Center** (www.homeloanlearningcenter.com), the **Federal Reserve's** consumer help page (www.federalreserveconsumerhelp.gov/

learnMore/home-mortgages.cfm), or the **Federal Trade Commission's** Mortgage/
Real Estate section (www.ftc.gov/bcp/menus/consumer/credit/mortgage.shtm).

The Mortgage Professor (www.mtgprofessor.com) offers a wealth of news
and tools.

If you're interested in a specific loan type, you can learn more about FHA
loans via the **U.S. Department of Housing and Urban Development** (www
.hud.gov/buying/loans.cfm) and about VA loans via the **U.S. Department of
Veterans Affairs** (www.benefits.va.gov/homeloans/eligibility.asp).

To find interest rates, check your local media, **Bankrate** (www.bankrate.com),
or **HSH** (www.hsh.com).

To learn how your credit scores may impact your loan interest rate or how
to improve scores and, thus, financing options, visit **Fair Isaac Corporation's**
myFICO Web site (www.myfico.com).

WHERE CAN I RESEARCH NEIGHBORHOODS?

Try **Zillow.com** (www.zillow.com), **Trulia** (www.trulia.com), **Housing Maps**
(www.housingmaps.com), **StreetAdvisor** (www.streetadvisor.com), **HotPads**
(www.hotpads.com), and if school districts are a concern, **SchoolMatters**
(www.schoolmatters.com).

WHERE CAN I RESEARCH HOME REPAIR AND HOME SYSTEMS?

Whether you're concerned about home maintenance and preservation or are
interested in learning about remodeling, there are dozens of resources out there.

Your home inspection report may provide a valuable starting point for
understanding your home's strengths and weaknesses, life spans of appliances
and systems, and costs to replace them. Inspection companies such as **Pillar
to Post** (www.pillartopost.com) and **WIN Home Inspection** (www.wini.com)
offer insights about various home systems on their Web sites. The **National
Association of Realtors' HouseLogic** (www.houselogic.com) site has valuable

tips, as does **This Old House** (www.thisoldhouse.com). If replacing appliances, consider reading *Consumer Reports* (www.consumerreports.org) for information on appliance durability and warrantees.

The **Federal Citizen Information Center** offers several downloadable guides to home maintenance and repair: www.pueblo.gsa.gov/results.tpl?id1=17 &startat=1&--woSECTIONSdatarq=17&--SECTIONSword=ww.

Do-it-yourselfers may want to check out **DIY Network** (www.diynetwork.com) or **ShelterPop** (www.shelterpop.com), as well as crafting publications. **Home Depot** offers classes on basic home tasks via the Home Improver Club (www.homedepot clinics.com), and **Lowe's** offers an online magazine with photo/video demos and articles on various home improvement and DIY tasks (www.lowescreativeideas.com), as well as woodworking shop classes via e-mail.

Remodelers may want to research the process via the **National Association of Home Builders** site (www.nahb.org), which offers consumer resources for remodeling as well as a quarterly online newsletter called *HouseKeys* for current and future owners interested in home maintenance. The **National Association of the Remodeling Industry** (www.nari.org) has consumer tips on what to expect and request when hiring remodeling contractors. To look at what typical remodeling projects recoup, *Remodeling* **magazine'**s annual "Cost Versus Value" report (www.remodeling.hw.net) may help. Debating whether to remodel or move? Visit **Remodel or Move** (www.remodelormove.com).

If energy efficiency or energy consumption is a concern, visit **Green Building Advisor** (www.greenbuildingadvisor.com) and **Energy Star** (www.energystar.gov) for guidance on materials, energy-efficiency enhancement and audits, and more. **Building Green** (www.buildinggreen.com), targeted toward professionals, also offers insight into the latest materials and issues with green construction and remodeling.

WHERE CAN I FIND A CONTRACTOR?

For light handyman projects, smaller hardware stores or independently operated building materials stores often have phone numbers of nearby contractors available on relatively short notice. Your Realtor will likely know numerous contractors, but many people find contractors via word of mouth. Otherwise, consider consulting **Angie's List** (www.angieslist.com), where customers review local service providers. **HGTV** offers a contractor listing service at www.kudzu.com/hgtv.do.

WHERE CAN I GET INSPIRED ABOUT THE TYPES OF PLACES I MIGHT LIVE ONE DAY OR GET DECOR IDEAS?

Well, where can't you get inspired? **HGTV** (www.hgtv.com) will inspire cable subscribers, but online you can turn to **Apartment Therapy** (www.apartment therapy.com), **Curbed** (Curbed.com), **ShelterPop** (www.shelterpop.com), and **Zillow Blog** (www.zillow.com/blog). Consider magazines including *Architectural Digest* (www.architecturaldigest.com), *Atomic Ranch* (www.atomic-ranch.net) *Better Homes & Gardens* (www.bhg.com), *Coastal Living* (www.coastalliving.com) *Dwell* (www.dwell.com), *Martha Stewart Living* (www.marthastewart.com), *Real Simple* (www.realsimple.com), *Southern Living* (www.southernliving.com) and *Sunset* (www.sunset.com).

ENDNOTES

CHAPTER 1

[1.1] Robert T. Kiyosaki and Sharon L. Lechter, *Rich Dad, Poor Dad: What the Rich Teach Their Kids About Money That the Poor and Middle Class Do Not!* (New York: Warner Business Books, 2000).

[1.2] Chris Steller, "3rd District Update: Madia Ad Swats Back, Paulsen Plays Bachelor Card, KSTP Gives DCCC Mailings An 'F,' " *Minnesota Independent*, October 1, 2008, minnesotain-dependent.com/11188/3rd-district-update-madia-ad-swats-back-paulsen-plays-bachelor-card-kstp-gives-dccc-mailer-f.

[1.3] Margaret Johnson, "Fussy, Hysterical, Wine-Sipping Pols," *Slate*, September 16, 2010, www.slate.com/id/2266921.

[1.4] Matthew Amster-Burton, "The Renter's Manifesto," Mint.com, April 13, 2010, www.mint.com/blog/goals/rent-vs-buy.

[1.5] Jane Hodges, "Home Shoppers Take Fresh Look at Renting," MSNBC.com, July 27, 2010, www.msnbc.msn.com/id/38415637/ns/business-real_estate.

CHAPTER 2

[2.1] Daphne Merkin, "A Passion for Property," *New York Times*, September 10, 2006, www.nytimes.com/2006/09/10/realestate/keymagazine/910relead.html?pagewanted=all.

[2.2] Kenneth T. Jackson, *Crabgrass Frontier* (New York: Oxford University Press, 1987), 50.

[2.3] Meghan Daum, *Life Would Be Perfect If I Lived in That House* (New York: Knopf, 2010).

[2.4] Jim Cullen, *The American Dream* (New York: Oxford University Press, 2003), 138.

[2.5] Jim Cullen, *The American Dream*, 141–42.

[2.6] John P. Dean, *Home Ownership: Is It Sound?* (New York: Harper and Brothers, 1945), 41.

[2.7] LeeAnn Lands, "Be a Patriot, Buy a Home: Re-imagining Home Owners and Home Ownership in Early 20th Century Atlanta," *Journal of Social History* 41, no. 4 (2008): 943+, chnm.gmu.edu/jsh.

2.8 Douglas Rushkoff, *Life Inc.: How Corporatism Conquered the World, and How We Can Take It Back* (New York: Random House, 2011), 56.

2.9 Kenneth T. Jackson, *Crabgrass Frontier* (New York: Oxford University Press, 1985), 51.

2.10 The Federal Housing Administration historical background portal.hud.gov/hudportal/HUD?src=/program_offices/housing/fhahistory.

2.11 Jim Cullen, *The American Dream* (New York: Oxford University Press, 2003), 151.

2.12 U.S. Department of Housing and Urban Development, *Urban Policy Brief*, no. 2, 1995, www.huduser.org/publications/txt/hdbrf2.txt.

2.13 Edward Glaeser, "Debating the Securitization of Mortgages," *New York Times*, July 27, 2010, economix.blogs.nytimes.com/2010/07/27/debating-the-securitization-of-mortgages.

2.14 Fiserv Case-Shiller Home Price insights: "For Many U.S. Markets, the Return to Peak Home Prices Will Be a Long, Slow Road," April 8, 2010, investors.fiserv.com/releasedetail.cfm?releaseid=457516.

2.15 Anna Momigliana, "Italy: Over 30 and Still Living with Mom," *Christian Science Monitor*, January 27, 2010, www.csmonitor.com/world/2010/0127/italy-over-30-and-still-living-with-mom.

2.16 Statement of Dr. Michael J. Lea, director of The Corky McMillin Center for Real Estate at San Diego State University to Committee on Senate Banking, Housing and Urban Affairs Subcommittee on Security and International Trade and Finance, *Congressional Quarterly Weekly*, September 29, 2010.

2.17 John P. Dean, *Home Ownership: Is It Sound?* (New York: Harper and Brothers, 1945), 171.

2.18 Karl Case, "A Dream House After All," *New York Times*, September 1, 2010, www.nytimes.com/2010/09/02/opinion/02case.html.

2.19 Agustino Fontevecchia, "Dr. Doom Bullish on Housing? Nouriel Roubini Buys a $5.5 Million Manhattan Condo," Forbes.com, December 17, 2010, blogs.forbes.com/afontevecchia/2010/12/17/dr-doom-bullish-on-housing-roubini-buys-a-5-5-million-manhattan-condo.

CHAPTER 3

3.1 James Truslow Adams, *The Epic of America* (Boston: Little, Brown and Company, 1931).

3.2 David Kamp, "Rethinking the American Dream," *Vanity Fair*, April 2009 www.vanityfair.com/culture/features/2009/04/american-dream200904.

3.3 Jane Hodges, "Home Shoppers Take Fresh Look at Renting," MSNBC.com, July 27, 2010, www.msnbc.msn.com/id/38415637/ns/business-real_estate.

3.4 Richard Florida, *The Great Reset* (New York: HarperCollins, 2010).

3.5 Wendell Cox and Hugh Pavletich, 7th Annual Demographia International Housing Affordability Survey: 2011, www.demographia.com/dhi.pdf.

3.6 Grace W. Bucchianeri, "The American Dream or the American Delusion? The Private and External Benefits of Homeownership," 2009, www.real.wharton.penn.edu/~wongg/research/The%20American%20Dream.pdf.

CHAPTER 4

4.1 "Bricks and Slaughter," *The Economist*, March 3, 2011, www.economist.com.

4.2 U.S. Census Bureau press release on American Housing Survey 2009, August 19, 2010, www.census.gov/newsroom/releases/archives/housing/cb10-124.html.

4.3 Danielle Hale, "Did You Know: Net Worth, Home Owners vs. Renters," National Association of Realtors press release, November 16, 2010, www.realtor.org/research/economists_outlook/didyouknow/dyk111610dh.

4.4 U.S. Census Bureau press release on American Housing Survey 2009, August 19, 2010, www.census.gov/newsroom/releases/archives/housing/cb10-124.html.

4.5 The Federal Reserve, "A Consumer's Guide to Mortgage Settlement Costs," www.federalreserve.gov/pubs/settlement/default.htm.

4.6 Alana Semuels, "Homeownership Loses Its Luster," *Los Angeles Times*, February 19, 2011, articles.latimes.com/2011/feb/19/business/la-fi-renters-20110219.

4.7 *IRS Publication 523 (2010) Selling Your Home*, www.irs.gov/publications/p523/index.html.

4.8 *IRS Publication 936 (2010) Mortgage Interest Deduction*, www.irs.gov/publications/p936/ar02.html#en_US_2010_publink1000230008.

4.9 Gary N. Smith and Margaret H. Smith, *Houseonomics* (Upper Saddle River, NJ: FT Press/Pearson Education, 2008).

4.10 IRS 2010 Tax Table, www.irs.gov/pub/irs-pdf/i1040tt.pdf.

4.11 Charles Farrell, *Your Money Ratios: 8 Simple Rules for Financial Security at Every Stage of Life* (New York: Avery, 2010).

4.12 Fannie Mae, news release regarding National Housing Survey, February 28, 2011, www.fanniemae.com/newsreleases/2011/5314.jhtml.

CHAPTER 5

5.1 Stefan Theil with William Underhill, R. M. Schneiderman, Joel Schectman, Steve Friess, Tara Weingarten, and Daniel Stone, "The Urge to Splurge," *Newsweek*, December 6, 2010, www.newsweek.com/2010/11/29/the-urge-to-splurge-is-creeping-back.html.

5.2 "Senate Banking, Housing, and Urban Affairs Committee Hearing: A Comparison of International Housing Finance Systems; Testimony by Alex Pollock, Resident Fellow, American Enterprise Institute," September 29, 2010, www.aei.org/docLib/Testimony-Comparison-International-Housing-Finance-Systems-Pollock.pdf.

5.3 Harold Bubil, "Realtors Redefining Ownership," *Sarasota Herald Tribune*, November 14, 2010, www.heraldtribune.com/article/20101114/COLUMNIST/11141001.

5.4 Sheila Bair, remarks to the Housing Association of Non-Profit Developers Annual Meeting, Tysons Corner, Virginia, June 7, 2010, www.fdic.gov/news/news/speeches/chairman/spjun0710.html.

5.5 Warren Buffett, Berkshire Hathaway Shareholder Letters, www.berkshirehathaway.com/letters/2008ltr.pdf (p. 11) and www.berkshirehathaway.com/letters/2010ltr.pdf (p. 16).

5.6 Fannie Mae, press release, April 6, 2010, www.fanniemae.com/newsreleases/2010/4989.jhtml.

CHAPTER 6

6.1 Katherine Salent, "New Homes' Siren Song: How Emotions Suck Us In," *Washington Post*, May 23, 2009, www.washingtonpost.com/wp-dyn/content/article/2009/05/22/AR2009052201484.html.

6.2 Diane Wedner, "Borrowers Spend 10 Hours Shopping for Cars, 5 for Home Loans," WalletPop, May 7, 2010, www.walletpop.com/2010/05/07/borrowers-spend-10-hours-shopping-for-cars-5-for-home-loans.

6.3 Ben Johnson, "Apartments Stage a Comeback as Renters Return in Surprising Numbers," *National Real Estate Investor*, June 23, 2010, nreionline.com/property/multifamily/apartments_stage_comeback_0623.

6.4 U.S. Census Bureau press release on American Housing Survey 2009, August 19, 2010, www.census.gov/newsroom/releases/archives/housing/cb10-124.html.

6.5 The Harvard Joint Center for Housing Studies, "The State of the Nation's Housing 2010," 32, www.jchs.harvard.edu.

[6.6] Dawn Wotapka, "Realty Check: 'Extreme Makeover' Downsizes Its Dream Homes," *Wall Street Journal*, April 6, 2010, online.wsj.com/article/SB100014240527023040174045751 65840903285032.html.

[6.7] Larry Hannan, "'Extreme Makeover' Home in Foreclosure," *Florida Times-Union*, February 1, 2011, jacksonville.com/news/metro/2011-01-31/story/hastings-family-extreme-makeover-about-lose-home-television-show-built.

[6.8] U.S. Department of Housing and Urban Development (HUD), "Housing in America: 2009 American Housing Survey Results," 4, www.huduser.org/portal/periodicals/ushmc/summer10/ch1.pdf.

CHAPTER 7

[7.1] Based on calculations from Fair Isaac and Informa Research on Fair Isaac's site, www.myfico.com/HelpCenter/FICOScores.

[7.2] "Existing Home Sales Rise in March," Marketwire, April 20, 2011, www.marketwire.com/press-release/existing-home-sales-rise-in-march-1504782.htm.

[7.3] "On-time Rental Payments Now Help Boost Credit Scores" (undated Experian press release), www.experian.com/rentbureau/rental-payment.html.

[7.4] U.S. Department of Housing and Urban Development, "Report to Congress on the Root Causes of the Foreclosure Crisis," January 2010, 16, www.huduser.org/Publications/PDF/Foreclosure_09.pdf.

CHAPTER 8

[8.1] National Association of Realtors Profile of Home Buyers and Sellers 2010.

[8.2] National Association of Realtors Profile of Home Buyers and Sellers 2007, 10.

[8.3] National Association of Realtors Profile of Home Buyers and Sellers 2010, 71.

[8.4] Diana Olick, "Negative Home Equity Is Worse Than You Think," CNBC, December 15, 2010, www.cnbc.com/id/40682173/Negative_Home_Equity_is_Worse_Than_You_Think.

CHAPTER 9

9.1 Jorge Atiles, Andrew Carswell, Russell N. James, and Cliff A. Robb, "Housing Costs Among Low-Income Renters and Homeowners: Rent v. Buy and the Hidden Costs of Low-Income Homeownership," Szilárd Kis and Istvan Balogn (Eds.), *Housing, Housing Costs and Mortgages: Trends, Impact, and Prediction* (New York: Nova Science Publishers, 2010).

9.2 *ibid.*

9.3 "U.S. Apartment Rents Poised to Climb More Than 5 Percent in 2011," MPF Research press release, January 6, 2011, www.realpage.com/company/news/us-apartment-rents-poised-to-climb-more-than-5-percent-in-2011.

CHAPTER 14

14.1 Jane Hodges, "More See Walking on Mortgage as Viable Plan," MSNBC.com, December 20, 2010, www.msnbc.msn.com/id/40704053/ns/business-real_estate.

14.2 Bob Okon, "Renters Find Out Their Homes Are in Foreclosure," The *Herald News*, December 19, 2010, heraldnews.suntimes.com/news/2884105-418/foreclosure-bowen-rent-thakkar-houses.html.

14.3 Charles V. Bagli, "A Rent Spike May Loom at Stuyvesant Town," *New York Times*, December 14, 2010, www.nytimes.com/2010/12/15/nyregion/15stuyvesant.html.

CHAPTER 16

16.1 HUD Releases 2009 American Housing Survey, July 1, 2010, portal.hud.gov/hudportal/HUD?src=/press/press_releases_media_advisories/2010/HUDNo.10-138.

CHAPTER 17

17.1 Freddie Mac, Remodeling site, www.freddiemac.com/corporate/buyown/english/purchasing/owning/remodel.html.

CHAPTER 19

19.1 Apartments.com press release, September 14, 2010, www.apartments.com/pressroom/RenterAttitudes

CHAPTER 20

20.1 National Association of Realtors, Home Ownership Matters site, www.realtor.org/topics/homeownership?wt.mc_id=rd0093.

20.2 Barbara Kiviat, "The Case Against Homeownership," *Time,* September 11, 2010, www.time.com/time/business/article/0,8599,2013684,00.html.

20.3 Rebecca Tuhus-Dubrow, "Rethinking Rent," *Boston Globe,* March 22, 2009, www.boston.com/bostonglobe/ideas/articles/2009/03/22/rethinking_rent.

20.4 "Bricks and Slaughter," *The Economist,* March 3, 2011, www.economist.com.

20.5 Department of the Treasury and U.S. Department of Housing and Urban Development, "Reforming America's Housing Finance Market," February 2011, 3, www.treasury.gov/initiatives/Documents/Reforming%20America's%20Housing%20Finance%20Market.pdf.

20.6 John Cranford, "Political Economy: Home Fires," *Congressional Quarterly Weekly,* November 14, 2009.

20.7 National Multi Housing Council 2010 Annual Report, "Renter Nation," 6, www.nmhc.org/Content/ServeFile.cfm?FileID=8660.

20.8 Lorraine Woellert and Rebecca Christie, "Treasury Report Calls for Winding Down Fannie, Freddie," Bloomberg, February 11, 2011, www.bloomberg.com/news/2011-02-11/obama-administration-calls-for-ultimately-winding-down-fannie-freddie.html.

20.9 Tami Luhby, "Slash Mortgage Deductions for the Rich? Fat Chance," CNN Money, February 15, 2011, money.cnn.com/2011/02/15/news/economy/mortgage_interest_deduction/index.html.

20.10 Bethany McLean, "Who Wants a 30-Year Mortgage?" *New York Times,* January 6, 2011.

INDEX

A

Adams, James Truslow, 45
American Dream, 45–46, 89, 97, 240
Appliances
   energy-efficient, 196
   replacing, 193
   warranties on, 202
Appreciation, 28, 230
ARM (adjustable rate mortgage), 37, 133–34
Auctions, 176

B

Bair, Sheila, 78
Balloon mortgages, 134–35
Bankruptcy, 104
Bear Stearns, 38
Better Homes in America movement, 34
Broker fees, 114, 166
Brown, Chris, 125
Budgeting, 83. *See also* Sustainable housing
Buffett, Warren, 78–79
Bulk sales, 176–77
Bush, George H. W., 36
Bush, George W., 36
Buyers
   co-, 51, 143
   credit scores of, 99, 106–7
   first-time, 47, 92–93, 113, 118, 121, 235
   move-up, 96–97
   self-employed, 143–44
   singles as, 51
   as sustainable consumers, 77–83, 230
   unmarried, 143
   women vs. men as, 52
Buyer's agents, 150, 153
Buyer's market vs. seller's market, 56, 165, 219
Buying. *See also* Closing costs; Down payments; Mortgages
   cohousing, 161
   co-ops, 161
   distressed properties, 136, 170–73, 175–81
   for-sale-by-owner homes, 160
   information sources on, 242, 245–46
   in multifamily buildings, 160
   negotiating and, 167
   in new-construction communities, 160
   offers, 153, 162–65
   rent-to-own, 161
   single-family homes, 159
   upfront costs of, 115

C

Calculators, rent vs. buy, 44, 246–47
Capital gains taxes, 48, 65, 217
Capra, Frank, 35
Carlin, George, 46
Case, Karl, 40
Cecala, Guy, 172
Chen, Celia, 38
Cities vs. suburbs, 243
Clinton, Bill, 36
Closing costs, 61, 115, 167

ACKNOWLEDGMENTS

I thank my agent, Danielle Svetcov, my editor, Kate Woodrow, and Lisa Tauber at Chronicle for giving me the chance to explore this topic and for their encouragement and responsiveness.

I also thank the National Association of Real Estate Editors for their support and a long-ago book research fellowship that got me started down this path. And Zillow's Katie Curnutte, who, one day over lunch a few years ago, took the words right out of my mouth when she said that rent versus own would remain a hot topic for years to come.

I'm lucky I have a wonderful group of writer and writer-tolerant friends who have offered moral support, advice, and reading time throughout this project. Thank you in particular to Kristina Shevory, Jake Engle, and Derek Scheips. I also appreciate writer friends who have helped with brainstorming, eyeballing work, or motivating in the form of their own productivity, including Michelle Goodman, Diane Mapes, Jennifer Worick, Joni Blecher, Megan McMorris, Elise Glassman, Stephanie Rabinowitz, David Partikian, Mark White, and Rob Salkowitz.

I'm grateful for editors at the *Seattle Times*, MSNBC.com, the *Wall Street Journal*, and Real Estate Forum. And I thank dozens of experts and spokespersons in the field, such as National Association of Realtors' Walter Molony, who have given of their time in interviews and pesky requests to explain the finer points. If I called you, you know who you are!

I thank the Vermont Studio Center for providing me and other working writers fellowships to focus, Tully's Coffee on Alki Beach for opening daily at dawn, and Alki Mail & Dispatch for letting me wander in and chat awhile. Seattle Public Library, I'll return the books soon.